PRAISE FOR BING WEST'S GRIPPING WAR NARRATIVE

# *THE VILLAGE*

"Unquestionably the best book to come out of the Vietnam war—human, compassionate, suspenseful, dramatic."

—Charles B. MacDonald,
author of *Company Commander*

"A superbly honest, readable work that goes beyond journalism to become good literature."

—Peter Braestrup, author of *Tet*

"This is the way Vietnam should have been fought—by tough volunteers who lived alongside the Vietnamese. . . . It will take the sternest idealogue to remain unmoved by West's perceptive and human treatment of the men who fought it. . . . It's an account of brave men at war in a far country, honestly told."

—*Washington Post Book Review*

"One of the small handful of truly great books to come out of the Vietnam war."

—Keith William Nolan, author of
*The Battle for Saigon* and *A Hundred Miles of Bad Road*

"Pure Hemingway in the best sense of that characterization. . . . West brilliantly portrays the drama of a war few Americans have known."

—*Pacific Affairs*

"Professional reading for professional growth."

—*Commandant's Reading List*

"A fantastic, down in the mud and crud book of enlisted Marines fighting to defend a village. . . . West tells of some of the victories and the tragic cost. And he tells it well."

—*Leatherneck Magazine*

**Books by Bing West**

The Pepperdogs
Small Unit Action in Vietnam
Naval Forces and National Security: Sea Plan 2000

# THE VILLAGE

# BING WEST

**POCKET BOOKS**

New York   London   Toronto   Sydney   Singapore

POCKET BOOKS, a division of Simon & Schuster, Inc.
1230 Avenue of the Americas, New York, NY 10020

ISBN: 0-7434-5757-9

First Pocket Books printing January 2003

10  9  8  7  6  5  4  3  2  1

POCKET and colophon are registered trademarks of
Simon & Schuster, Inc.

For information regarding special discounts for bulk purchases,
please contact Simon & Schuster Special Sales at 1-800-456-6798
or business@simonandschuster.com

Cover design by Jon Valk; cover photo courtesy of the author

Printed in the U.S.A.

To Mrs. Brannon,
and to the other mothers,
in order that they may better understand
what their sons did

# CONTENTS

Foreword by James R. Schlesinger,
Former Secretary of Defense ................................................. ix

Author's Preface ................................................................. xiii

*Book I* The Setting ......................................................... 1

*Book II* Night Patrols ..................................................... 59

*Book III* Defeat ............................................................. 125

*Book IV* "Work Very Hard—Never Look Tired" ............. 155

*Book V* The Challenge ................................................... 197

*Book VI* Acceptance ...................................................... 237

Epilogue: 1967 ................................................................ 323

1968 ............................................................................... 331

1969–70 .......................................................................... 343

1971 ............................................................................... 347

2002 ............................................................................... 349

# Contents

# FOREWORD
by Former Secretary of Defense
James R. Schlesinger

It is now some eighteen years since a young, ex–Marine captain joined us at the RAND Corporation. I for one found his writing absorbing. It was different from the torrent of Vietnam analysis in two respects. First, it was descriptive and concrete—simple vignettes that hinted at, but did not state, larger conclusions. The writing was sparse: stripped of those grandiose strategies or clichés (it is sometimes difficult to identify which is which) that frequently pass for wisdom at higher levels of government. West left the theorizing about grand strategy to others; not for him that American proclivity to impose the big picture from above. Second, his prose had a haunting quality—noticeably different from the rather sterile bureaucratese one so frequently encountered in RAND memoranda.

The splendid thing about this volume is its lack of pretense. West provides a remarkable portrait of the ethos of the Vietnamese countryside and a sense of what life in conditions of war was really like. Binh Nghia is a microcosm—with the generalized and parochial distrust of all outside forces characteristic of such a village. Since the war raging about the village was primarily a civil war, certain rules of the game to limit damage or reprisal against family and bystanders were unavoidable. The famous "hearts and minds" of the Vietnamese villagers could scarcely be won unless the government could provide security. Therein lay the crux of the pacification program. The *village* war would determine the outcome of the *civil* war. The ultimate failure of the Viet Cong in the village war meant that Hanoi could only triumph through direct invasion: the eighteen line divisions of the North Vietnamese Army that finally crushed the GVN in the spring of 1975.

The American attempt to shore up South Vietnam led to divisions in this country of a type that we had not seen in this century. Other wars—the War of 1812, the Mexican War, the Spanish-American War—had caused domestic divisions. But none had dragged on for a decade, and so those earlier tensions had been more rapidly dispelled. For the nation, Vietnam did not provide the unifying and exhilarating affect of World War II. Returning veterans were staggered, quite understandably, to discover that, having served God and Country, they were not received on their return with the usual acclaim. Protests about the war spawned ideologies, rather narrow minded ideologies at that. Put briefly, *everything* about Vietnam had to be rejected. The result was a *shunning* of this excellent book. Fashionable journals declined to review it.

I can well recall at the time West's disappointment at this rather unfair treatment. His work was largely descriptive and certainly nonideological, but it had been swept up in the larger ideological passions. Yet, as the bitterness of that earlier debate fades, this little study has finally come into its own. I can recall telling West in the early 1970s: do not worry; this is the classic description of the war; your book will eventually receive its just due—a decade from now, indeed half a century from now, those interested in the war will be reading your book to discover what it was really like. I believe that experience has justified that prophecy.

JAMES R. SCHLESINGER
JANUARY 1985

Dr. Schlesinger was Secretary of Defense in 1975, when South Vietnam fell. Prior to that, he was Director of Central Intelligence.

# AUTHOR'S PREFACE

This is the story of fifteen Marines who lived and fought for two years inside a Vietnamese village. There was shooting almost every night; from across the river a seasoned Viet Cong battalion attacked repeatedly. In this village, the South Vietnamese farmers planted rice during the day and after dusk patrolled with the Marines.

When this book was first published, emotions over America's role in Vietnam were heated and some critics refused to review *The Village*. Others wrote that Marines could not have lived for years protecting villagers from the Viet Cong and from the North Vietnamese. Yet despite the skeptics, at the height of the Vietnam War a dozen U.S. Marines did live in the village and were generally accepted by 6,000 Vietnamese farmers.

This is the story of one squad of Marines who spent over two years in the village of Binh Nghia (BEEN-KNEE-AH) and experienced some of the most intense and sustained small unit fighting throughout Vietnam. Reasonably, the Marines were too far outnumbered to survive and push out the guerrillas. The squad, despite its losses, never believed that. To stay alive, they used the tactics of the guerrillas.

To understand the reasons for the continuous combat and to decide whether to leave a Marine squad alone in such a village, the Marine command had sent me—an infantry captain—into The Village in 1966, although a squad ordinarily was led by a sergeant. While I led many of the patrols described in detail in the book, this story belongs to the men of the squad. So in writing the story I functioned simply as an unnamed character and also as the camera's eye. I tried to describe how we fought—not why—and I let the descriptions stand alone, without editorializing about the emotions and the hardships.

*The Village* is a description, as best as I could relate as a participant, of what war is like when you fight guerrillas, and of how Americans behaved when they volunteered to fight among the people. It was a bloody and intensely personal war. The Marines fought well while they were there; the village remained intact, out of bounds both to American air and artillery strikes and to North Vietnamese force and rule.

When I returned to The Village in 2002 (see the last chapter), I was greeted warmly by those who had fought on both sides. The marker to the Marines who had fallen was still there. Sometimes we underestimate how others see us.

BING WEST
SEPTEMBER 2002

To my wife, Kate, special thanks are due for shielding me from the household tasks I properly should have been doing when I was writing and for encouraging me to write on the many weekends when we both would have preferred doing something—anything—else.

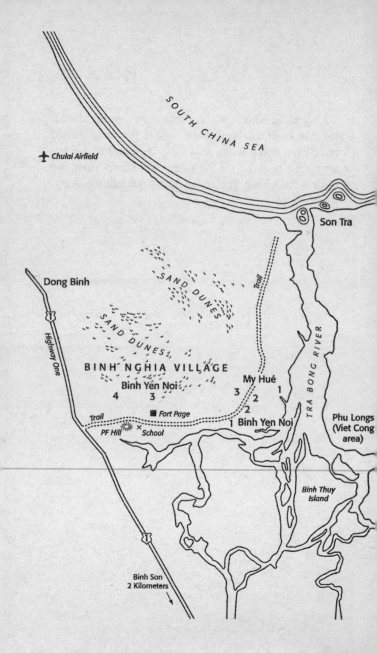

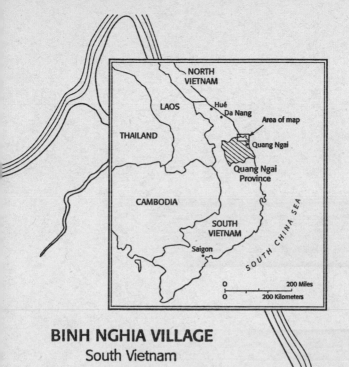

NORTH
VIETNAM

LAOS

Hué
Da Nang

THAILAND

Area of map

Quang Ngai

Quang Ngai
Province

CAMBODIA

SOUTH
VIETNAM

SOUTH CHINA SEA

Saigon

0        200 Miles
0        200 Kilometers

# BINH NGHIA VILLAGE
## South Vietnam

0          1          2 Miles
0     1     2 Kilometers

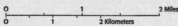

N
W ← → E

# BOOK I

# THE SETTING

# 1

Ap Thanh Lam wanted to go home. In the last six years of fighting, he had stayed overnight in his home village only once. And that night he had hidden in the shadows of a thicket and left as soon as he had killed his man.

Lam was a policeman—a professional who shunned politics and avoided discussions about ideology. He owed his training to the Viet Minh, in whose Security Service he had worked after World War II. He had broken with the Communists in 1954, and subsequently had fought against them. The Saigon government, though glad of his services, held him suspect, refused him promotions and transferred him frequently. But Lam was given what he valued most: freedom to operate as he chose. A middle-aged man with an unmistakable air of authority, Lam looked and acted like a cop. Even in friendly conversation he gave the impression that part of him was holding back, watching, listening, judging, respected by the villagers because he did not tax them and hated by the Viet Cong because he could trap them.

Lam rarely accompanied the Army into Viet Cong hamlets. Instead, he let the Viet Cong come to him. When he had a tip that a VC leader might be visiting a government-controlled hamlet, he told no one. That way, there was no chance of a leak. Even his squad of special police frequently did not know where or why he was taking them. The trapped Viet Cong rarely fought. The surprise was too great. A door would suddenly be kicked open and there would stand Lam, backed up by a dozen police with submachine guns.

In May of 1966, Lam was told that Truong My, an important VC cadre, would be sleeping with his wife on a certain night in the VC village of Binh Nghia (pronounced "Been Knee-ah"). Ordinarily, Lam would not have acted on that information. Trying to slip undetected into a VC hamlet was too dangerous. Most likely his police would be spotted by the hamlet sentries and end up in a firefight with the local guerrilla platoon while the VC leader escaped.

But Binh Nghia was different. It was Lam's home. He knew the back paths and hedgerows, the gates and the gaps in the fences, the backyard runs of the children and the houses of VC families.

The evening Truong My was due home, Lam put on the black pajamas and conical hat of a farmer and stuck a snub-nosed .38 revolver in his waistband. Unaccompanied, he left district headquarters and padded barefoot to the bank of a nearby river, where he climbed into a small sampan.

It was dusk when Lam reached the village. The VC sentries saw his sampan turn into the bank, but before they could walk to it, Lam had ducked into a nearby thicket. The sentries walked back to their outpost position without raising the alarm, having assumed Lam was a farmer returning late from the district market.

Lam stayed crouched in the thicket for several hours, patiently waiting for the families to finish their dinners, for the children to go to bed, for the dogs to curl up under the houses, for the women to wash the dishes, for the men to finish their strong moonshine wine, for the lights to go out. The Viet Cong did not mount strong patrols inside their hamlets at night; instead, they guarded its perimeters. By midnight Lam was walking slowly through the back-yards with no worry about an ambush and with only mild concern that he might accidentally bump into some VC on the move.

The home of Truong My was near the house in which Lam had been born and where his mother still lived. Lam and Truong My knew each other, but not well, for Lam was ten or fifteen years older. Although since choosing sides neither man dared visit his home on a regular basis, their families were immune from the violence. The relatives and children of both sides were equally vulnerable to reprisals, so no man dared strike the family of another, lest his own family suffer ten times over.

At one in the morning, Lam passed by his mother's house. Its lights were out, but lanterns were still flickering in a few other houses and it was toward one of them that Lam carefully walked. When near the hedge which surrounded the house, he stopped and stood for several minutes in the darkness, listening to the low drone of conversation from within the house and watching for any movement outside in case Truong My had brought a bodyguard home with him.

Once satisfied that Truong My and his wife were alone, Lam moved rapidly. Revolver in hand, he walked up to the gate in the hedge and felt along its hinges for any booby traps. Finding no trip wires, he untied the rope latch, opened the gate and entered the front yard. Without pausing, he proceeded across the porch and kicked open the front door.

Truong My was sitting at a table in the center of the room, a small cup of tea in front of him. His wife was off in a corner, tending the hearth. The wife was startled. Truong My was not. In the second during which the door had come banging open, the Viet Cong leader knew what would be next. It took Lam only an instant to cross the threshold and level his pistol. But in that same time

Truong My had come to his feet, kicking his stool behind him and thrusting the table toward Lam.

Then the first bullet hit him, but it didn't stop him, and he had momentum, and he was close to the doorway leading to the back of the house. But Lam was firing again, and again, and Truong My never reached the doorway. He died in his home while his wife watched.

Lam was not through. He ran to the house next door. There he found a farmer and his wife, who had heard the shooting, shepherding their sleepy children toward the family bomb shelter. At gunpoint, he led the parents back to Truong My's house, where he forced them to pick up the body and follow him at a fast shuffle to the river bank. With his dead enemy draped over the bow, he was paddling downriver toward the district town before the Viet Cong guerrillas in the village of Binh Nghia could organize a search for him.

The corpse lay on display in the district market all day, an object lesson intended to lessen the prestige of the Viet Cong and to demonstrate the power of the government forces. For a week afterward, the district buzzed with the news of Lam's exploit. The Viet Cong district committee swore they would revenge the killing of Truong My, their fury adding to Lam's reputation.

In June, Lam again moved in a spectacular way. He had been closely watching one of the leaders of a local political party. The man had been busy haranguing crowds and organizing support for a Buddhist struggle movement against the Saigon government. Acting on an informer's advice, Lam had the man seized at his home, where a quick search revealed correspondence which identified the prisoner as a member of the Viet Cong Current Affairs Committee. Yet the prisoner spent less than a day in jail before his political friends convinced the district chief it would be unwise to press charges.

There the matter did not end. To teach Lam not to act so independently, the political party started a whispering campaign against him, alleging that he was in the secret employ of Premier Ky and the Saigon clique. These were serious charges, for the Saigon government was never popular in Lam's province, and if Lam was considered a spy for the Ky regime, many of his sources of information would dry up.

Lam's temper was quick, and when he heard what the local political party was rumoring about him, he barged into the district chief's office and laid down an ultimatum.

"Do you know what is being said about me?" he yelled. "That I work for Ky—that I am not loyal to my province. Those idiots out there would rather see the Viet Cong take this province than work together. They won't believe what their eyes tell them. Well, I'm not going to put up with it. Either you get them to shut up or I'm going to arrest the next politician who hints that I'm getting paid to spy for Saigon. And if the arrest won't stick, I'll cut his tongue out before I let him go."

"You can't," the district chief replied. "And I can't. Neither of us is powerful enough. Let it die down. It might be better if you worked somewhere else for a while."

"Like where?"

"How would you like to go home to Binh Nghia? Your mother would be glad to see you. I gather you didn't stop by to say hello when you went in after Truong My."

"What are you driving at?" Lam asked. "You know I wouldn't last half an hour in the village without troops. And you don't have troops good enough to clear that village."

"I may have," the district chief replied. "Younger Brother thinks he can get some American Marines. The Americans don't like Viet Cong in the village right at the end of their airfield. They will help us if we send in some police and organize a militia. If you want, you can be in charge. It's up to you. It's your village."

Major Richard Braun was called Younger Brother by the district chief whom he advised. Although an affectionate term, it signified that the adviser was in the position of learning, not teaching. Braun didn't mind, since he had no intention of meddling in the Byzantine politics of the Vietnamese. Instead, he took pride in his thorough knowledge of infantry tactics. Every outpost in his district was registered to receive illumination and artillery support. He knew whom to call for night medevacs. He kept close liaison with the neighboring American units.

Braun's reputation for effectiveness attracted senior officers. In early June of 1966, Lieutenant General Lewis W. Walt visited Braun. Walt commanded the Marines in Vietnam, a battalion of whom were working in Braun's district, which was called Binh Son.

Binh Son is far from the seats of Vietnamese power. It lies in Quang Ngai, the southernmost of five violent provinces called I ("Eye") Corps, three hundred miles to the north of Saigon and four hundred miles to the south of Hanoi. Quang Ngai is one of the few provinces in North or South Vietnam where, even in times of peace, the population has had to struggle against starvation. Unyielding jungle and sharp mountain ranges penned the rice farmers and their families along the narrow green plain bordering the sea, where there was not enough land for a growing population.

Hunger fed politics, and in 1930 famine struck Quang Ngai when a high wind washed the rivers across the rice crops and drove the fish from shore. The French colonial government allowed the local Vietnamese satraps to collect their normal rice taxes from a starving people. Secret antigovernment societies flourished during the next ten years, and the people strongly supported the Viet Minh in their struggle against the French after World War II.

In 1960 the Viet Cong movement started to gain momentum, and four years later the Viet Cong could realistically claim control over most of Quang Ngai's villages and over all the jungle, allowing their main forces to establish a huge base camp in the mountains. The main VC forces then turned on the South Vietnamese regular forces. The latter, so organizationally muscle-bound that they had been unable to wrestle the guerrillas for control of the rural population, found they lacked the strength to win the conventional battles they had been structured to fight. In a series of brilliant battles and marches, the Viet Cong main forces bloodied and befuddled the Army of the Republic of Vietnam (ARVN) units and threatened to seize the capital city of Quang Ngai.

Against that background came the introduction of American combat troops into southern I Corps. Near Quang Ngai's northern border, in Binh Son district, stretched a barren coastal sand spit four miles long. There in March of 1965 troops from the 1st Marine Division splashed ashore unopposed and began to lay the steel matting for the jets which would fly in close support of the infantry. During the next year the Americans built and expanded their airfield, called Chulai, and clashed with the Viet Cong main forces in several sharp but inconclusive battles. In the populated sections of Binh Son and other districts, the Marines built battalion outposts. General Walt made it a habit to ask district advisers like Braun what he thought of the U.S. battalions.

Braun told Walt that the Marines would be more effective if they worked with the Vietnamese instead of just beating the bushes on their own looking for the VC. Walt asked for a specific recommendation.

"Well, General," Braun replied, "I'd like to see us try a combined unit, a group of Marines and Viets who would eat, sleep, patrol and fight as one unit—not two."

"If you had them, where would you put them?" Walt asked.

"There's a big village not far from here. It sits along a river which the Cong use to move supplies back up into the mountains. As a matter of fact, it's just south of Chulai airfield. The government forces were chased out of the village a couple of years ago. A platoon of Cong live there regularly now, and sometimes a company or more come in to resupply or rest."

"Why pick there to start?" Walt asked.

"I didn't, sir. The district chief did. He has this outstanding police chief who's being bad-mouthed by some of the local politicians. These pols make the Mafia look like a bunch of Trappist monks. The district chief's afraid this police chief will say the hell with it and transfer to another district. But his family's from this village and his mother still lives there. The district chief says he'll stick around if we make a play for that village. The police want some Americans along if they're going in there. They don't think too much of the local troops in this district."

"How many Marines do you want?"

"The police chief would like a full squad, sir, between twelve and fourteen."

"I'll see that he gets them," Walt replied. "By the way, what's the name of that village?"

"We call it Been Knee-ah, sir."

The residents of Binh Nghia lived in seven separate hamlets, four of which were called Binh Yen Noi and three called My Hué. Sometimes the villagers distinguished numerically among them by referring to My Hué 1 or My Hué 2, etc. It is a large village, encompassing four square miles of land, bordered on the east and south by a tidal river, and on the west and north by an expanse of sand dunes. While the village is clean and neat, its five thousand inhabitants are not rich. The soil is shallow and sandy, and in the fall the brackish overflow from the river leaves a salt crust upon the rice stalks. The scrub grows spindly and keeps the cows and other foraging animals thin. Fish is the final foe of famine for many villagers, but the sea bottom is sandy and weeks can go by without a good catch.

Binh Nghia belonged to the Viet Cong. By 1964 the National Liberation Front was the full-time government in five of the village's seven hamlets and controlled boat traffic moving toward the fishing beds at sea. The village chief and hamlet elders walked three miles each afternoon so they could sleep inside the district compound. In the fall of the following year came the Big Flood of I Corps, an inundation by the rain and sea which exceeded any catastrophe in living memory. Binh Nghia was cut off from outside military aid as bridges were washed away and roads flooded under. The regular military forces of the Saigon government were occupied with guarding and repairing the district towns and the province capital city, leaving the village militia to cope by themselves. Two strong local-force Viet Cong companies roamed from outlying hamlet to hamlet, village to village, destroying or dislocating the Popular Forces (PF) militia and declaring the villages liberated. Binh Nghia proved no exception. By 1965 the government of South Vietnam (GVN) had conceded all its seven hamlets to the Viet Cong.

Not so the two dozen militiamen whose families still

lived in the village. With no place to go and no reason to run farther than they had to, they had flocked to the top of a steep hill surrounded by open rice paddies, about a half-mile outside the village. During the daytime, when there was some assurance of reinforcements from the district, they would dart forward, nosing around the edges of the nearest hamlet, sniping at any exposed VC cadres. At night, knowing they were without support, untrained and cherishing no hope of success, they abandoned the village to huddle at the top of the hill. There they awaited the night when the enemy, annoyed by their pestering defiance, would choose to accept the dozen or more casualties necessary to assault and finish them.

To the men of the 1st Marine Division who were stationed in the district, Binh Nghia was just another village, with nothing peculiar to mark it. If the Marines approached on a large-unit sweep, they would find no traces of the enemy. If they happened to pass through one of its hamlets on a small patrol, they would likely receive some harassing fire from distant treelines. The villagers were uncommunicative, but not sullen. Among the Americans, Binh Nghia had no special reputation.

Still, when the call went out for volunteers to live with the Vietnamese forces in the village, the response was enthusiastic. General Walt had asked the commander of the Marine battalion in the district to select twelve men. The first rifle company polled produced over one hundred volunteers. The primary reason was comfort. For the Marine riflemen, assignment to the village would be an escape from the routine harassments of duty in a rifle company. Many thought they would be out of the dust or mud. They would sleep on cots instead of the bare ground. There would be no more jungles to hack through or mountains to climb—no more leeches, vipers or trench foot. There would be no first sergeant barking at stragglers. Life in the village would be sweet and easy. Or so it was rumored.

General Walt had laid down two stipulations concerning the volunteers. First, they had to be seasoned combat veterans. That was not a difficult requirement to meet. The Marines had been fighting the 2d NVA (North Vietnamese Army) Division on and off since midspring, and most of the riflemen had been engaged in at least three rough operations. Second, Walt asked the battalion officers to send only men who could get along with the villagers. Major Braun had been emphatic on that point, and it slowed the selection procedure. It took eight days to pick twelve men. The officers were aware from their own surveys that over 40 percent of the Marines disliked the Vietnamese. The problem was particularly acute among the small-unit leaders—the lieutenants and sergeants—whose opinions had considerable effect on their men. In addressing the problem, the Marine command had written that its surveys "suggest that of our squad leaders graduating from NCO Leadership School less than one in five marches (*sic*) forth with a positive attitude toward the ARVN and PF, and that probably one-third go forth with a strong dislike for the local people. This is not just academic. It is costing us lives."

The noncommissioned officer chosen to lead the volunteer squad was known to like the Vietnamese. His name was William Beebe and he was a career Marine. Only twenty-one, he had been in the service for four years, although he was still a corporal. Of medium build but with powerful, tattooed arms, Beebe was a scrapper and a stickler for alertness in the field. On large-unit sweeps, his squad frequently took the point and scouted ahead, with

Beebe easily distinguishable from his men by his habit of shouting and waving his arms. He was forever signaling his men to spread out and pay attention to where they were walking.

But Beebe had another side. He disliked rules and details, and somehow he could not imagine himself making out pay rosters and guard rosters and equipment rosters the way the first sergeant did. When not on an operation, he would run the risk of buying a bottle of local whiskey for his squad. Hard liquor in Vietnam was against regulations, and Beebe had been caught and fined more than once. While his tactical performance was excellent, his relaxed attitude toward garrison regulations had prevented his promotion to sergeant. The village volunteers thought they had the right kind of leader in Beebe. Life in the village would be sweet and easy.

# 2

On June 10, 1966, a dozen Marines left behind an American base camp with its thick barbed wire and canvas cots, solid bunkers, soupy ice cream and endless guard rosters, and went to live with some Vietnamese in the Vietnamese village of Binh Nghia.

Their destination that day was the stumpy hill where the village militia, called Popular Forces or PFs, huddled each night. The Marines never climbed that hill. At its base, they were met by Lam, who had with him fifteen police and eighteen PFs. Lam had decided to abandon the hill outpost because it took twenty minutes to walk from there to the nearest hamlet. With the arrival of the Marines, Lam felt his force was strong enough to move closer to the village.

The police chief had selected as his new headquarters a three-room adobe villa which sat at the outskirts of the third and largest of the hamlets called Binh Yen Noi. The villa, which had been deserted by a rich landowner in 1950 when the Viet Minh had first taken the village, looked south across a wide expanse of paddies. Its back-yard was a short expanse of shrubbery which ended near the back door of a thatched house.

After explaining that the first order of business was turning the villa into a fort, Lam asked if the Marines could provide the necessary materials. Beebe replied that he personally could requisition none, and since his company commander was leaving shortly, tiny supplies requested by the company would take weeks and perhaps months before arriving. Unfazed, Lam said they could build their own defenses without outside help. He promptly called a meeting of the villagers, explained that his men and the Americans had come to stay, and asked for volunteers to build the outpost. About forty villagers responded, a majority of whom were related to the PFs.

Beebe expected the police would force the other villagers to cooperate. Instead, Lam himself set to work and his men followed. All that first day under the hot sun the combined force and the villagers toiled, digging a wide moat around the villa, filling sandbags and propping them up as an inside wall, splitting sections of bamboo into thousands of short, sharp stakes and studding the moat walls with them, erecting a high, spindly bamboo fence thirty yards outside the moat on the theory that the wood would cause the premature detonation of recoilless rifle rounds aimed at the fort. They worked with shovels, hoes, axes and knives. Slats were not nailed to the rickety fence; they were tied with bamboo cord. The mud scooped out of the moat served both to fill the sandbags and to cement them in place. Several Vietnamese, obviously specialists at the task, were busy sinking a deep well in what had been the courtyard of the villa. Boys and some young women spent the day shuffling back and forth from the nearby treeline to the open fort, carrying buckets of fresh water. The boys liked to follow after the Americans, although they would jump to carry water to any policeman who shouted at them. They paid no attention to the local PFs, however, and dawdled when asked to bring them water. It was obvious the villagers did not respect the Popular Forces.

At twilight, Lam called a halt to the work. Most of the villagers went home, the women in one group shuffling ahead to prepare the evening meal, the men in another group ambling slowly behind and talking animatedly among themselves. A few women stayed at the fort, bustling about in a clatter of pans, shrieking to each other, preparing fires and setting plates down in the dirt. Then they, too, departed and a quiet peace fell over the scene, as the men scooped rice and chunks of meat from the simmering pots and sprawled among the sandbags to enjoy the evening meal. There was no wind and the crickets were starting to chirp. Across the paddies in front of the fort the sky was pink and red and soft.

While the Marines enjoyed the meal and the sunset, Beebe conferred in private with Lam. By the time he rejoined the Marines, several of them had fallen asleep.

"Let's wake up," he said. "Here's the word. We're expected to go out tonight. The police will pull guard here. All we have to do is patrol with the PFs."

"All?" Lance Corporal Gerald Faircloth said. "All? We

spend the day like a bunch of ditchdiggers and now we're supposed to have patrol duty at night too?"

"Shut up, Faircloth," Beebe said. "We haven't been here long enough for you to start bitching. The police aren't infantry. They can take care of the fort, but that's all. It's up to us and the PFs to handle the patrols. Anyways, only four of us have to go out tonight. You're one of them."

"Is that supposed to make me feel better?" Faircloth asked.

Faircloth was a hard young man, not given to smiling or socializing easily. He stayed to himself and bothered no one. And on the other hand, no one pushed him. Tall and wiry, he had the hand-and-eye coordination of a basketball forward. He was an expert with a LAW, or Light Anti-Armor Weapon, a three-foot piece of fiberglass tubing enclosing a self-propelled rocket which could stop a tank or blow up a bunker. On operations, Faircloth had been his company's antibunker specialist. Beebe wanted Faircloth along on the first village patrol.

For the patrol's point man, Beebe selected Corporal Phillip Brannon, an experienced tactician with an outgoing personality. Unlike Faircloth, Brannon enjoyed joking and horseplay and by his grinning, gangling manner invited practical jokes and childish horseplay. Not that he was all fun and games. He claimed that back home in West Texas he had hit a running jack rabbit at seventy yards with a .22 rifle, and those who had watched him fire his M-14 automatic rifle believed him. Not that Brannon was given to bragging. Self-deprecatory in his humor, he had the knack of communicating with the Vietnamese despite a limited vocabulary. Brannon loved to pantomime, and by exaggerated motions of clumsiness and wry expressions of face, he evoked the language of laughter. But Beebe had

not placed him at point because he made people laugh;
Brannon walked first because he carried a fast rifle.

Beebe himself was going on the patrol, and PFC L. L.
Page pestered him to be the fourth Marine. Page was the
youngest of the group, of average height and less physically tough than most of the volunteers. Beebe felt responsible for him. Page had desperately wanted to go to the village, and Beebe thought it was a good idea because Page,
with his unassuming manner and lack of egotism, wore
well in close quarters. Beebe had argued with the battalion
officers that he could teach Page tactics while they were in
the village. So Page went on the first patrol.

Wanting the PFs to make a good impression, Lam had
asked Nguyen Suong to go on the patrol. The Popular
Forces had no formal rank structure and the district chief
had never even appointed a leader for those at Binh Nghia,
supposedly because he did not want to waste a good man
on a suicidal assignment. Suong had gradually emerged as
the unofficial PF leader. Of medium build and mean eyes,
Suong was distinguishable mainly by his gold front tooth
and the sharp creases in his green utility uniform. His neat
dress deceived the Marines.

"He doesn't look like a field soldier to me," Brannon
said. "He's too clean."

Lam insisted otherwise.

"Well," Beebe said, "let's get going and find out what
has people so shaken up about this ville."

The four Marines stood in a group waiting while Suong
talked rapidly and forcefully to two PFs. The PFs were
shaking their heads and replying nervously, but Suong
kept jabbing his finger at them and answering in strong
tones. Beebe looked quizzically at Lam.

"Those two have not seen much combat," Lam said.
"Suong say to them that they be safe with Marines."

Finally, one of the PFs walked reluctantly past the Marines and stood in front of them. He was to be the guide. Brannon stepped up behind him. Each time the PF would turn nervously around, Brannon winked and smiled. The PF did not seem encouraged. Beebe stood behind Brannon, followed by Suong, Page, another PF and Faircloth.

"Di-di," Beebe said, gesturing at the point PF.

In the dimming light, the patrol passed through the incomplete breastworks in front of the fort onto the main path which led eastward straight across open paddies for a quarter of a mile before turning north and disappearing into a black mass of trees which surrounded the hamlet of Binh Yen Noi. The same treeline paralleled the path all the way to the fort, passing not thirty yards to the rear of the moat. But before entering cover, Beebe wanted to see how the patrol looked in the open.

It looked miserable, more like the parody of a heel-and-toe race than a combat patrol. No sooner had the PF at point struck the main path than he hurried eastward at a pace better suited to a cross-country race. Brannon tried to keep up, while at the same time juggling his equipment to keep it from rattling, forcing his gait to have the grace of a drunk ostrich. For the first few steps, Beebe had held his pace to a crawl, placing his weight carefully. Before he could adjust, a fifty-yard gap had opened between him and Brannon, whom he could barely see. Fearful of having the patrol split into two segments less than a minute after leaving the fort, Beebe broke into a trot, the speed of which increased for each man back in line, finally forcing a flabbergasted Faircloth to run as fast as his legs would carry him to join up with a column rapidly disappearing into the darkness. Hearing the footsteps pounding up behind him, the point PF broke into a run to stay out in front, where he assumed he was supposed to be. With momentum begetting more momentum, the patrol was thundering toward the black and ominous treeline with all the stealth of a berserk elephant, the equipment of the men jingling and jangling with every step.

"Catch him, Brannon, catch him," Beebe wheezed.

"Catch him hell," Brannon panted back. "It'd be a lot easier to shoot him."

"What's the word for 'stop'?"

"I don't know. But I know the word for 'water.' Will that help?"

"Screw it. Hold it up. I'm not going up against that treeline like this."

The two Marines jogged to a halt and leaned forward, hands on knees, to catch their breaths. Suong came panting up, followed at a few seconds' interval by each of the other patrol members.

"I don't believe it," gasped Faircloth, trying to untangle the straps of two LAWs from his neck. "I just don't believe it."

"What'll we do now?" Page asked. "Go back in?"

"Go back?" Beebe replied. "Page, you're out of your gourd. We just came out. I'll camp out here before I'll go back and face those others. We can't go back in. We'll have to wait."

The men sat down along the side of the road and waited. Five minutes passed, ten minutes.

Brannon spoke. "Don't look now but here comes Native Dancer. Walking. Slowly walking. Vee-re slowly walking. Like he's all alone and doesn't like it."

Up the path from the treeline, in a half-crouch, with his rifle at the ready, came the PF point. He was moving slowly and making no noise.

"Now that's good movement," Brannon said. "He does everything right. He just does it sort of backward."

Suong went forward to talk with the point. When he came back, he pointed at the treeline and whispered, "VC, VC."

"I think it's a crock," Faircloth said. "He's just trying to cover up for that guy screwing up."

"You're probably right," Beebe said. "But at least Suong's taking point. Let's go."

They entered the treeline, and the visibility dropped from fifty feet to five. Houses were spaced near the path, which was overhung with coconut and banana trees and bordered by thorn thickets and broad-leafed shrubbery. In places the vegetation so overgrew the path that no light from the sky entered, and in those black tunnels each patroller proceeded by sound and guess only. He could see nothing.

Suong moved quickly, too quickly for the Marines, who feared an ambush at any second and who were sure that the noise of their passage was traveling ahead of them. Once in the hamlet, the PFs wanted to stay close enough to the Marines to touch them at all times. If a PF felt a gap was opening between him and a Marine, he would run to close it, heedless of the crackling branches breaking under his feet.

After several minutes, Suong turned off the trail where there was a gap between two houses and waited until the others were bunched close behind him. Then he dropped to his hands and knees and crawled forward until he had passed the houses and was kneeling at the edge of a clean-swept backyard. After motioning Beebe to creep alongside him, he stabbed his finger toward the other side of the yard.

Understanding that they had arrived at their ambush position, Beebe gestured to Faircloth and Brannon to lie down between the PFs facing the yard. He motioned to

Page to twist around and watch the direction from which they had just come. Beebe and Suong lay side by side in the center of the small line and waited.

From the houses around them, they heard the murmur of voices, the clatter of pots, and occasionally the sharp, hacking coughs of the sick. Lights from the fires and the lanterns in the houses winked unevenly at them. The air close to the ground was windless and musty, smelling of decayed leaves, old fires and many humans. Without wind, the mosquitoes were hovering around the men, probing for a piece of skin where sweat had wiped away insect repellant, their buzzing near the ears a distraction from concentration on the job at hand.

So Beebe never heard the Viet Cong. He would never have seen them either had Suong not suddenly begun nudging him hard and pointing across the yard. Where Beebe had been looking blankly for an hour, he now thought he saw a shadow move. Straining to mark the spot, he slowly started to lift the rifle to his shoulder when a noiseless figure darted across an open corner of the yard and disappeared behind a house. Thoroughly startled, Beebe half-rose to his knees and his rifle barrel clanked on the ground. At the sound, a second figure appeared where the first had just been and disappeared in the same instant.

That was all. Nothing more untoward occurred during the patrol. But it was a shaken group of Marines who returned to the comparative safety of the fort.

"How'd it go?" a Marine asked when the patrol returned.

"Unbelievable," Beebe replied. "The PFs can't move and we can't shoot fast enough. I can see now why the PFs are scared shitless to go out there. It was like playing a game of blindman's buff, only the other guy can see. I don't know who we're up against, but they're good, man, they're very good. It's their turf."

"I still get shaky thinking of those first few nights," Beebe said later in an interview. "I had had a lot of stuff thrown at me in my year in Vietnam. Those guys I brought down to the fort had, too—at one time or another we had been pinned down in the paddies, mortared, had those B-50 rockets go whooshing over our heads, even gone after 50-caliber emplacements. It was nothing compared to that ville. That was the most scared I've ever been in my life. The PFs would be shaking. You'd reach out and you could feel them quivering. But they'd go as long as we did. Well, not always. Of course, there were times when I didn't want to go myself. Nobody did. You had the idea the VC were fussing with your mind, that they knew exactly where you were, that they could read the label on a suit in a dark closet."

# 3

The days quickly took on a routine, with activities following a regular pattern. The fort took priority at first and consumed much energy and attention. Within three days, however, the defenses were basically complete, although no credit was due to technology, not even barbed wire. The fort could have been built the identical way a century before.

Once the digging was finished, the men gladly laid aside their shovels and devoted full time to their combat tasks. The Marines were uncertain of their PF allies and frightened by their unseen adversaries, but there was not one of them who wanted a steady diet of digging. To them, the village night patrols brought an element of excitement and physical challenge not unlike a strenuous athletic contest. These men knew the results of firefights—the splayed bodies, the sobbing cries, the gritted curses—but they would rather face the chance of death than fill sandbags all the dull day long.

The police wanted no part of the night patrols. Although well trained and not afraid to run ambushes, they left such military chores to the Marines and the PFs. When it could be avoided, Lam preferred not to run a random chance of losing one of his police. His men were day people, specialists in the intelligence rather than the operational field of war. They were in the village only temporarily, and far enough overstrength in number to keep them safe while they were there.

The police were not so much interested in the enemy soldiers as they were in the people who connected the VC with the villagers and in those who supplied intelligence, food and recruits for the VC units. To combat their enemies, the police relied chiefly on the unraveling method. Once one enemy agent was captured, it was hoped that he would divulge information leading to someone else, and so on. But the Viet Cong did not oblige by organizing their apparatus in such a simple and vulnerable way. In their first four days in the village, the police questioned over fifty suspects, acting on gossips and tips provided by the PFs, their families and friends. Not one arrest was made, as Lam quickly discovered that all known Viet Cong had left those hamlets close to the fort. Only the part-time helpers and sympathizers had remained behind and, although the PFs disliked them, the police were not interested in them. Some such Viet Cong sympathizers were questioned and some were beaten, but all were released.

Lam was convinced that the only real enemy left during the daytime in the Binh Yen Noi hamlet near the fort were secret cadres whose identifications were not known to the villagers. It was rumored that the known village Viet Cong had been ordered to the hamlets of My Hué, four kilometers northeast of the fort. There they would be safe during the day and could roam throughout the village at night. The Viet Cong so dominated the three My Hué hamlets that any stranger ran the risk of being denounced as a GVN spy. The villagers were organized into committees, the better to watch each other while working for the common cause of the National Liberation Front. A local guerrilla squad kept a twenty-four-hour watch on the approaches to the My Hués, and fired warning shots when GVN forces came near.

About a week after the fort was built, Lam directed a raid against My Hué. He selected a secluded spot on the main trail to the marketplace and at night surrounded it with police, Marines and PFs.

When the villagers passed by in the morning, they were met by the police, who took them into a small ravine, asked a few quick questions and searched those who seemed suspicious. It was two hours before news of the dragnet drifted back to My Hué and the traffic ceased. By then the police had questioned over two hundred people and had taken grenades or small-arms ammunition from thirty.

Some of the ammunition had been intended to resupply a Viet Cong company operating outside the village, although the amount captured was too small to have any combat significance. Lam was also sure none of the porters was a high-ranking cadre. The VC did not risk their leaders so casually.

The thirty captives were bundled into boats and taken downstream three miles to the district headquarters, where the district chief gave them the choice of one month in jail or ten days at his indoctrination center, which he called "political education sessions," a technique he had learned while a Viet Cong commander. All chose the indoctrination center.

And after ten days of GVN lectures, discussions, harangues and exhortations, the odds were that at least two or three of the villagers would return to My Hué in the secret political or financial employ of the district chief. This compromised all of them in the eyes of the Viet Cong, and finding thirty replacements to run the risk of another police check point would not be easy. Lam knew, however, that the Viet Cong would nevertheless replace their losses, and would keep on replacing them after each police raid. The raids only bought time, while affecting the localized perceptions of the villagers concerning the relative strengths and chances of success of the two opposing sides. Sooner or later, GVN forces would have to attempt to enter and hold My Hué, not just cut it off from the outside.

The police believed that the Viet Cong, for their part, would have to attack the combined unit or lose influence among the villagers. Lam was convinced that enemy scouting parties were circling close to the fort each night. The local schoolteacher, Ho Chi, claimed that many of the children told of hearing Viet Cong soldiers nightly passing near their houses in the hamlet.

A short, wiry man with a toothy grin, Ho Chi was fond of practical jokes, with a complaisant Brannon as his special butt. Twice Ho Chi's size, Brannon would respond to a prank by seizing the schoolteacher, forcing him to the ground and sitting on him. This was the signal for the PFs to assault the big Marine, who lost ten wrestling matches in ten nights before refusing to play the game any more. Ho Chi's English was scarcely better than Brannon's pidgin Vietnamese, and on top of that he was a notorious liar. Even when he did understand what he was supposed to say, he frequently would say something else and twist a conversation beyond unraveling. He was the only man in the fort who could make Lam laugh.

The Viet Cong were the one subject concerning which Ho Chi could be relied to talk with rigid honesty. So great was his fear and hatred of them that sometimes his voice would shake during a translation. A bachelor, Ho Chi had lived alone with his father near the tiny schoolhouse, just off the main trail three hundred yards west of the fort. One night, a year earlier, the Viet Cong had entered his house looking for him. He was not there, for rarely did he dare go home in the evening. His father, however, was there, and they killed him. Ho Chi said they acted out of anger and frustration. There was no reason for them to kill his father. After that, Ho Chi had slept in the district compound until the arrival of the Americans, when he, along with about a half-dozen village and hamlet officials, decided it was just as safe for them to sleep in the fort and cut out the long commute to district. Ho Chi said he was not a brave man, and he was petrified at the Marines' teasing efforts to drag him outside the fort on one of their night patrols. Yet, six days a week, he walked down the road to his schoolroom and taught the children, an act for which he was marked for assassination.

Less than a week after the Americans had come to the village, Lam told Ho Chi to tell them that they, too, were marked.

The Marines laughed. What was surprising about that?

"No, no," said Ho Chi. "It is not just fighting. The VC are paying for your heads."

"You mean, my head?" Brannon asked, gesturing with both hands grasped around his throat.

"Yes," said Ho Chi. "That's it. VC pay five thousand piasters for you, much more for Lam," he giggled.

"I'm worth more than you make in two months, Ho Chi," Brannon teased. "Maybe you take my head, huh?"

Ho Chi did not want to joke. "Some PF are VC."

The Marines looked around. Lam and the PFs who were listening nodded their heads. Brannon seized Ho Chi by the shoulder while pointing across the paddies toward the small stream.

"VC right there, Ho Chi?" Brannon laughed. "VC right in front of fort? Maybe VC looking at us right now, huh?"

Brannon meant no harm by the remark, intending by a preposterous exaggeration to break the tension, expecting Ho Chi to swat him and initiate a wrestling match which would divert the attention of the combined unit.

Instead, Ho Chi replied, "Yes, there are VC there."

"Oh hell, Ho Chi, right in front of the fort?"

"Yes. VC. VC."

"Bullshit. I'll walk out there right now and prove there ain't no VC."

"No you won't, Phil," Corporal Franklin Lummis cut in. "You're not leaving this fort alone. I got the first patrol out. As soon as it gets a little darker, we'll walk down there together."

A short, muscular young man, Lummis had grown a thick, black mustache which greatly impressed the Vietnamese and gave him a threatening appearance and the occasional nickname of "Pancho Villa." Lummis had a dry, cryptic sense of humor, which the volubility of the amiable Brannon gave him the occasion to exercise. The two frequently worked together.

"I'll go along, too," Corporal Paul Fielder said. "I have

the late watch and I don't think I could get to sleep anyways."

Quiet and steady, Fielder had the trust of all at the fort. Despite his tall size and husky build, he did not throw his weight around even when provoked. He did his work without being told, and if there was another chore that he saw before anyone else, he did that too. Fielder was well on his way to becoming the second-in-command of the Marines at the fort. He was also the most anxious among them to go home, to his wife and newborn son.

"I want one more Marine on that patrol," Beebe said. "If Lam thinks there are Cong close to the fort, we'd better play it safe."

"I'll go," PFC John Culver said.

The Marines' nickname for Culver was "Combat," in reference to the ironic contrast between his open, round face, which was more boy than man, and his wild nature in firefights. There was no doubt about it: Culver liked to fight. Only, he didn't think. Sometimes he hadn't backed off, even when his squad was badly outgunned. He also liked to play poker, at which he invariably lost. Culver needed a type like Lummis or Fielder to steady him.

The patrol set, they settled down to wait for dark. Twilight was the best time of day at the fort. The heat which burned a tanned man's skin went with the sun, and although the mugginess remained behind, there was a faint breeze just steady enough to blow away his sweat, provided he did not move. After the night's assignments had been made, the Marines would collect their combat gear and sprawl out on the trench walls to oil their rifles and recheck tracer-laden magazines and rest their full stomachs. While waiting for their patrols to leave, they would doze or exchange small talk and joke with the PFs. From dozens of houses in the treeline behind the fort would drift the faint smell of cooking fires, and now and then the exasperated shriek of a harried mother calling for her child would reach the fort.

"It's time," Lummis said.

A simple patrol. Four Marines and two PFs. Out from the fort, straight across the paddies two hundred yards to the stream, a two-hour wait, and back in. Nothing to it. The Americans had now been in the village six days. This was the thirtieth patrol dispatched. The patrollers doubted they would encounter any enemy so close to the fort.

Walking on the paddy walls without any sort of concealment, they crossed a series of three rice paddies, each the size of a basketball court, and reached the stream bank. Parallel to the stream ran a low, thick dike, built by the farmers to prevent flooding in the paddies. The tide was out when the patrol reached the dike, and there was a four-foot slope from the paddy down to the water's edge. The routine ebb of the tide permitted vegetation exposure to the sun, and a narrow belt of swamp plants and mangrove trees ran from the edge of the dike down and out as far as the high-water mark, a distance of some twenty yards. The massive water buffalo, driven to the stream to soak after plowing the nearby paddies, had, by their bulk and daily habits, trampled clean a small swath in the swamp's undergrowth. From the edge of the buffaloes' inlet, the stream could be seen fifteen yards away, with a sand bar jutting up farther out in the river.

Lummis led the patrol over the dike and into the dark hollow of the inlet. It may have started as a lark, as a means of showing Ho Chi, the schoolteacher, that there was no bogeyman, but in the dark next to the water with the bushes rustling and clouds crowding the sky, the patrollers forgot the light mood in which they had left the fort.

Lummis set them in fast.

"I'll put the PFs on the left," he whispered. "Brannon, you and Fielder peel off right. Culver and I will take the middle."

A storm was coming. The wind was rising, blowing into their faces and humming against their ears, blotting out the ordinary night sounds and making it impossible to hear a soft footfall. The broad leaves on the thick shrubs were scraping against one another. The bushes were dancing and bobbing and swaying, giving the image of men leaping up and ducking back down. The wind was whipping across the stream and tiny wavelets were lapping and popping at Lummis' feet.

To his right Brannon had crawled atop the dike wall. There he lay in the mud on his stomach, his automatic rifle resting on its bipods in front of him, his chin propped on his fists. Below him, Fielder sat with his back resting against the dike wall, his head at Brannon's elbow, his rifle pointed into the dark swamp, so close at hand the muzzle could touch the bushes.

The rain started. At first a light spattering, followed by a steady downfall, and finally a heavy, continuous sheet of water. It seemed the raindrops were attached to each other in steady streaks, like from the faucet of a shower, slanting down with enough wind-given force to sting the cheeks of the patrollers and force them to squint and shield their faces. The nearby bushes quivered and sagged as the branches tried to shake off the tormenting streams of water. The din of the rain beating on the undergrowth, splatting in the mud and murmuring in the guzzling paddies, drowned the ears of the patrollers. They could not hear. They could not see.

Then came a white gash of close-passing lightning and a roaring clap of thunder over which a man's shout could not be heard. The cacophony of the elements decided Lummis. He pivoted around, with the intention of gathering his men and going back in. And there was Brannon on the dike, propped up on his elbows, his rifle stock against his cheek, his silhouette appearing in the lightning blazes. Like a pointer on a bird, he was frozen on the dike, with his taut body in a puddle of mud and water, most of his weight supported by his arms, leaning, straining forward, willing his body to melt and mold into the stiffness of the rifle's wood and steel.

Lummis froze. And without words, the message communicated to the others. In the lightning, Brannon had seen something move farther down the dike. Rigid as stone, he held his fix. Fielder rolled on his shoulder, to shield one ear from the rain, trying amid nature's sounds to distinguish a man's noise. Brannon broke his point momentarily to tap Fielder on the head and gesture at the swamp, then reset his bipods so that the rifle muzzle was pointing past Fielder's nose at the bushes.

The ambushers were being stalked. In the first flash of lightning Brannon had seen a man crawling up the dike, with others crouching some distance behind him. Having seen Brannon at the same instant, the crawler had rolled off the dike into the swamp, with his men following. The patrollers now had to wait out their enemy. To back off into the open paddies would invite attack, and the enemy could fire first from behind the protection of the dike wall. Minute after minute, the patrollers waited motionless, knowing that the enemy did not know exactly where they were, gambling that they could still get off the first bursts of fire.

As quickly as it had come, the thundershower was passing overhead, taking with it the intermittent light and part of the din. The rain slowed but still pattered on, and the wind stopped gusting and blew fair and steady. Lummis began to wonder about Brannon. He knew it was irrational to relax just because the squall had passed, yet he felt himself doing so.

Not so Fielder. Half-sitting, half-squatting next to Brannon, his left leg had gone to sleep and he had a cramp in his right thigh, yet he refused to unbend or straighten up. Listening for a careless foot in the swamp, he had twice heard a cracking sound like wood breaking. With the wind bending the mangrove bushes, he was not sure enough to act on the sounds. Still he knew it was not his imagination, for after the second cracking noise he had heard Brannon click off his safety. Sensing that the enemy was coming, Fielder laid aside his rifle and took a grenade from each of the breast pockets of his green jungle jacket. He took one of the hand bombs and quietly slipped off the elastic which was attached for added safety around the base of the spoon. Next he peeled off a piece of Band-Aid which held down the pull ring and kept the grenade from jingling when he walked. Finally, he pulled straight the bent-back edges of the holding pin and eased it halfway out of the grenade, so with a simple movement of his fingers or teeth he could complete the pull which would release the spoon and ignite the grenade's three-second timer. He repeated the process with the other grenade and sat there, listening, not seeing, a grenade in each hand, ready to go.

On the river, ducks and geese started squawking, the flutter of wings sounding quite close to the inlet. Within half a minute the racket died down.

Then it came, and only a professional could have called it a warning. The grenade was already out of the hand of the Viet Cong, already in the air, already seeking flesh and bone, when the slight pinging sound of the spoon flying loose traveled ahead of the thrown bomb and warned the tense Marines.

"Incoming!" yelled Brannon, his shout mixing with Lummis' scream of "Grenade!" and the patrollers were diving flat when a white flash whipped across their eyes. A sharp crack slapped their ears, followed by the bee hum of shrapnel sailing past before losing death speed and plopping down harmlessly into the paddy water behind them, like a handful of pebbles tossed into a shallow puddle.

Less than two seconds passed before Fielder shouted "Outgoing!" as he jerked at a loose pin and lobbed a grenade out and over the bushes around him, as if he were making a hook shot with a basketball. The grenade landed with a soft splat, and there was a delay of a few seconds marked by a quick rustle of bushes near where the grenade had hit. Fielder was in the process of pitching his second grenade when he heard the movement. Opening his palm, he let the spoon fly from the grenade, then lobbed it twenty feet at the sound. He had barely let it go when his first grenade went off, which in turn covered the sound of his second grenade landing. Its blast seemed to follow before the bushes had stopped dancing from the shock wave of his first grenade and Brannon was shouting.

"Beautiful—that was beautiful. Right in there. Right on the bastard. Beautiful."

Then Lummis was bellowing, "Brannon, shut up. All right, let's rip this place apart just in case there are others."

On both flanks, the Marines and PFs emptied magazines into the swamp. Red lines of heavy tracers cut back and forth through the bushes which stretched ten meters to the open river.

After about ten seconds, they stopped firing. Someone cursed. The clatter of empty magazines being changed drowned out his voice.

"Knock it off and sit still. Listen for them," Lummis said. "We probably got that one, so listen for groans. Anybody hit?"

"Yeh. Culver took some shrapnel. No big thing though. It hit him in the head."

"Wha-at?"

"I don't feel too bad," Culver spoke up. "But I'm bleeding like a stuck pig. I caught a piece in my forehead."

The sound of the firing had carried clearly to the fort and Beebe had immediately called the nearest artillery position, asking for illumination. While Lummis was bandaging Culver's head, the first flare blossomed over the patrollers.

"Look," said Brannon, "there's a boat."

Beached on the sand bar not fifteen yards out in the stream was a round wicker-basket boat. One or two Viet Cong had been paddling downstream under cover of the storm when the bank had suddenly erupted with fire. They had then beached their craft. The Marines did not know whether they were lying flat and unseen on the sand bar or had swum off.

"Hose down that sand bar," Lummis said.

Fielder and Brannon began firing, the red arcs of the tracers skimming across the water, a few hitting rocks on the sand bar and angling off in wild and spectacular flight.

"How's Culver?"

"He'll be O.K. There's blood all over him, but he was only nicked."

"Another Purple Heart the easy way," said Culver. "One more to go and I go home."

"Hey," Brannon shouted, "let me try for that boat with a LAW. I never get a chance to fire one."

"All right, Brannon," Lummis answered, "but don't screw up. It's our only LAW."

"Relax, I'm a pro," Brannon said. "Watch this."

Brannon extended the LAW and knelt in the inlet near the spot where the incoming grenade had gone off. Sighting in carefully at the round wicker boat not thirty meters away, he squeezed the firing mechanism. Nothing happened. He realigned and squeezed again. Nothing. He tilted the tube upward off his shoulder to inspect the faulty trigger. The LAW went off with a roar, the rocket streaking out across the paddies.

"Great shooting," Lummis growled. "That's gonna land in district headquarters."

The patrol leader walked to the water's edge with his grenade launcher. He fired once and the M-79 shell splintered the boat. "Let's go home," he said, "before we shoot down a jet."

"What about that guy in there?" Brannon asked, looking toward the mangroves.

"You want to go in there stumbling around looking for him?" Lummis replied.

"No."

It was raining again as the patrol turned back toward the fort and the men splashed noisily along the paddy dikes. By the time they reached the fort the flares had gone out. Beebe was waiting to debrief them and they clustered briefly in the courtyard, heads bowed, the water running in rivulets from the brows of their hats.

"That's it for tonight," Lummis said. "Let's pack it—"

He was silenced by the quacking of ducks in the stream not two hundred yards across the paddies directly in front of the fort.

"Son of a bitch," he said softly. "No sooner are we in than they move right in front of our noses. That really frosts me."

The squawking and fluttering of the ducks became

louder. Lam walked out into the rain and mud, clad only in his white underwear. Ignoring the weather, he stood listening for a moment before shaking his head and smiling at the disgruntled Marines.

"Tiki, tiki," he said. "Small. Not many, two, maybe four."

Lummis turned to Brannon.

"Want to go out again?"

"Sure," Brannon said. "Why not?"

"You can go out after the last patrol comes in," Beebe said. "But don't go farther than we can support you."

# 4

The patrollers straggled off to sleep. Ordinarily most of the Americans and Vietnamese slept outdoors on cots, air mattresses and sandbags, with the light breezes keeping away the bugs. But the rain had driven everyone indoors and the men were sleeping side by side in a hall about the size of a small living room. The air was dank and smelled of wet, dirty clothes and too many bodies.

Lummis found a niche by the door, shrugged out of his wet gear, took off his shirt and boots, lay down and fell asleep. At four, the Marine sentry came in search, tripping over men and shining his flashlight into several cursing faces before finding Lummis, who in turn woke Brannon. They put back on their sopping shirts and boots, struggled into their web gear heavy with magazines and grenades, threw two LAWs apiece over their shoulders, picked up their automatic rifles and walked out of the fort.

"We'll be in the cemetery, Theilepape," Lummis called to the sentry. "You'll hear if we get into it."

Cold, sullen, in ugly temper, Lummis walked down the trail toward a cemetery a quarter of a mile away. Brannon lagged several yards behind, watching their rear. The clouds had passed and the stars were shining down, bringing a brightness to the night and promising a brilliant dawn. They reached the cemetery and turned right, passing cautiously between the mounds of earth until they neared the bank of the stream where they had fought six hours earlier. Then they sat down some yards apart with their backs against tombstones and, with a clear view over the calm stream, waited to add to the dead.

For an hour they sat and no boats came by. Gradually it grew light, and in the hamlet to their left the fishermen stirred and emerged from their houses and began pushing their boats on wooden rollers toward the empty waters. They stopped momentarily when they saw the two ambushers looking at them, but then proceeded again, their bustle disturbing a huge rat who scurried along the high-tide mark in the mud past the ambushers. Brannon thought of shooting the rodent, but let it go lest the fort go on alert at the burst. They stayed past six in the morning, not from any hope that some bemused Viet Cong would paddle by in the light, but to watch the dawn come.

At the start of another day, Lummis rose to his knees, picked up his rifle and flipped the bipods back alongside the barrel. Seeing that, Brannon followed suit, and together they walked back out to the trail, bearing with them the stink of the muck and the bites of mosquitoes and chiggers. Lightheaded from lack of sleep, their movements were sluggish as they trudged back.

Just outside the fort's fence, they met Gerald Sueter, the squad's Navy corpsman. Since he had medical duties in the Binh Yen Noi hamlets each morning, he was not assigned any late-night patrols. Sueter's day started when many of the Marines were going to sleep.

"Since you two are up," he said, "why not come down to the market with me? You might be able to grab a hot bowl of soup for breakfast."

"That beats C-ration coffee," Lummis replied. "Let's go."

All three were fond of the early morning, before the heat. Since first light lifted the village curfew, they passed dozens of people, some going to work in the fields, others driving cows, some getting an early start to the district market. The Marines exchanged courteous morning greetings with the men. They said fewer words to the women, who always seemed in a great hurry, quick-shuffling along the trail with shoulders hunched under the weight of water cans or bundled firewood balanced on stubby poles. They refused to look directly at the Americans, although Brannon, in complimenting a few good-looking girls, set up a titter among some older women.

Clean-shirted children, happily forgetting they were on their way to school, were soon swarming after the Americans, gawking at Sueter's hefty size, trying to pinch the hair on Lummis' forearms and challenging Brannon to recite more words in Vietnamese than they could in English.

A few youngsters, mostly indentured orphans, did not attend school. These were the poor, illiterate buffalo boys in dirt-stained clothes who with tiny reed switches drove their enormous beasts to the hot paddies or the wide river. Whenever the buffalo plodded past, the Marines left the dung-spattered trail and stood well out on the paddy dikes, fearing the horned charge their strange American smell often provoked.

The Marines also stepped aside whenever they heard the jingle of a bicycle bell and with a wave of his hand a PF would pedal past, hurrying home from the fort to breakfast with his family and begin a day's work.

Or at least that was the government's plan for the Popular Forces: they would be primarily farmers or fishermen and only part-time soldiers. In Binh Nghia few PFs had the stamina to patrol and walk guard at night and then toil in the hot fields by day. Most needed to sleep sometime. Yet they were paid only part-time wages—$20 a month, half the wage earned by the police or the soldiers of the regular Vietnamese units. Most of Binh Nghia's PFs were lucky: they were bachelors. They could eat and sleep at home and use their meager salaries to buy cigarettes and beer—when they didn't gamble it all away. For those five or six PFs who were married, life was much harsher; not only did they have little money to spend on themselves, but their wives had to work doubly hard to support their families.

At a leisurely pace, the three Marines followed the main trail to market. East of the fort for a quarter of a mile their path ran straight, bordered on both sides by dark green paddies, before taking a sharp left turn and veering north when it struck close to a wide river called the Tra Bong. At the bend the trail entered a treeline, and for over a kilometer the trail was lined with cool thatched houses, separated by bramble fences and smooth dirt paths worn into grooves by generations of use. Interlacing the main thoroughfares were hundreds of less distinct tracks, the backyard roads beaten by the foraging domestic pigs, the cows and water buffalo plodding to and from their stalls, and the children playing among the houses.

The marketplace was a loose collection of a dozen wooden sheds without walls, jammed with women trading and selling rice and piglets and chickens and fish and fly-encrusted pork. Brannon and Lummis sat down at a food stall to practice their Vietnamese by ordering breakfast while Sueter was engulfed by a wave of potential patients. The three Americans stayed in the hamlet for several hours.

Such contacts between the villagers and the Marines were not unusual. During the daytime the Americans liked to get away from the confines of the fort and stroll in the Binh Yen Noi hamlets, which were considered relatively safe in full light. But at night no hamlet was safe and for the villagers there was the constant danger of being caught in the middle of a firefight in the dark. When they heard a night patrol passing, many mothers gathered up their families and went to sleep in their bomb shelters.

On the tenth day and the fortieth night patrol after the Marines' arrival, Corporal Leland Riley, a slender young man with pale, sharp eyes, was leading a four-man defensive patrol across the paddies in front of the fort. From the villagers, the PFs had heard that a large enemy force planned to attack that night. Beebe had sent Riley out to provide advance warning.

Riley was walking point along a low paddy bank with his men strung out behind him when he saw a group of figures moving toward him from his right.

"Down," he hissed, sliding down into the shallow water amidst the rice stalks so that only his head, shoulders and rifle showed above the bank.

The shadowy figures also stopped moving and started murmuring to each other in soft Vietnamese.

"VC," Riley said, and loosed a long burst from his M-14 automatic rifle. The Viet Cong sought the cover of another paddy dike and swiftly returned fire.

From the flashes of the weapons and the colors of the tracers—those of the Marines showed as red and the Viet Cong's white—the watchers from the fort could judge exactly where the lines were.

"Riley, hold your position," Beebe radioed. "I'll get artie. You just hold where you are."

Beebe called an artillery battery four miles away. He was specific.

"I have about thirty VC in the rice paddies at coordinates 589973. My patrol is one hundred meters east, so be careful."

A few minutes later, Beebe received the message, "Round on the way."

This was followed by the familiar banging sound of a shell impacting, but none of the Americans or Vietnamese in the fort saw any explosive flash in the paddies.

Beebe looked at Lam, who shook his head worriedly.

"Cease fire, cease fire. We lost your round," Beebe yelled into the radio.

"Watch it," came the reply. "There's a second one already on the way."

Crr-ump. A white flash followed by a shower of sparks burst from the dark treeline behind the fort.

"You stupid bastards," Beebe yelled. "You're three hundred yards short."

The firefight in the paddies sputtered out, as the Viet Cong, knowing their position was exposed, pulled off. But from the treeline behind the fort came the glow of a fire, and Lam took six PFs and ran to the spot.

Hit by one of the artillery rounds, a thatched hut was blazing. Of the family of five, three had survived, although wounded. The mother and her daughter had been killed. Beebe called in a helicopter to evacuate the father and his two boys. Lam told the villagers that he had been standing next to the Americans when they had called for artillery, and that he would have done the same. The error had not been made at the fort. But two women were dead because of firepower gone awry, and the black ashes of the house could be seen by patrols coming and going from the fort, a constant reminder which for seventeen months affected, if it did not actually determine, the American style of fighting in the village of Binh Nghia. The Marines saw too much of the villagers, and lived too closely with them, not to be affected by their personal grief. Besides, the Americans had to patrol with the PFs, whose own families were scattered throughout the hamlets and who were naturally concerned about the use of any weapon which might injure their relatives. The rifle—not the cannon or the jet—was to be the primary weapon of the Americans in Binh Nghia.

The morning after the artillery accident, Beebe was ordered to Marine headquarters at Chulai airfield to testify before an investigating board about the tragedy. When he returned to the fort, he saw a large crowd of PFs and Marines gathered outside the main room. He asked what was going on.

It was a simple story. Lam had gone out that morning to take his usual stroll through the hamlet in order to pick up pieces of information about enemy movement during the night. Upon being told that there were some Marines having breakfast at the marketplace, he had decided to walk that way and join them. He wasn't paying particular attention to his immediate surroundings. Suddenly a woman yelled to him to look out. Instinctively, he ducked just as a carbine cracked behind him. The bullet passed by his head, missing by inches. The sniper was crouched in a doorway only a few feet away, and as he tried to get off a second shot, his carbine jammed. Lam was on him in the same instant, pistol-whipping him to the ground and knocking him out. Lam had then carried the man to the fort and was now questioning him.

Inside, the hall which had been jammed with sleeping men the night before was now empty, except for a desk, several chairs, a table and two benches. At the desk sat Lam, his thin face so pale it seemed rubbed with chalk, and on the floor to his right sat a small man with a wispy mustache, clothed in faded black shorts and a black shirt. He looked like a meek and tired old farmer. His arms were bound behind him and there was a purple and red welt on his forehead and he was plaintively explaining something to Lam, who seemed to be concentrating all his attention on the fiberglass tube of a LAW which had been fired. As the prisoner babbled on, Lam picked up a knife, hacked off the front and rear sights of the LAW, then gently turned the smooth tube in his hands. Satisfied with how it felt, he bonked the prisoner over the head, almost playfully, as a teacher might rap an unruly seventh-grader over the knuckles.

The prisoner looked up apprehensively. Lam asked a question. The prisoner started to give a querulous reply. Wham. Without even looking down, Thanh smashed the man across his shoulder blades. The man stopped talking. Thanh repeated his question. The man started over again with his pat explanation. Wham. Wham. The tube smashed down again and again. The interrogation had begun.

Ho Chi watched the proceedings for several minutes, walked over to the group of gawking Marines and shook his head.

"Too tough," he said. "That man will not talk."

After beating the man for two hours, Lam came to the same conclusion. All he could tell the Marines was that he was sure the man was a long-time member of the Viet Cong Secret Security Section.

The man would admit nothing. Late in the afternoon, he was taken out of the village by four policemen. They didn't say where they were going.

Lam was worried. It was not just that someone had tried to kill him. That had happened frequently. What bothered him was his lack of information. The enemy appeared active and aggressive in the village, unafraid of the combined unit. Lam wanted to know what the VC leaders were telling their men, what their plan was for keeping control of the village, what sort of attacks he could expect.

# 5

Lam knew the man who could find out such information. He was Tran Quoc Phuoc, the district leader for the government pacification program. A natural politician, he was just the sort of man to hear and catalogue every rumor floating around the district. Phuoc wanted to run in the August election for representatives to the National Assembly in Saigon and was making a determined effort to get around the district and drum up support for his candidacy in the rural hamlets. But his travels were hampered by a lack of security.

Lam suggested to Phuoc that Binh Nghia, with its five thousand inhabitants, would make a better political base than the district town. Phuoc's wife and daughter lived in Binh Yen Noi and he could see them every day. He would have Marine or police protection if he wanted to visit dangerous hamlets like My Hué. In return, Lam was interested only in what Phuoc might learn about the Viet Cong.

Attracted by the prospect of votes, Phuoc agreed to come. He brought with him twenty RDs, or Revolutionary Development workers. According to a government theory, the RDs were to help the villagers in their daily work tasks while convincing them that they should be openly loyal to the GVN and uncooperative with the VC. Although the RDs carried weapons, their task was not to beat the enemy by force. They were supposed to show the villagers that the Saigon government cared for them and that the Viet Cong were to be shunned. The theory called for the PFs to protect the RDs.

Within a few days it was apparent that the RDs were of little use. Few of them were from the village, many were in their teens and none was married. In trying to direct their efforts, Phuoc frequently looked like an exasperated Boy Scout master with a high-spirited troop. Send the RDs to work in the fields, and he would find them trying to coax the girls into the bushes. Set them on their knees in the hamlet to plant small vegetable gardens, and they would sneak off to an abandoned hut to drink beer. Scatter them at night in four-man teams among the houses of Binh Yen Noi to trap VC, and, if they felt it safe, they would cluster together, light a lantern and play cards. If they heard a suspicious noise, they would blow out the light and remain huddled together, inviting a grenade. Good-natured young men by day; frightened children by night.

Their leader was different. Phuoc was in his thirties, a pleasant, intelligent man who knew the people and the Viet Cong. Tactics and fighting did not interest him. The second day he was in the village, he suggested that his men be combined with the PFs under the leadership of the

Marines. Phuoc's talents lay in talking and listening, a business to which he devoted most of each day. He believed he could outthink the Viet Cong, and that the people would warn him of their approach. So, like Lam, he would stroll around the hamlet in the early morning, talking with the farmers on their way to the fields and stopping by the market to gossip among hundreds of women who congregated there. Unlike Lam, he carried no weapon.

The night patrols remained the responsibility of the Marines and PFs, and Beebe usually let the patrol leader choose his own men. It was generally agreed that Brannon's patrol group was the best, because it had Luong. Nguyen Van Luong did not look impressive. He had a flat face, slightly protruding teeth and a squat body scarcely taller than his M-1 rifle. He was middle-aged and had fought for the Viet Minh against both the Japanese and the French. He drank too much and hated to farm or fish. But he could worm his way through a dry thicket without breaking a twig and he could spot a Viet Cong on nights so dark other patrollers could not see the man in front of them. Luong loved to play jokes, and that was what attracted him to Brannon. In turn, Luong's reputation attracted followers among the PFs. In particular, the younger of two brothers named Khoi attached himself to Luong. Khoi was a pleasant, unobtrusive youth and Luong didn't mind his company.

About four nights after the arrival of Phuoc and the RDs, Brannon's group was slated for a short patrol through Binh Yen Noi. Beebe had decided to go with them. While waiting to get started, Brannon was, as usual, clowning with Luong. This annoyed Beebe, who was phoning in the patrol route to company headquarters.

"Brannon," Beebe yelled, "why don't you and Luong get out of here? Go play in a paddy or something."

Unfazed, Brannon replied, "O.K., we'll start heading toward the ville. You and the others can catch up. Let's di-di, Luong."

The two best shots in the combined unit left, and Beebe leisurely finished sending in his list of map coordinates. Brannon and Luong had been gone fully five minutes before Beebe took Khoi and started out after them.

Wanting to overtake Brannon before he reached the shadows of the hamlet treeline, Beebe moved at a fast clip, with Khoi lagging behind. It was cloudy, but there was enough light to see about fifty yards out into the paddies. Beebe was not worrying about security, since Brannon was somewhere on the road out in front.

Brannon and Luong had walked away from the fort side by side, wisecracking and goosing each other with their rifle barrels. Both came alert as they neared the dark tree-line. To their left were paddies, the trees were in front of them, and the cemetery marked by grass lumps and white tombs lay to their right.

"Dung lai," Luong said.

Brannon stopped. Luong was backing up. No lights and no sounds were coming from the hamlet. It was too early for such quiet. Luong saw movement behind a gravestone. Squatting, he fired. Brannon flopped down on the trail beside him, and brought his automatic rifle in line to follow Luong's tracers. The rounds pinged off the tombstones and clattered skyward. Panicking, a man left the shelter of a tombstone and stood erect to run. The bullets drove him down dead. A weak return fire rattled harmlessly back from among the graves. They heard Beebe coming up behind them at a run.

"Let's move in," Brannon yelled. "There are only a couple of them."

The three patrollers started into the cemetery, alternately dashing forward, flopping down and firing. Fire from the graveyard had stopped. Concentrating on where they had last seen the flash of a weapon, they ran right by an enemy soldier lying flat in the weeds.

Khoi was late coming up, and he didn't know what to do. He stood there, all alone in the road, listening to the bursts of fire and the shouting of his companions. Unintentionally, he was blocking the escape route of the enemy soldier. So the soldier shot him three times in the back.

At the same time, the sentries at the fort started firing at shadows and Brannon and Luong spent several minutes shouting in their respective languages back to the fort for a cease-fire. During that time Khoi's ambusher slipped off. He made a run of it straight across the paddies, and despite the barking of several weapons he got safely away. It was not until the firing had ended that Luong found Khoi sprawled on the road.

Marine headquarters was concerned about the incident because the division's intelligence section had translated some enemy documents which singled out the combined unit in Binh Nghia as the principal target for attack by VC district forces. In addition, the village guerrillas were ordered to seek contact against the Marine night patrols. This order went contrary to established Viet Cong doctrine, which was to avoid fights with strong forces and not to use guerrillas in steady combat. The enemy documents thus explained why the Marine night patrols were shooting or being shot at every night; they also indicated that the combined unit was weak, and could be destroyed piecemeal outside the fort.

Phuoc had more information. He had listened to what the villagers were saying after the death of Khoi and,

putting that together with what Lam had picked up, concluded that the Viet Cong had marked Binh Nghia for a
special effort. The reasons, he told the Marines, were personal as well as military. Binh Nghia bordered the Tra
Bong River, which the enemy used regularly to transport
rice and other materials. The Marine patrols were threatening this supply route. Perhaps more importantly, the
presence of Lam and the Americans had enraged the Viet
Cong district committee. In May, Lam had to sneak into
the village. In June, he could casually stroll through the
central marketplace. And all he had for backing was a rag-
tag outfit which included a handful of Americans. The
entire force scarcely outnumbered the Binh Nghia guerrillas, and directly across the river the Viet Cong kept a
main-force battalion. The situation was intolerable. A
dozen Americans could not just move in and live among
thousands of Vietnamese and call a village pacified. The
district committee had to defeat the attempt and disprove
the theory that a few Americans could work among many
Vietnamese. They had to strike at the fledgling government effort in Binh Nghia lest it become the first in a
series. The Americans had to be forced out. The combined
unit had to be destroyed.

Phuoc said the local Viet Cong were tough and well led.
The VC district chief was Le Quan Viet, a curt, hard man
with one arm who for a decade had ruled an area across
the river called the Phu Longs. In 1964, Quan Viet's name
had become known throughout the district when he captured the final five government-supporting hamlet chiefs
on his side of the river. For a week he displayed his captives in a series of hamlets, and then one noon in the main
marketplace of the Phu Longs he beheaded all five. In
Phuoc's opinion, if Quan Viet and his council were determined not to lose control of Binh Nghia, then the death of

Khoi was but the first of many. Phuoc was to be proven correct.

On June 20, Lummis drew the early-evening patrol. With him, he took two PFs, plus Combat Culver and Larry Page, who usually patrolled under Beebe's personal guidance. It was to be a short patrol, due back before midnight. At dusk, the patrol crossed the moat at the front of the courtyard (the fort's only entrance and exit), and cut back along a narrow paddy dike to enter the treeline immediately behind the fort. Taking a side trail, the five men moved slowly until they reached a spot where two paths crossed. There they spread out in a semicircle and settled down to wait. To see better, most sat up. Page was considered luckier than the others; he had a coconut tree against which he could prop his back.

It was a quiet evening and they were close to the fort. The hours passed dully. Lummis dozed off a few times, each time jerking himself awake, aware that if he were slipping off to sleep, the others were too.

Perhaps they were asleep, or perhaps those awake could not hear the bare feet in the hard-packed dirt of the trail. None saw the enemy soldiers. Yet suddenly they were there in the midst of the patrollers. Lummis came alive first, giving a startled grunt and swinging his rifle upward at a figure standing next to him. The enemy leaped backward with a yelp, and for a few seconds the chaos was total as a dozen rifles exploded in a circle not twenty feet wide, with the patrollers firing up and the Viet Cong shooting down and some enemy soldier screaming at his men and Lummis yelling, "Stay down! Stay down and fire high!"

It was over in seven seconds. No more firing, just the quick fading of running feet, and silence.

"Sing out," Lummis said quietly. "Is everybody O.K.?"

The responses came back from the dark amidst the metal whackings of magazines being changed.

"I didn't hear Page. Page. Page? Page, answer up."

Nothing.

Lummis crawled over to the coconut tree. Page was still sitting upright. Lummis' order to get down had come too late for him. The youngest of the Marines was the first of them to die.

The Marines named the fort after him.

For a while after Page was killed, the night patrols did not venture farther from the fort than half a kilometer. This upset Lam, who insisted that it was up to the Marines and the PFs to dominate the night. If they could not, the village would remain under Viet Cong control. No police work, no RD promises, no political popularity of Phuoc, could compensate for the lack of military superiority within the seven hamlets.

Beebe agreed to push the patrols, but privately he doubted if the patrols could move as far as the My Hué area at night, let alone ever see the PFs fulfill Lam's expectation of controlling those three hamlets. Although they had been patrolling with the Marines for a few weeks, the PFs still hung back, a sure sign of how they rated the Marines in comparison to the VC. Far from inspiring confidence, the Marines seemed to be acting as a magnet for increased and more effective enemy violence. The RDs and the PFs and the police had seen no proof that they were safer for the presence of the Marines. And the people in the village had scarcely been affected by the Americans. A few villagers were richer for selling beer. That was all. The PFs, lacking any sort of military training, did not know how to move or shoot. What they did know, they had learned by trial and error, and many of their tactics minimized the short-term risks of death while ensuring an eventual total defeat. By coughing and kicking their feet on patrol, they hoped the VC would hear them coming, and, fearing a larger force, let them pass unmolested. By bunching closely together, each had a chance, if the VC did fire, that the bullets would hit someone else. In return, the VC faced little danger that the PFs would hit them, a fact demonstrated when the Marines lined up the PFs for target practice and watched slack-jawed as they missed a mud dike five feet high at fifty yards. Not only had they never been taught how to shoot; they had not been issued any ammunition for practice. Thus those with experience, such as Luong, the ex–Viet Minh, were frustrated in their attempts to help the others. And above all, fear of the Viet Cong was close to paralytic.

Lam was relying on the Marines to provide the antidote to that fear, while the Marines were relying on Lam for leadership. Beebe was due for rotation, having been in Vietnam for thirteen months. He did not want to leave at such a time but was forced to choose between an extension and his marriage. He chose his marriage and expected to be leaving within a few days. Lam promised to help his successor in whatever way he could.

The police chief had undertaken a propaganda campaign to convince both the villagers and the PFs that the deaths of a PF and an American had not weakened the resolve of the combined unit. The government forces had come to stay. Although Lam gave his pitch at the village marketplace and in the hamlets, many villagers expressed skepticism, since government forces rarely patrolled farther than the hamlet nearest the fort. So Lam called a meeting of the hamlet chiefs, most of whom he had recently appointed, to discuss better patrol schedules and other means of protection. To demonstrate the degree of his confidence, he invited the officials to come not to the fort, but to his mother's house, where they could discuss the matter over morning tea.

The night before the meeting, Beebe sent patrols through the hamlets of Binh Yen Noi every two hours. None made contact. The next morning the villagers went about their routine chores in a routine manner, a nearly infallible sign that no Viet Cong were lying in ambush near the meeting house. Still, Beebe offered part of his squad for bodyguard duty, but Lam refused, saying that since there was no danger it made no sense to show fear of the Viet Cong. Those hamlet chiefs who had not stayed overnight in the fort would have to travel unescorted from the district town. Lam said the least he could do was walk alone from the fort to his own house. After all, every morning he made his rounds alone. Beebe complained that every morning the police chief did not tell people which house he would be visiting the next day, as he had in this case, and still the Viet Cong had nearly succeeded in killing him.

Lam went alone and nothing happened. It seemed Beebe had worried for nothing. Lam's mother had risen early to reclean her spotless house, set out cups and biscuits, and prepare a thick, tasty soup for her son's guests. The officials arrived early and by nine o'clock Lam and his eight guests were engrossed in a spirited conversation, while Lam's mother puttered about in a back room.

Next door, a four-man VC assassination cell from the district Security Section was hiding. By different paths they had pedaled to that house the previous day, all posing as farmers. They had remained there overnight, the homeowner later pleading that they would have killed his entire family had he betrayed their presence.

At nine in the morning, the four men left that house and swiftly approached Lam's back door. Each carried a pistol.

Lam's mother saw them coming and shrieked an alarm. At her yell, the men sprinted forward.

Lam was the only armed man in the house. As his guests leaped toward the windows and front door, he drew his revolver and crouched to fire. He just wasn't fast enough. The Viet Cong came through the door too quickly and all were firing as they came, while Lam had waited for a clear target rather than risk shooting his mother. There were other men still in the room, clawing to get out the windows, but the Viet Cong paid them no heed. Every weapon was firing at Lam, and even after he went down the four Viet Cong converged over his body and stood shooting the corpse. Then, for good measure, they dropped two grenades next to Lam's body and ran out the back door. The blasts knocked out one wall and collapsed part of the roof. Lam's body was totally mangled.

When the police and Marines arrived, neighbors had already dragged Lam's stunned mother from the wreckage. In deep shock and grief, she could tell them nothing. But the villagers said the killers had bicycled toward My Hué. It took an hour to gather a large enough force to enter that hamlet, and when the angry police did push in, hoping that someone would fire at them, all they met were frightened villagers who claimed the four men had crossed the river to the safety of the VC stronghold called the Phu Longs.

The next day, in an impressive ceremony, the villagers buried Lam in the cemetery near the fort. Beebe missed the funeral. He was flying home. With Lam dead and Beebe gone, only Phuoc remained as the symbol of leadership within the combined unit, and he had no interest in military matters. The district chief was considering withdrawing the unit before more men were killed and the villagers who attended Lam's funeral were plainly frightened. The Viet Cong were claiming victory. Within a week they had killed three times. They had butchered the strongest man in the combined unit in his own house. It was obvious who held the initiative.

Before he left for the airport, Corporal Beebe had given his commanding officer an end-of-tour report. It read in part:

> On June 10th, 1966 one squad of Marines from Company C, 1st Battalion, 7th Marines were picked to join the Popular Forces unit at Binh Yen Noi. It is obvious to those who have initiated and followed the PF program that it has been a success. Since the Marines have begun their instructions, the confidence and skill of the PFs have risen considerably. The PFs are now a well-organized efficient combat unit. This program has also strengthened the relationship between the Marines and the PFs and civilians in the area. The effect of this has been the strengthening of the defensive posture of the area.
>
> ROBERT A. BEEBE
> CPL USMC

The Viet Cong had a problem. In a war in which events were rarely significant in and of themselves, what counted were the perceptions of people about those events. The villagers and the PFs who knew the history of Binh Nghia could clearly see the power of the Viet Cong manifested in the deaths of Khoi, Page and Lam.

Not so the Marines. Ignorant of that history and of the nature of the war, volunteers for the Marine Corps and for Vietnam, veterans of dozens of firefights, volunteers for the village, it never occurred to them to view the blows as the brink of defeat. They were saddened and shaken by their losses, but, not knowing the past, they did not view the events as a prelude to the future. There is no evidence that at the end of June the Marines shared the Vietnamese view of the situation in the village.

# BOOK II

# NIGHT PATROLS

# 6

Sergeant Joseph Sullivan replaced Beebe as squad leader. A tall, proud man who had been promised a promotion if he performed well in the village, Sullivan fitted the stereotype image of the Marine NCO. He was strict, single-minded and dauntless. He was sure of himself and of his duties.

"The reason," he said, "most of the Marines volunteered to come down here—well, not most of them—all of them—is the excitement. And you have a sense of independence down here. There's no harassment and no paperwork. You're always in contact with the Viet Cong. You know you have a job to do. You go out at night and you do it."

Sullivan attributed the troubles at the fort to a lack of tactical aggressiveness and insisted that the unit carry the fight to the enemy. Instead of trying to defend the Binh Yen Noi complex of hamlets, the PFs and Marines had to launch patrols into the My Hué hamlets at the far northern end of the village and they had to ambush the river night after night. The Viet Cong had to learn fear and they had to learn they could not row supplies past the village. Then, Sullivan believed, they would leave Binh Nghia alone.

His first night in the village, Sullivan led a patrol to ambush at a river crossing. He weighted the patrol heavily with Americans—two PFs and six Marines. It was to mark Sullivan's style in the village. He did not like to rely on the PFs, and he found communications with them particularly hard.

"Sometimes," he said, "it is difficult to get the PFs to open fire on the VC. So we use the PFs as our eyes and ears. It is the Marines who do the actual fighting. You cannot always depend on the PFs to advance with the Marines."

Still, Sullivan put a PF at point in the belief that a Vietnamese soldier could spot a Viet Cong at night before an American could. At dusk, the patrol filed out of the fort, passing across the stagnant moat studded with bamboo stakes and through the tall bamboo fence.

The PF at point turned left and walked twenty yards to an outer fence. Three unarmed villagers, serving as gate openers and sentries, looked at them blankly for a moment. Then one noisily pushed open the gate; another lifted a wooden mallet and began tapping against a bamboo pole: tap—tap—tap—tap—tap—tap—tap. Supposedly, this was the villagers' signal that there were no Viet Cong nearby. If there were, the first beater to see them was supposed to change the tempo of his signal, and all other listening posts would repeat the warning. The Marines did not like the system and looked at each other uneasily, bothered by the racket of their exit. The beaters, from Viet Cong families, were impressed into service. Why they should risk their lives to warn a GVN patrol was beyond the understanding of the Marines.

In column, the patrollers moved east across the rice paddies and entered the main street of Binh Yen Noi. The street was a straight, narrow dirt path leading northeast, overshadowed by palm trees and thick brush and lined with thatched huts. The villagers were still awake and the Marines heard chatter from many houses. Lights shone from some doorways and fell across the street. The Marines hurried across these lighted patches.

The villagers knew a patrol was passing. It seemed to

the Marines that some warned the Viet Cong by signals. In one house, a man coughed loudly and falsely. Farther on, an old lady shifted her lantern from one room to another as the patrol neared, then shifted it again after the patrol passed. The PF at point hurried on.

"That really bugs me," PFC Sidney Fleming whispered to Brannon. "We should go in there and shove that lantern down her throat."

"The PFs must know what they're doing," Brannon replied.

"Bullshit. They're scared."

"So am I. You should be too. Some PF's liable to shoot you for a Cong."

A skinny, impressionable young man with a wispy mustache and jaunty air, Fleming believed the Viet Cong were invisible at night because they wore black pajamas. So on patrol he insisted upon wearing a black beret, black chinos and a gaudy black shirt with a button-down collar.

About two hundred yards past the marketplace, the path veered close to the river and the underbrush had been uprooted to shape a mud landing for sampans. As the patrol drew abreast of the tiny cove, they noticed a large boat beached bow first and lighted by lanterns which glowed dully. Three or four men, busy tossing sacks of grain onto its deck, did not stop their work or even look up as the patrollers filed by within thirty feet of them. The PF at point paid the scene no attention and hurried on into the darkness. The Marines did likewise, some shielding their eyes so as not to lose their night vision to the lanterns.

The patrol reached the far end of the town and for a quarter of a mile followed the dikes between open rice paddies, before turning right and walking about fifty yards to the river. The villagers used the area as an outdoor commode, and the bank was carpeted with human waste.

The patrollers settled down to wait. Droves of mosquitoes descended on them. They did not dare slap them away. A few unfortunates disturbed some red ants. They crept to other positions, cursing under their breaths and praying the ambush would soon be sprung.

The Viet Cong tried to accommodate the wish. No sooner were the Marines in position than firing broke out from the hamlet they had just passed. Green and white tracers streaked high over the Marines' heads. Sullivan identified the weapons.

"Automatic carbine. Two Russian blowbacks, an M-1. Lie still. Don't return fire. They're trying to get us to give away our position," he whispered.

The Viet Cong fired three bursts in the general direction of the patrol, then stopped.

One hour passed. The Marines heard a few splashes near the far bank but saw no movement. Downriver in midstream a light flashed on and off, on and off, in a slow, steady pattern.

"I'm going to nail that boat," Faircloth whispered.

"Save it," Sullivan whispered. "We want to get more than just a boat."

A second hour went by. More scattered probing fire came from the Viet Cong in the hamlet. Sullivan suspected the patrol might have passed an enemy outpost, which was now trying to locate the Marine position so their main force could avoid it.

"We'll hold here and hit the main body when they cross," he whispered. "We got a pretty good position here. It would take a couple of companies to get at us and I don't think they could do it even then."

During the next hour the Marines heard a few splashes downriver and saw a dull light bobbing along the far bank. By midnight, when the patrol still had not fired, the enemy lost caution and started to move freely. Frequent splashes and the mutter of low voices carried clearly to the Marines. There came the distinct clunk of a heavy bundle striking the bottom of a boat.

Corporal Riley, who had the sharpest eyes of the patrollers, whispered, "I see them. Two—three boats and a bunch of them on the bank—right across from us."

"Yeh, LAWs up," Sullivan whispered.

Faircloth slowly extended two rocket tubes.

"See them?"

"No," whispered Faircloth. "Wait—now I do."

"Fire when ready."

In rapid succession, Faircloth fired his rockets, the explosions slapping the ears of the patrollers and carrying across the water with a flat, plunking sound like someone striking an off-tune guitar string. Then came the chatter of the automatic rifles, as all six Marines started firing, placing their shot groups where they thought they saw or heard the enemy. Hundreds of red tracers skimmed across the river and swept the opposite bank.

Water splashed some Marines in the face.

"What the hell?" yelled Brannon. "Hey, we're getting some incoming."

But the return fire was too low to cause concern to the patrollers.

"Cease fire! Shut up and listen up," Sullivan shouted.

Silence. A few seconds went by. Then a distinct splashing was heard near the other bank. Someone was wading out of the water, trying to climb the bank. Riley and Brannon fired, their tracers converged, then swept back and forth. Again there was silence.

Next came a sound like paper ripping, followed by a loud pop. A flare burst over the river, and began its squeaking, dangling descent beneath a small parachute.

Having heard the firing, a sentry at the fort had called for artillery illumination from a Marine company outpost a mile west of the village. With the light, the Marines could see the other river bank clearly. Nothing was moving. The tall saw grass was still.

"Check those boats," Riley said.

Pulled up on the bank were two dark, canoelike shapes.

"Check them, hell. Blast them," Sullivan replied.

The other two LAWs were quickly opened and fired. The first hit to the left, but the second one exploded dead on. Short bursts from the automatic rifles further splintered the hulls.

The last flare died out. It was twenty minutes past midnight.

"We put a hurting on some of them," Brannon said.

"Let's head back in," Sullivan said.

Upon the patrol's return, a dozen men were waiting in the courtyard to listen to the debriefing. Most wanted to know about the firefight, and it was only in a passing comment that Fleming mentioned the boat.

"Man," he said, "I never seen a tracer like that warning shot that VC sentry fired off. It was sort of a light, eerie green and it just seemed to float over our heads, like a flying saucer."

"Where was the sentry?" someone asked.

"At the market. Near where a big boat was being loaded."

Nguyen Thang Thanh, who had taken over the police after Lam's death, had been slouching at the edge of the crowd, only half-listening. At the word "boat," he straightened up and seized one of the PFs, speaking fast and excitedly. The PF answered nervously and Thanh bore in, drilling him with question after question.

The next morning Thanh left the fort with a strong

force of PFs and police. They returned near noon, driving in their midst two men and three women, their faces bruised and their arms bound behind them. Throughout the afternoon Thanh methodically beat and slapped the captives.

It was the first time the Marines had seen Thanh in action. His arrival the previous day had created a stir among the glum police, who had nudged each other, giggled nervously and hastily straightened their uniforms. Thanh had spoken less than three sentences the entire day and had ignored the Americans. Over six feet tall, he was thin as a reed and wore black pajamas with sleeves too short, revealing knobby wrists and skinny forearms. His eyes were hidden behind glasses tinted smoke-gray and his walk held a slight mince. To the Marines, he did not compare favorably against their memory of the respected and courteous Lam. On his chest Thanh had tattooed the words "Sat Cong"—"Kill Communists." The PFs claimed the Viet Cong had slain his wife and all his children except one, a four-year-old boy whom he had brought with him to the fort and who knew how to shoot a pistol.

The Marines watched as Thanh beat his prisoners. When one woman refused to talk, he rubbed a wet cloth with lye soap and pressed it against her face. The woman struggled to breathe and sucked into her throat the stinging lye. He drew back the cloth before she suffocated, let her gasp for air once, then slapped the rag back against her face. Eventually, the gagging woman started to speak in sobs and Thanh extracted the information he sought.

He then explained to the Marines that the boat they had passed the previous night near the market belonged to the Viet Cong. When the patrol walked by, the enemy had been loading it with rice for their main forces in the mountains. The chore was particularly pressing since the Viet

Cong had the 3rd NVA Division to feed as well as their own. Thanh explained that members of VC committees had either bought and hoarded the rice themselves or taxed it away from the other villagers. Although the boat the Marines had walked by had drifted downstream unscathed, Thanh said the Marines' fire had destroyed two sampans and caused a third to overturn.

Of his five prisoners, Thanh believed none was valuable. They were only workers doing as they were told. The PFs knew them all. They came from two separate families, both of which had relatives in either the district or mainforce Viet Cong units. The only formal political ties to the Viet Cong to which any would admit was membership in 1964 in the Farmers' Liberation Committee. That was a totally harmless admission, since in 1964 the Viet Cong controlled the entire village and had organized the populace into a myriad of committees.

Satisfied he would learn nothing of further value from the five, Thanh put them in two sampans and sent them downriver to Binh Son with only one guard. There was no reason for them to try to escape. If they were successful, they could never return to their village and their families. The district chief, on the other hand, would lecture them for ten days at his indoctrination center and then let them go home. Once back in the village, they would thereafter be carefully watched by the PFs and their families. If there was among them a secret party member, he would continue to aid his cause. But as for the others—the peripheral helpers of the revolution—their usefulness to the Viet Cong was finished. None of them would want to be brought before Thanh a second time.

# 7

A few nights later Brannon wanted to return to the grave-yard where Khoi had been killed. Returning from two successive patrols, he thought he had seen movement in that area. Sullivan agreed to take a look and told Faircloth to bring his LAWs and join them. The sharp-eyed Riley volunteered, as did Luong. The sixth member of the patrol was PFC Fleming, dressed in his black outfit.

At midnight the patrollers went out through the squeaking gates and past the clattering beaters. They followed the trail for a few hundred yards before cutting right and tip-toeing along a paddy dike. Several times a patroller slipped off and splashed noisily into the paddy. To Luong and Brannon, running a tandem point, the splashes had the effect of fingernails being screeched along a blackboard.

"Nobody here but us Cong, Luong," Brannon hissed.

When they reached the burial mounds, the patrollers spread out in line, slipped off their rifle safeties, and in crouching postures slowly advanced. In less than a minute Luong was satisfied they were alone in the graveyard, and to communicate that fact he audibly snapped the safety of his M-1 back on and stood erect with the weapon over his shoulder, muzzle first. Exasperated, Sullivan insisted the Marines keep searching for another five minutes before acknowledging that Luong's judgment was correct.

The graveyard had been dug outside the Binh Yen Noi hamlet in a marshy corner between the Tra Bong River, which ran north from the district town, and a tributary stream which ran east past the fort. At the intersection of the streams, fishermen had built bamboo fish weirs. From the graveyard, three lighted lanterns were visible in the vicinity of the weirs. Although night lights on the river were forbidden since they could serve as beacons for the Viet Cong, some stubborn fishermen persisted and the PFs, knowing the economic necessity of night fishing, refused to enforce the order.

"As long as we're here," Sullivan whispered, "why don't we watch those lights for a while?"

The patrollers settled in behind the gravestones. If the Viet Cong tried to move up the tributary, they would have to pass through the weirs.

After an hour of waiting, the patrol was alerted by the disturbed squawkings of ducks and geese. Also hearing the geese, the tender of the lanterns on the weirs juggled and moved the lights. Next a light shone through a clump of bushes on the far bank and the Marines heard the dull sound of wood scraping against wood.

"They're carrying a boat over the fish traps," Sullivan whispered.

Riley had been watching to the rear.

"There's someone moving in on our right flank," he whispered.

"Cut him off," Sullivan hissed.

Riley and Brannon moved down the bank to prevent an enemy probe.

Faircloth was listening to the paddle splashes near the fish traps.

"I think I can hit that next boat when they climb the traps," he whispered, clutching his LAW.

"Go ahead," Sullivan replied.

Faircloth knelt on his left knee. He placed the short fiberglass tube on his right shoulder. The tube wavered up and down, then steadied. He squeezed the lever. Flame spurted from both ends. One hundred yards away there was a bright flash. The Marines started sweeping the river with automatic-rifle fire. Riley emptied a magazine into the bushes along the bank to his right. Overhead, a mortar flare blossomed.

"There they are," Riley shouted.

The firing caught two Viet Cong in a round wicker-basket boat trying to cross the river behind the fish traps. In the sudden light, they were easy targets. They dove overboard as Riley and Brannon opened fire. The tracers ripped through the boat and whipped the water. Standing on the bank, the two Marines changed magazines and waited to see if the Viet Cong would resurface. They did not. The light boat rocked to and fro. The surface of the river was calm and shone brightly under the flare.

"I guess that's that," Riley said.

Brannon did not have a chance to reply. Bullets hummed between them. Both were diving off the bank before they heard the sound of the machine gun. They sprawled in the rice mud behind the paddy dike. Without lifting his head, Riley yelled, "It's coming from the other side. They've got us spotted. Get them off us."

To the Marines crouching fifty yards away, the acrobatics had provided an interesting spectacle. Since their main position had not been seen by the Viet Cong, they were not under fire. Not wishing to expose their position by chancing a random burst of small-arms fire at the machine gun, Sullivan's group took their time preparing to open fire.

Faircloth extended another LAW. He gauged the distance at one hundred yards, under good lighting from the mortar illumination. Having hit point targets at two hundred yards, Faircloth was confident. He sighted in, then paused.

"So that's what they were doing in those bushes with a

light. Setting up a gun to cover their movement," he said, as if discussing a subject of purely academic interest.

"Come on, come on," Sullivan replied, before yelling to Riley and Brannon: "You two just stay put."

"I don't believe it," Riley groaned. "Will you guys fire?"

Faircloth fired. The explosion was muffled by the bushes. The chatter of the machine gun stopped.

"You two dingers can come home now," laughed Sullivan.

Crouching low, the two Marines trotted in from the flank. The patrollers formed a hasty circular perimeter, lay down and waited to trap any infiltrator who might have crept close during the firing. The last flare hissed out. For ten minutes they lay still, listening. They could detect no human movement.

Then from the weirs came a deep groan which floated across the waters like a distant ship's foghorn.

"My God," Brannon said, "they're rising from the dead."

"We'll see about that," Fleming replied, squirming to bring his weapon into a steady position. "Let's see how long the dead can swim with an assful of lead."

The groan turned into a cry like a dog wailing, then the wail stopped, to be replaced by a few words: "Nghia Quan—dung ban."

At the words, Luong who had also been waiting to shoot, jerked up and said urgently: "No shoot, no shoot. No VC. No VC."

Fleming relaxed his firing position as Luong walked to the water's edge and shouted. Out of the darkness a trembling voice responded. Luong shouted again, giving instructions. His voice was followed by the sounds of someone half-tripping over the wooden weirs, half-splashing in the water. A few minutes later a figure appeared waist-deep in the black water, hobbling painfully toward the shore, jabbering nervously all the while. It was a thin old man, clad only in tattered shorts. His body was lean and taut with lumpy, vein-striped muscles formed by decades of hard work. One calf was gashed and blood was streaming down his foot.

Luong knelt and peered at the wound under the feeble rays of a flashlight. Satisfied with the examination, he slapped the man encouragingly on his trembling thigh and swiftly bound the wound.

"That's a million-dollar wound the old man has," Brannon said. "Someone should shoot me like that so I can go home."

With Luong supporting the injured man, the patrol returned to the fort, where Sueter, the Navy corpsman, attended the fisherman. A tall, relaxed young man with a friendly bedside manner, Sueter laughed as the old man, who enjoyed being the center of attention, insisted on showing him how he wanted the bandage wrapped.

"It's a clean wound," Sueter said. "If he'd keep it dry, it would heal in a couple of weeks, but I know he'll be out on the river again tomorrow night."

"Not if Thanh has anything to say about it," Sullivan replied.

With his wound tended to, the old man had begun to scold the PFs, many of whose fathers he knew, for allowing the Americans to fire at the Viet Cong as they were crossing his fish traps.

But when Thanh stood before him, the old man stopped talking. As were some of his Viet Cong counterparts, Thanh was a fanatic. He pursued his cause of anti-Communism with the divine absolutism which characterized religious excesses in the Middle Ages. To him torture was a methodological problem, not a moral dilemma.

Softly the police chief began asking questions, abruptly dismissing many of the old man's faltering replies with a wag of his hand, as though he were brushing aside frost on a window, the better to see in. The old man talked and talked and talked, and Thanh listened and looked and probed. The others sat and listened, the Marines bored and yawning at what they could not understand, the PFs listening carefully and murmuring to each other.

The old man described the enemy troops who had crossed his fishing weirs. His description confirmed the report that the politician Phuoc had given to Lam a few weeks earlier: VC district force troops were moving into the village nightly to attack the combined unit. The district Party committee had agreed to devote a priority effort to its neutralization or destruction. Binh Nghia would be controlled by the Party.

Thanh told the old man to go home in the morning and to spread the word that the old ways were finished. The enemy's use of the villagers as signalers and porters must stop. A villager could continue to work for the Viet Cong, but he was now put on notice that the penalty could be death, as the Marines were instructed to shoot at anyone moving outside his house after curfew. There was no way the Marines could tell in the dark whether a person was a Viet Cong or a farmer forced to help the enemy that night. Thanh believed that the accommodation between the Viet Cong and most of the villagers was based, not upon political ideology, but upon the villagers' sense of self-preservation. The Viet Cong were stronger than the PFs, and it was wiser to obey the stronger side. He wished to upset that accommodation by weighing in with an outside force which posed the ultimate threat—that of death—to a villager who undertook the simplest act to help the Viet Cong, such as carrying a sack of rice or waving a lantern.

Thanh was partially bluffing. If a villager could be identified, as was the old fisherman, he would not be jailed, let alone executed, provided the police and the PFs believed he had been impressed into service by the Viet Cong. The villagers knew that once they could talk to the PFs, they would be safe. But Thanh was pointing out that there was little chance of talking with one of the American night patrols. For carrying a sack of rice, a man could die, not because the Americans wanted to kill him, but because they could not tell him from a Viet Cong in the dark of night.

The Viet Cong could not match that threat. For them to deliberately kill a villager who refused porter or signaling service would expose their own families to retribution. The choice was up to the villagers, and much depended on how active and aggressive they judged the night patrols to be.

# 8

Night after night three or four patrols went out, and night after night one or more of them made contact with the enemy. Each contact required a situation report, and every situation report was briefed to the generals at division and corps level. By mid-July, Fort Page was known throughout the high command as the scene of more night action than any other village in I Corps, and I Corps was the most violent area in Vietnam. Its reputation for contact was making the fort a celebrity stop, and in late July Marine headquarters wrote a capsulized history of the unit to pass out to high-ranking officers and visiting members of the press. The handout read in part:

> The PFs are now confident of their fighting proficiency and realize they are quite capable of denying enemy access to their hamlet. In short, they have come to realize the VC can be beaten and that they are capable of doing it.

Not all Americans shared that euphoric belief. The district adviser, Major Braun, was concerned with reports that as the Marines at the fort became more proficient in patrolling, they tended to shoulder more tactical responsibilities and to shove the PFs and even the police aside. Acting on Braun's concern, the battalion commander, Lieutenant Colonel John S. Woods, sent a lieutenant named Thomas J. O'Rourke to the combined unit. Ostensibly, O'Rourke would be in Binh Nghia to give tactical advice to Sullivan, not to command the Marines. Unofficially, Woods wanted O'Rourke to convince Sullivan and the others to work with the PFs and to make a report on the real situation in the village.

O'Rourke was readily accepted by the men. As the executive officer of Charlie Company, the unit which sat on the dunes behind Binh Nghia, he had known the Marines before they had volunteered for their independent duty. He had a reputation for tactical shrewdness, acquired by two years of infantry work in Southeast Asia. A former college halfback, O'Rourke was muscular and well coordinated, and in the field he pushed hard and insisted that his men sweat rather than take the obvious paths. But when not in combat he mixed easily with his men and could laugh at a joke about himself.

The night of his arrival, he decided to tag along on the

patrol Sullivan was leading. Nguyen Suong, the quiet PF with the gold front tooth, assigned the PFs while Sullivan selected the Marines. But when Suong called to one Vietnamese, Sullivan interrupted.

"Him number ten with Marines, Mr. Suong," Sullivan said. "Him no go with Marines."

"O.K.," Suong replied.

"What's the matter with him?" O'Rourke asked.

"Last night he was at point," Sullivan replied, "and he suddenly yelled 'VC, VC!' hit the deck and started blasting some bushes. So the Marines started firing too, including a machine gun and an M-79. After we had burned off a couple of hundred rounds, that idiot got up laughing and said 'No VC.' He pulled the stunt because he was tired of the patrol and wanted to go in."

"Is that all a PF has to do to avoid patrolling?"

"What else can we do?"

"Let's bring him and take along a tough PF who'll smack him if he goofs off. A couple of hours of sweating at point and he'll think twice about pulling a smart-ass stunt again."

"All right."

Suong was pleased by the reconsideration, since it would help him with discipline among the PFs. The reluctant patroller, whose name was Tam, was placed at point and O'Rourke took up a position right behind him, followed by Suong and Sullivan and several others. The patrol plan was to take the main trail into the Binh Yen Noi hamlets, past the market and on to an ambush site along the river.

In the open paddies just outside the fort, Tam moved slowly, giving each patroller time to shake down his equipment and adjust it against various squeaks and rattles. But when he entered the blackness of Binh Yen Noi,

Tam quickened his pace, seeking to escape the dark by running away. O'Rourke, holding to a slow tread, let him go. Tam did not go far. Within a minute he had scurried back to the cautious O'Rourke, frantically gesturing to him to walk faster. O'Rourke slowed down even more. For a few seconds, Tam stood rooted, terror telling him to flee that dark place, the shame of flight tying his feet. As the patrol fled past him, he made up his mind, and jumped into line just behind O'Rourke, giving the Marine the point position.

From inside a house, the sound of forced coughing reached the Marines. The patrol stopped. The coughing stopped. The patrol proceeded. The coughing started again.

O'Rourke stopped and turned to Tam, who shook his head and tried to push the lieutenant forward. The rest of the patrol came up and clustered around. The man coughed again, loudly, persistently.

"What do you think?" O'Rourke whispered, addressing no one in particular.

Suong spoke up, making no attempt to keep his voice low, acknowledging the patrol's presence had been signaled.

"Yes, yes. Very bad man. Number ten. Him warn VC."

"Let's take him in," O'Rourke said, gesturing as though he were grabbing the man.

"No," said Suong. "No good."

Tam nodded his head vigorously.

"That guy must have some clout if Thanh can't touch him," Sullivan said.

"Well, we'll make him a believer," O'Rourke said. "We'll put the fear of God into him, then he won't be so quick to spy on us next time."

Three Marines converged on the house, led by Lance

Corporal Robert Bettie, a tall, tough young man with a calm, self-contained manner. Bettie entered through the open front door. Inside the man calmly stood waiting. When Bettie hesitated for a moment, uncertain what to do next, the man spat out a window. Bettie swung, hitting the man in the face and knocking him down. He put his rifle muzzle on the man's chest.

"When Marines pass, you no talk, you no cough." Bettie made a loud false coughing sound. "You no warn VC no more. I come back sometime. I see."

It was doubtful if the man understood one word, but the message was clear. Bettie walked out of the house. Suong, who had been peeking in the doorway, was laughing.

Then ahead of them rang out four or five quick, insistent clangs from a metal gong, and the heavy tone rolled through the hamlet.

"I don't believe that," O'Rourke groaned. "Next, they'll be using sirens."

He paused, then: "Let's move."

"Still?" Riley asked.

"What did we come out here for?"

"Let me check with Top," Riley said. "She'll know if the Cong are in here."

"Good idea," said Sullivan.

Riley took point and led them down a side path toward the river, then turned left and crossed a paddy dike to enter a copse sheltering seven or eight houses. He walked up close to the house nearest the paddies and called in a low voice, "Missy Top? Missy Top?"

Vinh Thi Top was a cute eighteen-year-old girl with a pert manner and a quick smile. She had a full, well-shaped figure and often wore tight pants and a light, white cotton shirt. She never wore a bra and she loved to flirt and tease. Almost daily a half-dozen PFs and Marines swarmed around her house and her mother was quick to profit from her daughter's popularity. Top offered to do the laundry of those Marines who liked to hang around her house drinking beer and eating fresh peanuts. It was the mother who did most of the washing and pocketed most of the money, but everyone was satisfied with the arrangement.

Top made some extra money through sex, but she would go to bed only with men she liked and when she felt like it and asked no fixed price. She took what was offered more as a gift than as payment and sometimes a week or two would go by when she would sleep with no one. Any Marine was at a disadvantage in the competition for her favors, since he had to coax her to bed during the daytime, when it was hot and sticky, and the children were running about shouting and screaming, and no room had a lock and the PFs and other Marines always tried to peek in and watch and laugh. In that environment sex was limited, but the Americans liked to visit the homes of Top and other young girls anyway, just for the companionship and the escape it provided from the war which washed over the village at dark.

Top was one of the few villagers openly defiant of the Viet Cong. When she was fifteen, she had been kidnaped by the VC and forced to perform nursing duties in a hospital far back in the mountains. After several months, she escaped, only to be recaptured when she was within two miles of her house. But she persuaded her two guards to let her go before they had walked her back to the hospital. The district committee later punished the guards for immoral actions and ordered Top seized and returned to the hospital. But she proved too elusive. She never slept at home, and changed residence every night. Sometimes she would wait until dark before slipping into a friend's house, and the dusk patrol often passed through her front yard on the off-chance that she would still be home. If she was, she would whisper to them what she had heard passed from house to house about VC movements that night. It was an information technique the Marines had learned from the PFs, who had several such contacts in each hamlet.

Now at Top's house, Riley kept calling, "Top? Top?" while O'Rourke and the other patrollers stood back in the shadows and kept watch. Eventually, the thatched door to the house swung up and outward like a garage door and Top stepped outside.

"VC come, VC come," she said, pointing toward the marketplace. She placed her hand affectionately on Riley's arm, gestured to him not to shoot her, giggled and darted into the darkness down the path.

The patrol turned back toward the market. To get there they again had to silhouette themselves on the long paddy dike. They went across the open space at a jangling trot, forsaking quiet to regain some concealment.

Safeties off, they walked slowly up the trail, and when they reached the wide market, they spread out on line and gingerly moved across, ducking between the empty stalls, fingers on triggers, tense, waiting, expecting from somewhere a burst of fire or a hurled grenade.

Nothing. Through the marketplace, back into the dark, narrow trail, up through the hamlet and out into paddies. Nothing. Across a dry paddy and into the scrub growth along the river bank. Nothing.

O'Rourke was tense.

"Relax, Lieutenant," Sullivan whispered. "These people are always imagining there are Cong all over the place. All we have to do is watch the river."

Sullivan placed the men on line facing the water and motioned them to spread out and lie down. The night was dark with clouds and a boat could have passed by seventy yards from them without being seen. From the sounds, it was obvious that Viet Cong were on the river and on the far bank. The noise of loud splashes, as if someone had slipped off the bank, reached them and occasionally they heard the dull thunk of boat wood. Still, they saw no movement. One hour passed. Two hours. No one could pick up a definite target. Even Riley, squinting and bobbing his head, could not make out the boats he could hear moving in the shadow of the far bank.

Alone among the patrollers, O'Rourke had no concern with the river traffic. Worried about their rear, he had crawled forward to the river's edge, slowly pulled his body over the bank, twisted around and, half-lying and half-standing, set the bipods of his automatic rifle facing back across the paddy in the direction from which the patrol had come. Despite himself, twice he dozed off for a few seconds, lying in the soft, yielding mud with his head resting on his crossed arms. Each time he awoke in fear, imagining that a Viet Cong was standing just above him, about to shoot.

The second time he came awake, he peered at the shrubs along the trail with ferocious concentration, trying to squeeze the sleep from his brain. The harder he stared, the more he was certain two of the clumps were moving, yet so slowly that it was like watching the minute hand on a watch. So he fixed in his mind the location of the two objects, closed his eyes and held absolutely still for half a minute. When he reopened his eyes, the dark shadows were not where he had fixed them to be.

He looked around and saw none of the other patrollers. He had told no one he was shifting to stake out their rear, and now watching the slow stalk of the enemy, he felt more aggravated than afraid. The enemy was still over fifty yards from the patrol line, but if he fired, his tracers would pass by the unsuspecting Marines and they might fire back at him.

Riley solved his dilemma. Alerted by instinct, he had turned his attention from the river to look back over his shoulder. His eyes had immediately picked out the infiltrators and he glanced around to see if the other patrollers had spotted them. He could see only PFC Guadalupe Garcia, a shy, soft-spoken young Marine who was immensely popular with the Vietnamese. Riley crawled over to him.

"Lupe," he whispered, "they're behind us."

"I thought I saw something move back there about a half-hour ago," Garcia whispered in reply.

Both men rolled onto their backs and looked past their feet toward the paddy and the bush-bordered main trail.

"See them?" Riley whispered. To him the prone figures were easily distinguishable from the other shadows.

Garcia squinted and strained for several seconds before responding by holding up two fingers next to Riley's cheek.

"Yeh," Riley whispered.

"Better tell Sullivan."

"Sullivan hell. I'm going for O'Rourke. You watch those two and don't move."

As silent as a crab on sand, Riley scurried between the bushes along the bank to the spot where O'Rourke was supposed to be lying. It was empty. This made Riley stop crawling and cast his eyes about frantically for a few seconds until he saw O'Rourke's head and rifle. He crawled on his stomach up the embankment until his face was only inches from O'Rourke's.

"They're out there," he hissed, jerking his thumb over his shoulder.

By way of reply, O'Rourke only smiled and held up a

grenade. By now the other patrollers were crawling in toward the lieutenant, having seen Riley slip by. The activity among the patrollers alerted the two infiltrators, who froze among the shrubs. Blending with the dark shadows, they waited for the moment of danger to pass.

"Let me throw the grenade," Riley whispered.

"No," O'Rourke whispered. "Let them get closer."

"Aw, come on. I spotted them. Let me throw."

"All right. But let them move in first, so we don't miss."

Riley put down his rifle and picked up the grenade, holding it in his right hand and hooking his left forefinger through the pull loop. O'Rourke squirmed to snuggle his stock into his shoulder and placed his cheek along the wood of the receiver. They waited. Several minutes eased by.

Then, either having decided they had been detected or thinking better of their chilling game, the two shadows moved, fast and away. Riley responded while the two Viet Cong were still getting to their knees in preparation for their sprint to the rear. He jumped to his feet, jerked the pin and flung the grenade with the body motion of a javelin thrower. The Viet Cong were running at a diagonal to the Marines and Riley's excited throw carried the grenade right over the heads of the runners. O'Rourke let loose a long burst of tracers at the fleeing figures, and in three seconds it was over, with nothing to shoot at except blackness and the fading sound of fast feet.

"Damn," O'Rourke said. "I wanted them."

And with that he was off, weaving like the halfback he once had been, rifle held high, moving forward at a driving run to close behind the Viet Cong and cut them down. Sullivan up and moving. Then Riley. O'Rourke out fifty yards, seventy-five, one hundred. Down flat at a dike, rifle on bipods in front of him. Searching, listening, straining.

Nothing. Nothing but the hoarseness of his own breath and the pounding strides of the others coming up behind him. Sullivan flopped down, followed by Riley. All listened for a moment before admitting that the Viet Cong were gone.

"I think I hit one," Riley said.

"You mean you might have brushed one with that fast-ball of yours," O'Rourke replied. "The idea was to blow them up, not set a world's record for the longest grenade throw."

"Sorry, I got a little excited."

"No big thing. This ambush was compromised long before we got here. The VC were playing with us. We're just going to have to think these things through more. It's going to take more planning. Let's head back in."

When they returned to the fort, the Marine sentry yelled to Sullivan, "Battalion wants the report, ASAP, Sarge."

O'Rourke, distinctly out of spirits, said, "Let me have that damn thing. Horse Three, Horse Three, this is Charlie Five. Saw two VC, threw one grenade and fired sixty rounds. No friendly casualties. No enemy casualties. Over."

The radio sputtered.

"Horse Three, I told you what I saw. You can do what you want with it. Over."

The radio sputtered again.

"Aye-aye, sir. Out."

Garcia spoke up. "What did battalion want, Lieutenant?"

"They're claiming one VC probably killed and one wounded," O'Rourke replied. "The operations officer said no Marine can fire sixty shots at an enemy and miss."

# 9

By August the twelve Marines had engaged in seventy firefights and their dress reflected the experience they had gained. Brannon and several others bought camouflage uniforms sewn skin-tight so when they walked down a black trail their passage would not be betrayed by the swish-swish of pants' legs rubbing together. Sueter took to wearing black-and-green-striped shorts and a green T-shirt, paying in mosquito bites for his silent passage. Lummis favored Levi's and sneakers. Although no American could match Luong, who went barefoot whenever he had point, the Marines were improving. From the start, the Marines could shoot better than the Viet Cong. Long hours on the ranges of boot camp under the tutelage of stern drill instructors had seen to that. And after hundreds of patrols in the village the Marines were learning to move as well as the Viet Cong. The wish to keep on living was seeing to that.

Staying alive was a matter of minimizing one's own mistakes while capitalizing upon those of the opponent. Plus a little bit of luck and much common sense. Like the night O'Rourke tried to force the Viet Cong into error. He had a simple plan.

"Sullivan," he said, "I'll go out first by the main trail and set in near the market. You give me a fifteen-minute head start, then take the back trail up to the dunes. With both entrances to Binh Yen Noi covered, we stand a good chance the Cong will be tipped off about at least one ambush. If they are, they'll move in right by the other one.

When you get into position, fire a green flare. That way the Cong will think you're coming back in, but I'll know you're in position and it's safe to fire at anyone moving."

O'Rourke took Lummis, Fleming and two PFs and left the fort shortly after dark. The night was cloudy and the shade trees lining the trail beyond the marketplace cast the path in such pitch blackness that O'Rourke set his men in less than a foot from the trail. Lying on their stomachs, they waited, watching the skyline for the signal flare.

Fifteen minutes passed. A half-hour—forty-five minutes. No flare. An hour slid by. Thinking Sullivan had miscued, O'Rourke's exasperation grew to anger. He and his men would be forced to be in position all night, fighting off sleep and the mosquitoes, yet unable to fire even if they saw somebody.

He was bitterly musing on the stupidity of his position when the first of the patrol walked by. The man came silently up the soft trail and was standing directly above O'Rourke before the lieutenant heard him. Then he was so close that O'Rourke, looking up, could see his silhouette. He seemed too tall for a PF, and O'Rourke guessed Sullivan's delay had been caused by putting a Marine at point, who had become lost. The man glided cautiously on, and his place was taken by another figure, in turn replaced by a third. As the patrol passed, O'Rourke could easily hear the jangle of equipment loosely strapped to web gear, and such sloppiness increased his anger against the lost patrol. The patrollers were letting their point man do all the work. The others were just bumping along behind, making no special effort to be quiet. Not only that, but O'Rourke counted ten men and he had asked Sullivan to take out no more than six.

The last man in the patrol stopped to let out a smothered cough, his feet not a foot from O'Rourke's face.

O'Rourke had a strong urge to reach out, grab the Marine by his ankles, throw him to the ground and show Sullivan's entire patrol how heedless their passage had been. Only the fear that the Marine might shoot as he fell held O'Rourke back from tripping him.

The patrol passed on and O'Rourke waited for the green flare. Waited. And waited. No flare came that night, and at dawn O'Rourke led four furious and frustrated patrollers back to the fort. It was not yet six in the morning when he kicked open the door to Sullivan's private sleeping quarters and shook him awake.

"Sullivan," he said, "you're lucky I didn't kill you last night when you led that herd through the marketplace. And why the hell didn't you fire your flare afterward? My people were almost eaten alive waiting for seven hours because you screwed up."

Sullivan sat up on the edge of his cot and slowly rubbed the sleep from his eyes, while he tried to concentrate on what O'Rourke had said. At length, he replied:

"Sir, I don't know what the hell you're talking about. I never left this fort last night. I found we were out of green flares. You didn't have a radio and I wasn't about to go poking around the market looking for you. So I canceled the patrol.

"I don't know who you saw out there, but they sure as hell weren't Marines."

O'Rourke next awoke Thanh and Phuoc, and told them of his brush with the strange and well-armed patrol. They promised to investigate and O'Rourke went off to sleep. By noon the heat and the noise inside the fort had dragged him reluctantly awake, and he listened drowsily to the police reports. Several villagers had given a similar report: an enemy main-force unit had come across the river from the Phu Longs and entered Binh Yen Noi. One housewife swore they spoke with North Vietnamese accents.

The rumor upset the PFs, who were not sure how they should react to the news. Even Luong seemed uncertain and looked to the Marines for tactical advice. The Marines were less concerned because they had fought against North Vietnamese units several times before coming to the village and all were convinced that the Viet Cong made the more dangerous adversary on patrols in the hamlets. The North Vietnamese moved and fought in platoon-, company- and battalion-sized units, unsuited for the village war because they could easily be detected. The Marines doubted that the North Vietnamese would risk crossing from the Phu Longs in larger than squad size, since they would have to risk being trapped against the river with no route of retreat if they were spotted and a large U.S. unit was called in.

O'Rourke was particularly determined to persist in small-unit patrolling, despite the lingering doubts of some PFs and some Americans. Fielder, Sullivan's dependable second-in-command, shared O'Rourke's outlook and volunteered to take the first patrol out the next night. Fielder asked Suong to select two PFs who needed training to accompany him. He took only one other American— Combat Culver, who constantly gambled away his pay and tried to duck out of routine garrison chores, but who seemed afraid of nothing. Culver's trouble was that once he became engaged, he grew so absorbed in the battle that he forgot to think and had no feeling for when he was overmatched and it was time to withdraw. So Fielder put him at rear guard, posted a PF at point and left the fort slightly before nine in the evening.

The night was heavily overcast, with a rain falling so softly that the drops on the leaves did not interfere with the hearing of the patrollers. The low clouds shrouded the hamlet in dark gloom, and only years of familiarity with the trails permitted the PF at point to walk at a steady pace. Fielder, as second man, followed by keeping close enough to listen to the hoarse breathing of the PF, who seemed to require more air to breathe the deeper they moved into the hamlet. Culver, listening rearward at each dozen steps, kept falling behind and losing contact, then groping his way forward like a blind man until he bumped into the others. After being momentarily left behind for the third time, Culver's temper snapped and he broke the silence.

"Tell that damn point to slow it down," he hissed. "We're not trying to set any track records."

The request had the opposite effect. Noting that the Marines were tense, the point man became more fearful and sped off at a fast walk, as if he thought he could outrun the blackness which encloaked him. Not a light from a house shone as they hurried on, and the early evening chatter which usually floated from the homes was missing. The patrollers moved through a black and silent hamlet, sure sign that the enemy had come that way before them and that the villagers, anticipating a firefight, had all scrambled into their family bunkers—large, thick mounds of earth with a hollow center found beside or within each house in the village.

Suddenly the point stopped so quickly that Fielder bumped up against him. The path in front of them was piled high with dry brush, thorns and vines, a flimsy barricade blocking the path, with no way to step through or remove the tangle without making enough noise to alert anyone waiting on the other side.

"VC . . . VC," the PF at point kept insisting, "VC."

The blocked trail was a standard means the Viet Cong

had of signaling that they were in the hamlet and did not want to be disturbed. Assuming PF compliance, it was a means whereby the enemy could avoid an unwanted engagement. Unsure of the situation, Fielder looked to the PFs.

"No go . . . no go," they said. "Beaucoup VC . . . beaucoup VC."

The brush could have been thrown across the trail by two local guerrillas who wanted to visit their wives, or it could be a challenge to lure the Marines into bulling their way ahead to where a main-force ambush waited.

"Let's go on," Culver whispered. "We don't need them."

Fielder was not so sure. One of the few Marines who was married, he had a wife and baby waiting at home for him. He exercised a high degree of common sense which had won him the respect of the more reckless Marines.

"We'd get lost in there in a minute," he replied to Culver. "And it's for sure the PFs won't go with us. Let's go back. It's not worth it."

"O.K."

With obvious relief, the PFs hastened back to the fort. The Marines dawdled, knowing they had to face Sullivan. They arrived at the fort several minutes after the PFs.

"What do you mean you thought you'd get lost?" Sullivan yelled. "We have to show these people there is no place we won't go. No place. If they think there are Cong out there, then we go out—especially if the PFs want to come in."

"We don't go with people too scared to shoot, Sergeant," O'Rourke interrupted. "Fielder was right in coming in. Now let's take some shooters and get back out there."

Within ten minutes, a new patrol left the gate. Riley had

point, followed by Fielder, O'Rourke and Sullivan, with Garcia at rear guard. They moved back toward the barricaded path at a snail's pace, taking an hour to cover a quarter of a mile. When they were almost to the barricade, the clouds opened without warning. One moment there was a slight mist, and the next the rain was falling in thick, heavy sheets and the dirt path swelled into a small stream and the rush of the falling rain made it necessary for O'Rourke to talk to Riley in a normal voice.

"In this stuff we don't have to sweat our noise," he said, "so move out and let's get up that blocked path before it stops."

Within a few minutes they were at the spot where the previous patrol had turned back, and already the waters had washed away the flimsy brush barricade. The patrol did not stop, but moved on up the trail, each man straining to see in the dark and hear in the rain. Not one seeing or hearing anything. Too quickly, it seemed, they were through the hamlet and out on the open sands.

"If they were in there," Garcia said, "I bet they ducked into a house. I don't think they think we'd come back a second time in this stuff."

"Let's head for the front of the ville," Sullivan suggested. "We may catch them going back across the river."

The patrollers cut due east, moving quickly under cover of the rain, relying on Riley's eyes to alert them against any enemy traveling toward them. Within fifteen minutes they had covered a half-mile, stopping briefly when they hit the main trail just below the marketplace.

"Straight ahead to Top's house," Sullivan said, "then hang a right and follow the river bank to the big coconut tree."

As they moved forward, the rain slackened and soon petered out altogether, passing as quickly as it had started.

The patrollers walked across the paddy dike in front of Missy Top's, their boots sticking in the mud and giving off a slurping sound with each step. While on the dike they could see each other plainly, but once on the other side, the small bush-lined path between the houses was black and they had to grope their way forward. They knew the area well, however, and none had trouble. The sounds of the suction between boots and mud being broken kept each patroller informed of the whereabouts of the others. Slurp, slurp, slurp, they went up the trail. In contrast to the tension and silence of the earlier part of the evening, the sound struck Fielder as comical, and he started to giggle. From the houses came subdued chattering and chinks of light. Evidently the villagers had no reason to believe the Viet Cong were in their section of the hamlet. In nervous relief, Garcia joined Fielder in giggling. Slurp, slurp, slurp. Next, amusement at the absurdity of the evening spread to Sullivan, then to O'Rourke, and soon all four were giggling. Back from point slurped an annoyed Riley.

"Will you guys knock it off?" he whispered. "It's bad enough up front without a bunch of girls behind me."

"Sorry, Rile," O'Rourke whispered.

"The Cong aren't around here, Rile," Fielder whispered. "Look at the houses. And God knows if they're here, they've sure as hell heard us coming."

"We're here anyway," Sullivan whispered. "Let's set in on the river edge of the clearing."

Cautiously they moved across a small clearing about thirty feet wide and marked by a tall coconut tree on the river bank. Out of habit, they checked around the houses on either side of the clearing. One house seemed normal. But as they approached the other, a small dog tethered to the front door started yapping, only to be screeched into silence by a sharp tug on the rope around his neck as an occupant of the house opened the door and dragged him inside. Probing around the house, Garcia nearly stumbled over a man sleeping in a pile of wet hay next to the water's edge. He was snoring quite loudly. Garcia walked over and stood looking down at him. He was soon joined by the outer patrollers.

"I don't believe it," O'Rourke said. "How dumb does he think we are? He likes to sleep in the rain and he can't hear me standing right above him, right? Garcia, talk to him."

"What'll I say?"

"Ask him what he's doing here."

"He'll say he's sleeping."

Fielder and Sullivan chuckled.

"Every time we pick up some villager by ourselves we screw up, Lieutenant," Sullivan said. "The PFs or Thanh can do it, but we just end up pissing off some innocent farmer."

So they left the supposedly sleeping man and turned to watching the river, setting a simple ambush, with O'Rourke and Sullivan sitting under the tree peering at the water, Riley on one flank and Garcia on the other. Having the watch to the rear, Fielder looked for a spot from which to cover the ambush and noticed that in the center of the clearing lay a large log. Against this he snuggled, lying on his stomach in the mud, his body hidden in the log's shadow, his automatic rifle on its bipod pointing across the clearing at the trail they had just come down.

For an hour the five held their positions without stirring. A slight wind came up, just enough to push wavelets against the bank and smack spray on Sullivan and O'Rourke, just enough to rustle the bushes and blow odd smatterings of water off the leaves, just enough to push the wet clothes coldly against the bodies of the patrollers and keep them shivering, just enough to blow away the mosquitoes and gnats, and for that the Marines were grateful. They would rather be chilled than eaten. The cold also drove off sleep, and O'Rourke sensed they could hold the ambush until dawn if their shivering did not become too acute.

At a little past one in the morning, all the patrollers became aware of a shift in the night sounds. Since the rain, the frogs in the paddies had been contentedly croaking, here and there, off and on, following no set pattern. Then the croaking changed to complaining, in a swelling chorus of indignation that started from the south and, to the listeners, seemed to travel up the main trail to the marketplace, where it petered out.

Hearing the frogs, Fielder listened harder, knowing O'Rourke was counting on him to give first alarm from the rear. For several minutes nothing untoward entered his straining consciousness. Then he heard a sound unmistakably human.

Slurp.

His safety was off and his cheek along the rifle stock and he waited. The others could not move. Riley tried and came the closest to swiveling around, but he couldn't pull his rifle barrel through the foliage without telltale scratching sounds. Garcia was too far distant on the other flank to hear the footfall. Sullivan and O'Rourke heard it, and in their exposed position all they could do was slide slowly down the trunk of the tree and leave it to Fielder to take the shot.

Fielder was trying, but several minutes had passed since he had heard the foot in the mud. The noise had not been repeated. The enemy scout seemed to have stopped moving. Fielder knew better than to let himself believe that. So he reasoned the man had left the trail for firmer ground and was working his way forward among the houses. Directly in front of Fielder, on the side of the clearing, stood a thatched house whose small front yard was paved with flat flint rocks and enclosed by a patch of brambles trimmed like a hedge. If the scout was from the area, Fielder felt he would make for that yard, since from there he could scan potential ambush points along the river without making noise each time he shifted his position.

A few minutes later Fielder thought he heard branches rustling along the side of the house. He could not be sure it was not the wind. But he was sure of what he no longer heard, and that was voices from the house. Peering up at the brambles from across twenty feet, he thought he saw for a second a blob against the skyline. He waited, unsure, unwilling to fire prematurely and give away his position. He heard a twig break. Still, he hesitated. But he was primed, his body taut, ears attuned, finger resting lightly on the trigger, waiting, waiting for the next sound to fix the scout. A bush rustled as its branches were slightly parted.

Fielder fired, the strong recoil pounding the butt into his shoulder while he kept squeezing the trigger, trying to pick up the line of tracers and bring the bullets on target.

"There he goes!" yelled Riley.

A blur of black by the corner of the house, a brief, frenzied snapping and bending of bushes, and the enemy scout was gone.

"Damnit all to hell," yelled Fielder.

He had fired twenty bullets in one excited burst, yet missed because he had used a magazine which contained no tracers. Unable to see his fire, he had failed to lead properly when the scout ducked around the corner of the house.

"You had good position, too," O'Rourke chided him.

"Now they know exactly where we are. Rainstorm or not, they followed us here. That means they think they can take us. So it's not just a few guerrillas out there."

"What'll we do?" Garcia asked.

"Nothing. Let them make the first move," O'Rourke replied. "If we don't try to bug out of here, they have to come in after us. We'll play it by ear when they do. In the meantime, hold tight and listen up."

The Marines lay down in a small semicircle with their backs to the river and waited. Fifteen minutes, twenty, thirty, forty. One hour.

"Listen," Riley hissed, "the frogs."

The frogs were croaking that a force was walking south along the main trail. At a distance of about two hundred yards, the croaking drew abreast of the patrollers' position, then drifted by to the left before petering out. Several minutes later, two carbine shots rang out on their left, followed by two answering shots from the market off to their right. Then, simultaneously, from both directions the frogs started complaining.

"They've got us boxed and now they're moving in," Sullivan said.

Without a radio, the patrol was to use a red hand flare to signal for help. But in the heavy overcast it would not be seen by the fort. And once heavy firing broke out, illumination flares would be a mixed blessing if the patrollers were caught on the open river bank.

"We better get the hell out of here," O'Rourke said. "We'll go up the middle."

"Huh?"

"They're moving in from our flanks. The one place that scout has told them to avoid is the trail right out in front, because that's where he almost got blasted. As they come in, we go out that trail."

"What if that's what they're trying to get us to do?"

"Look, we're going across open paddies. If you were a Cong commander, would you figure us for the paddy route, or that we'd try to stay in this cover along the bank? And let me tell you, if they have enough troops to cover the left, the right and the front, we've had it anyways."

O'Rourke stood up and started down the dark trail they had come in, the others following. Slurp, slurp. Only now the frog cries were getting closer and the noise of their mud passage did not sound as acute. They moved swiftly back to Missy Top's house and in a tight bunch crouched together in its shadow. Between them and the main trail back to the fort stretched the open paddy. They waited until the croaking was behind them, the noise drifting steadily closer to their old position at the coconut tree.

"O.K.," O'Rourke whispered. "Let's get across. Riley and I will go first. Once we're off the dike, the rest of you follow. Get your ass in gear going across. There's no place you can hide out there if we're spotted."

O'Rourke went first. He started from a runner's crouch, hit the dike at a fast clip, and scampered across with the jerky motions of a drunk trying to walk a straight line. Riley tried to follow the act at the same pace and midway over slipped in the slickness of the mud and splashed bottom first into the paddy. The unmistakable sound made the waiting patrollers wince, but Riley was already scrambling up the dike and running on. Then Garcia, Fielder and Sullivan were crouching and running, each expecting at any moment the bullets to snap at them, none quite believing it when one after another they tumbled safely off the dike and into the ditch by the main trail.

"We did it," gasped Fielder. "You called it right, Lieutenant."

A few moments later rain started falling again, and in the downpour the patrollers walked back to the fort unmolested, leaving the enemy force to beat the bushes.

# 10

Early the next day Thanh and his police were at the marketplace trying to gather information on the enemy force which had prowled the hamlet the previous night. At the fort, Sullivan woke O'Rourke and asked him if he wished to go back to the spot where they had seen the man supposedly sleeping in the wet hay. Sullivan had something to show the lieutenant.

When they arrived, the old lady who owned the house where they had seen the sleeping man came out to meet them, followed by several shy children. She greeted Sullivan warmly but laughed off his questions about the sleeper. After a while he gave up asking.

"Maybe she just locked her old man out for drinking too much. Damned if I can get a straight answer out of her," Sullivan said. "Well, it's time for some refreshment anyways."

He pointed up the tree. She smiled and spoke to one of the barefoot boys, who half-shinnied, half-walked a full forty feet up the thick tree trunk to its crowned top, where he hacked loose and pitched down a light-brown coconut, then slid easily back to earth.

"Not bad climbing for a ten-year-old, huh?" Sullivan asked.

"Fantastic," O'Rourke said. "Does he do that often?"

"I come by here about once a week. You know, just to get away from the fort. The old mama-san and I get along. You might say that's my special tree. I pay a hundred piasters a coconut, and mama-san saves them all for me. You ever have coconut milk?"

"No."

"You'll like it. Come on."

The old lady was inviting them inside, and they stepped from the heat into the coolness of her front room, with a hard-packed, clean-swept dirt floor, a simple table, four rickety chairs and a large wooden altar decorated with faded family pictures, cupfuls of thin, charred prayer sticks and a Chinese calendar. To the left was the kitchen, with a stove hearth, a large kettle and several pots, and a sturdy chopping table. To the right was the bedroom, consisting of a clothes closet and a large bed with tight-fitted wooden slats for a mattress. The two men sat down at the table and the boy handed Sullivan the coconut, into the side of which he had chopped a drinking hole. Sullivan drank deeply of the cool, sweet liquid and handed the fruit to O'Rourke, who sipped cautiously at first.

"Hey, that's good," he said.

"Yes, it is," Sullivan replied. "You know, this isn't such a bad life. It's kind of peaceful sitting here, not sweating, looking at the river, knowing no Cong's sneaking up on you. I kind of like it."

The two leaders remained at the house for several hours, passing the time in tranquil talk. Neighbors dropped by to say hello, with the old lady acting as beaming hostess, and omnipresent children gathered to sit on the door stoop and peer at the Americans. Sullivan had brought his camera and offered to take a picture of the entire family. No less than eight children gathered around the woman for the photograph. Then she insisted that

Sullivan join them, which he did, with the neighbors joking that he was the father, and O'Rourke took the picture. The Marines declined an invitation to stay for dinner, but did give a boy money to buy two large beers, which they leisurely consumed before thanking the old lady for her hospitality and walking back to the fort.

That evening Suong decided to send out four close-in patrols to warn if any enemy forces were massing near the fort. Brannon hooted at the PFs as they left the fort, several of whom laughed and yelled back and gave him the finger as they walked out.

"Four patrols in Binh Yen Noi," Brannon kidded Suong. "Never happen. Maybe they go boom-boom, huh?"

Suong had to laugh. He knew the PFs would check with their friends in the hamlet, and if the villagers had not heard Viet Cong passing by, there was a good chance one patrol would be left on guard, while the others visited their girl friends. Phuoc had told the Marines that in 1963 on the nearby island of Binh Thuy the PF platoon commander had gone over to the Viet Cong and in three years had killed fourteen of his former comrades. He knew who was sleeping with whom, and his favorite technique was to hide in a house which he suspected a PF would soon be visiting, catch his man at a disadvantage and kill him with a knife. No such incidents had occurred in Binh Nghia, although Phuoc conceded that even if they had, it would probably not have stopped each individual PF from believing it would never happen to him.

But on this night there was strict attendance to business, for the patrols had not been gone twenty minutes when the crumping sound of a grenade exploding somewhere in the hamlet carried back to the fort.

"Now that's what I call a big boom-boom, Suong," Brannon called out.

Suong grinned and nodded. Whatever the prior intentions of the PFs on patrol had been, both knew that now no patroller would sneak off alone to a lovers' tryst.

No shots followed the grenade, and the listeners at the fort concluded that a patrol must have brushed near a startled guerrilla, who had thrown and run. The next two hours passed uneventfully, but shortly after ten in the evening from the direction of the marketplace drifted the muffled staccato of several weapons. One burst of firing, then another, then a few stray shots, then silence again. Another brush encounter.

By midnight all patrols were back in, none having observed or heard from the villagers any evidence of main-force activity, but two reporting that some small enemy groups were definitely within the hamlet.

"Let's wait a couple of hours for those guerrillas to settle down," O'Rourke said, "and then go out after them."

According to the PFs, there were about thirty armed and active guerrillas operating in the village. Some had secret hiding places there, but most had moved across to the Phu Longs and came back only at night. Almost every one of them could be recognized on sight by the PFs, with whom they had grown up. Over a period of time the police had pieced together a thick book listing Viet Cong known to be working in or near the village. When translated, the book provided close-up portraits of the enemy soldiers.

The enemy was well organized. Across the river, a man named Pham Van Hoi, alias Lien, was responsible for providing food and shelter for the guerrillas who could no longer stay in Binh Nghia twenty-four hours a day. Hoi, forty-two years old and with a ninth-grade education, had joined the Viet Minh in 1945 and had risen to village chief by 1953. But the next year he was expelled from the Communist Party for getting a girl pregnant and went back to work in his home hamlet as a farmer. Fear of arrest by Diem's police soon drove him to regroup to North Vietnam, where he received finance training and worked as a tax collector before infiltrating back to Binh Son district in 1962. Hoi managed the logistics in the Phu Longs, supplying both displaced guerrillas and itinerant main forces.

Although Hoi set the rice tax to be collected in Binh Nghia, it was doubtful if he would ever risk setting foot in that village while the combined unit was there. The combat tasks were left to the guerrillas and local force company, commanded by Nguyen Thi Son, described in government files as "about 45 years old, widower, no children, atheist, poor farmer, has a primary education. He is tall, large build, strong, active . . . is in habit of speaking quickly and after each sentence he clears his throat, lack of high serving spirit, quick-tempered, used to thunder out against people, local residents don't like him." Son attended to military matters, while Nguyen Suyen was "responsible for the Political Section" and for relations with the villagers. Prisoners questioned by government interrogators had described Suyen as "about 35 years old, married and has one child . . . is a poor farmer and an atheist. He is thin, slope-shouldered, looks down when walking. He is quiet, high-spirited, self-possessed and polite. All local residents like him. He has been a member of the Communist Party since 1950 and was arrested for a year in 1957. He can suffer all hardships and difficulties."

In his intelligence file, Thanh also had listed nonfighting members of the Viet Cong organization who still resided in the village, former members of front committees who were temporarily inactive, but who still might occasionally help the Viet Cong either because of threats or promises of reward, or out of loyalty. These were the little fish Thanh frequently arrested, beat and sent to short jail terms at district.

In contrast, the village also harbored a few true, dedicated, dangerous stay-behind agents, members of the Viet Cong Security Section. No one in the village, including the guerrillas, knew who they were. They would not be found participating in a random firefight; that was the chancy job of the guerrillas, whose persistent presence was a constant reminder to the people that the struggle for the village was still undecided.

At two in the morning a rover patrol set out to seek the guerrillas. O'Rourke thought enough time had elapsed to lull the enemy into a feeling of safety. If there was no action in Binh Yen Noi, he planned to strike out for the My Hués. So it was a large patrol which left the gate—six Marines in all, including Sullivan. As the Marines filed out, Luong, the ex–Viet Minh, rolled off the sandbags where he had been dozing and fell into line behind his friend Brannon. He didn't say anything, just grinned meanly and strutted along, his M-1 rifle, overly long for him, slung upside down beneath his right armpit. His presence changed the tone of the group. He only went on those patrols which he thought would make contact. With Luong in their midst, the Marines tried harder to make less noise.

Riley had point, and O'Rourke gave him his head, the patrol having no set route or destination. For two hours they roamed at a slow, slow pace, avoiding the main trails, using children's paths, slipping through backyards, Luong stopping by houses where low lights still burned to listen to the talk from inside. There was no wind and the patrollers kept moving to avoid the mosquitoes. In the warm air all soon were thoroughly soaked with their own sweat. First the point took them north toward the sand dunes, then east toward the market and the river, then south toward the cemetery, and northeast toward the dunes again.

"Rile," O'Rourke whispered, "head outside. We'll take a break on the dunes."

To go out on the dunes, or to come from the dunes into the hamlet, one had to pass through a large, groaning gate, one of seven official entrances in the mile of bamboo fence the Revolutionary Development workers had insisted the villagers build around the hamlets. Theoretically, it kept out the Viet Cong, who in reality could cut their way in at almost any point. Phuoc wasn't exactly sure why his RDs had to erect that fence; but it was one of the ninety-eight tasks his men had to complete according to Saigon regulations before the Binh Yen Noi area could be labeled pacified, and Phuoc, running hard for election to the National Assembly, was not about to cross some higher-ranking officials over something as trivial as a fence. Yet he was a shrewd enough politician to promise the people that he would, if elected, speak to the Ministry of Rural Reconstruction in Saigon about their silly fence-building project which took time away from planting rice and catching fish.

The PFs argued that there was some military value in the fence, for often the Viet Cong were too pressed for time or just too lazy to break down part of the fence, which was a noisy operation in any case, and so instead they would come through the gates. Even if the gate beaters did not sound the alarm at such times, sooner or later the information would drift back in rumor form to the fort.

This was not the hamlet's first experience with a fence.

Once before, in 1962, a fence had gone up, after Binh Yen Noi had been designated a Strategic Hamlet. Then the PFs had learned to approach fence gates with caution, since twice they had lost men in the procedure. Once the Viet Cong were waiting in ambush on the other side of the gate and riddled the point man when he walked through; the other time two guerrillas hid beneath the platform where the beaters sat and silently garroted the rear guard of a PF patrol, the sounds of his death being blotted out by the creak of the gate being shut by the beaters.

As Riley approached the gate to the dunes, Luong cut out of line and overtook him, grasping him by the shoulder and gesturing to the Marine to stay put while he went ahead. The beaters' all-clear signal—the wooden tap-tap-tapping—was a familiar background noise which followed the Marines through the hamlet on every patrol. It was so familiar that Luong had disappeared into the darkness before Riley realized he had heard no tapping from the post to their front.

The patrollers waited for Luong to make his stalk. Several minutes passed with only the usual night sounds: a dog somewhere yapping, a few crickets chirping, the slight scuffing of the restive Marines, a hacking night cough from a nearby house, a water buffalo with the patrollers' scent in his nostrils stamping and snorting. Then the Marines were jarred by Luong's deep-voiced roar, followed by panicked, breathless gasps and a thrashing in the underbrush. As one man, the six Americans charged forward, covering the thirty yards to the gate in a few seconds, coming with muzzles leveled, only to see three beaters cowering on their low bamboo platform and Luong furiously chopping with his machete at a thick bamboo plant. "Asleep" was all he said in explanation as he shoved past the dumbfounded Americans and began whacking at the beaters with his heavy switch. He stopped only when his arm grew tired, then shouted at one of the bruised beaters, who scrambled off his perch and swiftly pulled open the gate. Next Luong took and shoved him out the gate, so that he would draw first fire in case an ambush waited. Satisfied all was clear, Luong walked out onto the desert.

Several hundred yards out on the white dunes, O'Rourke called a halt. The open desert was the safest place to take a fifteen-minute rest. The men collapsed and lay breathing through dry mouths. They had left their canteens behind because they sloshed back and forth when half empty. During the day the temperature had risen to 109 degrees and the night was not much cooler. On the dunes with nothing but cactus and small bramblebushes and ridge after ridge of sand there seemed no escape from the thirst and the heat which had caked the dry spittle to the roofs of their mouths and had each man silently damning a climate which left him cold and wet and shivering one night and thirsty and hot and sweating the next.

All except Luong, who stood for a moment looking down at his prostrate companions, and then gestured to them to follow him. Unquestioning, they trudged after their new guide, fighting their way through loose sand ankle-deep up a steep slope and down the other side, following the course of a wash around two more ridges before coming to a flat space about the size of a football field, surrounded by dunes. There they saw the crumbled sides of what once had been a stone house, while a few feet away stood a stone well, and perched on the well's edge a rusty bucket trailing a short piece of frayed rope. Luong laid down his rifle, took off his crossed bandoliers of ammunition, stepped out of his sandals, rolled up his trousers, grasped the rope in his teeth, placed the bucket behind his back and climbed down the side of the well, disappearing into the blackness. A few moments later the delighted Marines could hear the bucket being dunked, and when Luong appeared, he was grasping a gallon of water. Twice he repeated the procedure, slaking the thirst of every Marine. Afterward they lingered longer than the originally allotted time, reluctant once their mouths were again wet to leave the soft and comfortable sands, to stop looking up at the stars, to walk away from a place which had brought peace and succor to them.

"It's four-thirty," O'Rourke said. "The hell with My Hué tonight. It'll be getting light in another hour. Let's go back in."

Reluctantly the men got to their feet, their sweat now dried and caked in white crusts on their shirts, their calf muscles cramped. In their first tentative steps back toward the hamlet they looked like tottering old men. As they entered the clammy dark of the hamlet's foliage, the patrollers revived almost despite themselves, instinct overriding fatigue. They avoided the main trails when they could, twisting their way laboriously through the backyards, often just guessing where they were, not especially concerned about directional errors because they were the only patrol out, resigned to enduring until light.

They had almost reached the back side of the marketplace when Riley halted suddenly. The patrol jerked up short and for several minutes nobody moved. Riley walked silently back to O'Rourke and whispered: "I thought I heard something on the path to our right. Did you?"

"I'm not sure," O'Rourke whispered. "We were still moving when you stopped. Go ahead, but take it slow."

They proceeded at a creep for a few minutes, when again Riley halted, this time going down on his knees, placing his rifle on the ground and flattening out. His head pointed toward a path six feet away. The other members of the patrol quietly lay down about ten feet apart and faced in the same direction. O'Rourke crawled to Riley's side.

"I know for sure I hear someone behind us. They're coming up this path," Riley whispered.

"Do you think they've heard us?" O'Rourke asked.

"No—too far away."

O'Rourke scooted back and warned the others. Sullivan and Fielder pivoted about to protect the rear and right flank of the patrol. Riley, O'Rourke, Brannon, Lummis and Luong faced the path and waited, having slipped off their safeties.

They heard the enemy approaching, not the steady noises of careless footsteps but the intermittent crunches and snaps of people walking cautiously but not cautiously enough. The middle of the path was obscured in dark shadows. The ambushers could not see any figures approaching; they could only gauge the distance by ear. O'Rourke thought he saw a man pass by him, but he could not be sure. He heard another man getting close.

Not one of the Marines could remember who sprang the ambush. All were agreed that the seven rifles opened up within the same second. Swinging his weapon back and forth, each patroller fired until he had emptied a magazine. It was strictly area fire at sounds. Not one Marine could actually see a target or be sure that he had hit anything. Then O'Rourke and Riley rose to their knees and heaved two grenades back down the trail in the direction from which the Viet Cong had come.

"Cease fire!" O'Rourke yelled. "Riley, block for us to the front. A couple of you guys search the area."

The action had lasted eight seconds.

Lummis and Brannon stepped out of the bushes, peering at the ground in front of them.

"One," Lummis said.

"Blown away?" O'Rourke asked.

"Yes, sir."

Luong walked forward and struck a match in front of the faces of the two men. He grunted once but said nothing.

"Get their rifles," O'Rourke said. "We'll head in by the main trail. Make sure you have fresh mags in those weapons. Fielder, take point."

It was growing light when they arrived back at the fort. Thanh was waiting, having heard the firing. Luong spoke to him, identifying one of the dead guerrillas by name. Thanh took out the book in which were recorded the name and affiliations of every adult in the village, with a special roster of those who had joined the Viet Cong. It contained about two hundred names. Thanh drew a neat line through one of them.

# 11

A few nights later, O'Rourke was again engaged. It was a short patrol designed to set up an early-evening ambush along the river in an effort to catch the enemy when they first entered the village. With the lieutenant were Garcia, Brannon and PFC John Glasser, a thin, bespectacled young man who handled the supply job for the combined unit. Choosing a likely vantage point on the river bank, O'Rourke placed Garcia and Brannon on the flanks, keeping Glasser, who had less experience, with him. The sky was overcast and visibility limited. There was little wind.

When they did not make contact in the first hour, O'Rourke judged it unlikely that any Viet Cong would be crossing near them, so he decided to tutor Glasser on the different night sounds they were hearing. When Glasser showed keen interest and whispered question after question, O'Rourke became absorbed in responding and neglected to keep close watch on the river.

After an hour of conversation, O'Rourke decided to abandon the ambush and shift farther up the bank, so he moved away from Glasser to signal to his flankers. That done, he crawled back to his original position to take one final look around. What he saw made him grasp Glasser's arm.

"Look," he whispered, "two of them."

"Where?"

"Right there, right in front of us."

Almost directly to their front, down the bank near the water loomed two figures, their outlines just barely visible against the background of the water.

"There?" Glasser whispered.

"Yes, can't you see with those glasses? Lie flat. I'll take them. Just don't move."

O'Rourke could hear Brannon and Garcia coming up behind him. He knew he should wait so that they could all fire together, but he was furious with himself for breaking the cardinal rule of strict attention when on patrol.

"Screw it," he thought. "I'll drop both of them myself."

As Glasser watched in amazement, O'Rourke lined his automatic rifle up on the crouching enemy and squeezed the trigger, hugging the rifle to his shoulder to hold down the recoil. The red tracers streamed forward in a blast of light and sound, struck their targets full on and ricocheted skyward in a screaming cascade of white and red.

O'Rourke had poured twenty bullets into two rocks.

Silence. The sound of embarrassment while O'Rourke realized what had happened. As he had talked, the tide had dropped, exposing the two enemy stones to his refocused attention and angry fire. Now Glasser was looking at him as Sancho Panza must often have looked at Don Quixote.

Predictably, Brannon was the first to speak: "Sure looked pretty, Lieutenant."

Then Garcia: "That was still some damn fine shooting."

Brannon again: "Yeh, and those rocks would have fooled me. It's like you keep telling us: play it safe."

Garcia turned to Glasser.

"You were lucky to be here, Glasser. That's some of the finest shooting you'll ever see. You remember that for your next patrol."

For a week O'Rourke lived with the fear that he would be forever nicknamed "The Rock," but the incident was never mentioned. Brannon and Garcia were looking after him.

In mid-August the frequency of contacts started to drop off, and the PFs heard from the villagers that the Viet Cong were starting to move by side trails to avoid contact with the combined-unit patrols. Then one day Thanh received information that a favorite enemy route was the narrow track upon which Larry Page had been killed two months earlier. That morning the police chief had arrested a short, muscular man garbed in tattered farmer's clothes who claimed to own a half-hectare of paddy just north of My Hué. He was not on the census rolls of the village, recently updated by the industrious Phuoc, and since Thanh was not in the habit of arresting every male he saw, it was apparent someone had informed the police that the farmer was not who he said he was.

Between them, Thanh and Phuoc broke down the man's

cover in half an hour. Not a trained agent, he was unused to deceit and once he was convinced his arrest was no accident, he acknowledged what Thanh already knew: he was an assistant platoon leader in the P31st District Force Company, sent by Le Quan Viet, the one-armed VC district chief, to contact some local guerrillas and to confirm their reports concerning the tactics and habits of the combined unit. Quan Viet had become leery of casual incursions into the village and had just about abandoned the idea that the combined unit could be intimidated into ceasing its patrols. The prisoner was to determine if there were routes which could be used for rice takeouts or for the passage of main-force units without bumping into a patrol. The hamlet guerrillas claimed there were, but Quan Viet was no longer taking their word for conditions in the village.

The prisoner gave many answers in refutation of assertions by Thanh, who responded to the man's defiance by knocking him down several times. But each time he struggled back to his feet, despite his arms being bound behind him, and stood at attention, with his heels locked together. The man had courage, and Thanh did not seem to resent his attempted spying the way he did the activities of the Viet Cong Security Section. When the questioning was finished, the PFs wiped the blood from the man's face and arranged for a guarded sampan to take him to district. Thanh did not go along, and it was reasonable for the Americans to assume that the spy, who was happier (and probably better) as a soldier, arrived safely at district.

Hearing that the safest guerrilla route was the track where Page had been killed, all the Americans clamored to be included on the next ambush sent there. Suong, however, advised that only a few could go without making too much noise, and he singled out as a guide a PF who disliked patrolling but whose family lived next to the path being used by the guerrillas. The PF would not go without taking a friend, so O'Rourke made the decision that he would go and take just one other Marine. That way each American would be paired with a Vietnamese who knew the village. If the track was as obscure and overgrown as it was described, they would only get a head-on shot at the Viet Cong anyway. For his steadiness, Fielder was chosen to accompany O'Rourke.

In keeping with a cover plan, they left the fort just after dark as part of a combined patrol of twelve men and followed the main trail into Binh Yen Noi. The night was clear, with a bit of light lingering from the sunset, and even in the shadows of the hamlet each man could see the outline of the patroller in front of him. It was a patrol designed to be a shade too early and a footstep too big. From most houses they passed, they could hear supper plates rattling, and several homes, trying to catch a slight breeze on a warm evening, had not yet closed their doors in keeping with the light curfew. Some children were still playing in their front yards, and a few men, home late from the fields or the sea, were stooped over washbasins alongside their houses. Fragments of conversation, with each word clearly distinguishable, floated by the patrol. Once there were the excited screams of children and a ball sailed over a hedge and bounced by the patrollers, with a little girl in fast pursuit. Retrieving the ball, she scooted back inside her yard without once looking directly at the armed men. At least two dozen villagers saw the patrollers passing. None called out, or waved, or in any way acknowledged what they saw, lest a watching neighbor interpret the action as active commitment to the GVN cause and denounce the waver to the Viet Cong.

That was the way of it. Anyone branded as an active

helper or spy for either side could not sleep in his own house at night but had to seek the protection of the armed camp which he supported. So the schoolteacher and the hamlet elders slept at the fort, while most of the hamlet guerrillas slept across the river in the Phu Longs. But when armed Viet Cong did slip into the hamlet, they would ask at certain sympathetic doors whether a patrol had passed and, with the shroud of night guaranteeing the informers anonymity, they would pick up information, just as the PFs did using the same technique at different doors. In case the Viet Cong were already in the hamlet, they would be informed that a large patrol had passed through, headed in the direction of the My Hués.

The patrol moved according to plan, paced by a point man who dallied so that they cleared the northern end of Binh Yen Noi under conditions of full darkness—minus four men. O'Rourke's party had dropped off in a patch of deep shadows and waited for several minutes for the main patrol to move well away. Then they were up and picking their way through the weeds and brambles, the PF guide in front following no path but just a general direction which took them toward the rear of the hamlet. As they went, the houses seemed to close in on them and they passed from backyard to backyard at turtle speed. It was like walking down an apartment corridor hoping no one would open his door and look out. There was no breeze and the air hung heavy with kitchen smells, and the four men were edging around the sides of houses so closely connected it sounded as though the conversation of one family would interfere with that of another.

In an hour they covered about three hundred yards, and on a map their route could best be duplicated by the doodlings of a two-year-old. Then in what seemed like just another in an endless series of backyards, the guide stopped, beckoned the Marines forward, and pointed toward the front of the house, where a square of light from the front room spilled onto the ground outside.

"There?" O'Rourke whispered incredulously.

"Hi—hi," the PF nodded in reply.

O'Rourke dared not risk further conversation, but he was plainly not enthusiastic about lying in ambush within fifteen feet of some stranger's house. He looked at Fielder and shrugged. Fielder shrugged back. So they started forward, O'Rourke in the lead, poking ahead with the toe of his boot, tamping the ground ever so slightly for twigs, nudging aside mats of decaying leaves, putting the heel down, shifting the body weight to balance on the forward foot, easing the rear leg out in front, and repeating the process again. The act required balance, strong thigh muscles and patience. One step a minute was good time.

They came to the patch of light which filled a small open space between the house and a bamboo thicket through which it would have been impossible to move in silence. O'Rourke handed his rifle to Fielder, squatted on his haunches and cocked his head sideways, squinting up into the open window, watching the bobbing head and shoulders of a woman appear and disappear as she went about some household cleaning task. He waited until she was turning away from the window and then, hunched over, scooted across the six feet of light. The next time she turned away Fielder handed over both rifles. The time after that Fielder crossed over.

They waited for the PFs to copy the procedure. Like two boys being encouraged to enter deep water for the first time in their lives, the PFs would crawl to the light's edge, peer anxiously across at the vigorously gesturing Marines, glance up at the window and scoot back deeper into the shadows at each approach of the housewife. It was a clever

act. O'Rourke knew they were not frightened of the
woman. They did not want to cross because they dreaded
being trapped alongside the Americans in a lopsided firefight with no escape except across a patch of glaring light.

After several minutes, the Marines gave up their pan-
tomimed entreaties and swiveled around to check out their
new surroundings. They had the house behind them, and
directly in front of them ran a large ditch which held only
a few inches of stagnant water and stank from garbage and
defecation. A single board spanned the ditch, the sides of
which were scantily decorated with hardy shrubs. By poking and peering at different angles, O'Rourke was able to
see a slight track leading away from the board on the far
side. By lying in wait at the corner of the house with the
patch of light just behind their feet, they could fire at anyone crossing the plank.

With a few hand signals, they reached agreement on the
plan and prepared for a long wait. Taking positions side by
side so that a whisper could be passed mouth to ear, they
gently extended the bipods on their rifles and set them
down, muzzles toward the track. Next they set down their
other equipment. O'Rourke carried in one sack a dozen
magazines, each separated from the other by a burlap
wrap. He placed the sack beside his rifle, and from the
eight pockets of his dark-green utilities pulled and placed
next to the sack three antipersonnel grenades, one illumination grenade, two hand flares and a flashlight. Fielder
wore a camouflage jacket tailored to include a dozen separate pouches. When loaded, it weighed over twenty
pounds. He slipped the jacket off and placed it beside his
rifle. In a green T-shirt, tanned arms and a face black with
grease paint, he still blended with the shadows.

Both lay down on their stomachs and waited. The hamlet was quieting down as most of the children in nearby

houses fell asleep. But in the house beside which they were lying the housewife was shrieking in such a shrill voice that neither Marine feared he would doze off as long as she was awake and talking. The stink from the ditch made breathing unpleasant, and even as they lay quite still, beads of sweat rolled off their faces. The sweat washed away their foul-smelling insect repellant, and the mosquitoes soon found them and came in droves from the ditch, humming around their ears, taunting them before biting. Rather than slap them with a human sound which carried for several yards, the Marines tried to brush them off or catch and squeeze them in their hands, accepting bites on their palms and fingers for the pleasure of killing some of their tormentors. The shrill housewife added to their discomfort by pitching a bowl of water out the window, the fright from the sudden splash jerking the tense bodies of the men with the force of electricity. After a while their elbows and forearms, bone-bruised from previous patrols, ached too much and they stretched their arms straight out, letting their jaws dig into a ground prickly with tiny pebbles and allowing the weight of their upper bodies to sag against their rib cages. But, after a time their chests ached too much and twitching could not defend against the merciless mosquitoes and it would be back up on their elbows, with hands pawing at the insect-filled air. For four hours they endured the bites, and the nagging wife who just wouldn't turn out the light and go to bed, and the fetid air, and the pain of an immobile body on an unyielding surface. They endured, sustained by the vision of their enemies walking across the ditch.

Shortly after midnight the crack of a branch alerted O'Rourke, who grabbed Fielder by the wrist and gestured with his head in the direction of the sound. Both listened intently and both caught the next sound, the unmistakable clank of metal on metal, as though a man with a rifle had stopped short and the next armed man in the column had bumped into him, their rifles briefly touching. Totally motionless, the Marines waited for the next move, O'Rourke slowly breathing through his mouth so that he could hear better.

Instead, they saw a man, or rather they saw where he had been. Across the ditch the bushes appeared darker than the gloom of the night around them, and yet one of the lighter patches between the bushes turned dark for an instant as a figure filled the space, then lightened again as he moved out of sight behind another bush. He was coming softly, and he was coming alone, a suspicious point man with courage and skill, sensing something wrong and dangerous yet not quite sure what or where it was, as skittish as a deer approaching some undergrowth where he had once been attacked by a tiger. O'Rourke was sure he was barefoot, for he seemed to flow along, as though he were skating rather than walking, sure of what was underfoot and concerned only with what lay on the other side of the ditch.

Once at the plank, the man stopped and just stood there, unaware that death lay ten yards away and that once he crossed the ditch his life would end. Yet something was gnawing at him, holding him back. For over a minute he stood debating with himself, then turned and walked back the way he had come, making a few careless noises, as if the unseen danger at the ditch were the less for having been briefly faced.

O'Rourke and Fielder silently slipped off their safeties and wriggled slightly behind their weapons to gain better firing positions, convinced the point was going back to bring up the main body and they might be able to cut down three or four of the enemy in their first burst. Then if the odds looked bad, they could run away while the Viet Cong were seeking cover and trying to regroup. They lost sight of the man, but a few moments later they heard faint whispers and they listened for the footfalls or slight rattle of equipment which would indicate the column was moving toward them. Instead, the whispering continued, became louder, more sibilant, the paradoxical sound of an argument in whispers.

Finally silence, and the point man gliding toward them again. Again at the plank and again the balk, a whisper from the dark to prod him on, the foot on the plank, the fingers on the triggers. Then abruptly he was gone, back once again down the track, a shadow among shadows, a blot among the bushes. And this time there was a murmur of voices, insistence against flat defiance, followed by a slight shuffling at a receding tempo, and nothing more except the usual night sounds. It was over.

"Nuts," hissed Fielder, in an expulsion of breath and anger.

"Umph!" came a gasp through the open window behind them, followed by the sound of a chair falling and a sharp puff of breath extinguishing the light inside the house. Despite themselves, both Marines let out snorts of laughter.

"Sorry," Fielder whispered.

"No harm done. No way that point man was coming back here," O'Rourke replied. "Let's find the PFs."

That did not prove to be an easy task. The Marines tried whispering the Vietnamese word for PF: "Nghia Quan? Nghia Quan?" No answer from the PFs. They tried tapping on their rifle stocks. No answer. Finally in exasperation they called out in low voices, "Nghia Quan?" No answer. The Marines were alone.

"They bugged out," Fielder said.

"They're probably at the fort," O'Rourke replied. "Let's go home."

When they did make their way back to the fort, they found the two PFs waiting for them in the paddy just outside the gate. Suong had not let them enter alone and they had been too fearful to return to the track. Although Fielder was irritated, O'Rourke accepted their apologetic presence calmly. Inside the fort, several soldiers were awake, waiting to hear the results of the patrol. O'Rourke told them what had happened.

"The Cong are getting shook," he concluded.

"I know that point man didn't see us, so the Cong are backing off because they don't know where we are. They don't like it out there so much any more."

A few days later, on August 10, 1966, O'Rourke flew back to the United States, leaving with a satisfied feeling that things were going well. The Americans were patrolling better, although they were not paying enough attention to the PFs. Sullivan tended to make decisions without asking advice, and Suong had complained to O'Rourke about the sergeant's style. Still, the individual troops got along well and there was no friction with the villagers. It appeared that if the combined unit persevered in their patrolling, the Viet Cong could gradually be deterred from entering the hamlets.

Certainly the district officials had been buoyed by the tenacity of the combined unit in continuing to seek contact with the enemy after Page and Lam had been killed. Shortly after O'Rourke's departure, a large Vietnamese and American inspection party from province came down to review the progress of the village noted in the reports from district. Phuoc's Revolutionary Development cadres turned out smartly dressed and lined up as an honor guard along the main trail to escort the dignitaries to the main marketplace. There, after a round of speeches and anti-Communist songs, the Binh Yen Noi area was officially declared an Ap Doi Moi, or pacified hamlet.

This resulted in a redistribution of the government manpower assigned to the hamlet. The police force returned to district, leaving behind only Thanh and two assistants. The RDs were sent back to Quang Ngai City, the province capital, to await reassignment. Phuoc was granted a leave of absence from the RD program to campaign full time for the National Assembly, and he moved back to Binh Son district headquarters, promising to visit the village often. Only the PFs and the Marines were staying, their combined force numbering thirty-five, if all the PFs came to work on the same day.

With fewer government troops in the village, the Americans expected that the Viet Cong might push harder, and in the last days of August they patrolled with special diligence, convinced they would contact the Viet Cong even more frequently than they had in mid-July.

The Americans were driven by a group ethic. They were judged by their peers and each knew what was expected of him and what he expected from the others. Their performances in the combined unit would serve no long-term goals, since only Sullivan planned to stay in the service. As far as the group was concerned, a man could be sloppy at the fort and try to duck distasteful chores and only be yelled at by the others or chewed out by Sullivan or Fielder. But on patrol no man dared let down, or suggest that the enemy be purposely avoided. That would finish him in the eyes of the others. While Beebe was in charge, a corporal leading a patrol had circled out onto the dunes instead of setting an ambush on the trail, as instructed. The patrol passed an uneventful night, as the corporal intended, but when he returned to the fort and told Beebe no one had come down the My Hué trail, the other patrol members turned their backs on him and walked disgustedly away. Beebe sent the man back to the battalion in disgrace.

The Americans liked the village. They liked the freedom to drink beer and wear oddball clothes and joke with girls. They liked having the respect of tough PFs like Luong and the admiration of the other PFs who could not bring themselves to challenge the Viet Cong alone. They were pleased that the villagers were impressed because they hunted the Viet Cong as the Viet Cong had for years hunted the PFs and the village officials. The Americans did not know what the villagers said of them in the privacy of their homes, but they observed that the children, who did hear their parents, did not run or avoid them, as they did Thanh. The parents were more than just polite. The Marines had accepted too many invitations to too many meals in too many homes to believe they were not liked by many and tolerated by most. For perhaps the only time in the lives of those dozen Americans, seven of whom had not graduated from high school, they were providing at the obvious risk of death a service of protection. This had won them open admiration and stature within the Vietnamese village society in which they were working and where ultimately most of them would die.

# BOOK III

# DEFEAT

# 12

The Marines' expectations of increased combat in late August did not materialize. There were a few brushes, one or two grenades pitched at them, and several sampans shot at. Most of the river encounters were of the usual variety with undetermined effects: a splash, a boat, a shot, a minute of heavy firing, a lull, the pop of illumination flares, a view of placid waters, darkness, silence. Only one encounter proved unusual.

Fleming had taken four men to set in an evening watch on the river above Binh Yen Noi. They had not even finished the clearing of twigs and stones from the ambush spot when two sampans came sculling by within seventy yards of the bank. Thinking they could capture the occupants of the boats, two PFs stood up and shouted to the rowers that they were trapped and to put into land. The response was a fast and accurate burst of fire which forced the PFs to go flat in front of the Marines' rifles and gained for the boaters several seconds of rowing time. Then the patrollers disentangled themselves and their angry bullets whipped the waters. The lead boat got away, leaving the slower sampan to absorb hundreds of rounds before slowly sinking without ever capsizing. The next day the villagers brought six bodies to shore. One was dressed in olive drab trousers and a camouflage shirt and was carrying a 9-mm pistol. Thanh sent the corpse to Binh Son for an identification check, while the other five were left on the bank for relatives to claim. Gossip among the river traffic would carry the word across the river and into the Phu Longs.

That afternoon the district chief drove to the fort to tell
the ambushers that the man with the pistol had been identified as a Viet Cong captain. The pistol was given to the
PFs, along with three carbines which had also been
retrieved. And that evening, since no one had come to
claim them, the five bodies on the bank were buried in a
common grave.

With the exception of that one river ambush, action in
and around Binh Nghia was light, and the month ended on
a quieter note than the Americans had anticipated. They
were not sure how to react to the lull in the tempo of violence. They had been in the village almost a hundred days,
had conducted over four hundred patrols, had fired or been
fired on over two hundred times.

The weeks and months of contact after contact had
exacted a price from the men. All had lost weight and all
longed for an uninterrupted night of sleep. A Marine was
lucky if he averaged four to five fitful hours of rest each
day, usually from four until nine in the morning. Few of
the Marines had learned how to slumber through the simmering heat and human noise which filled the fort during
the day. The battalion had given them a large squad tent
and cots, so the Marines had a room to themselves, but the
temperature under the canvas rose to over 100 degrees by
ten in the morning and stayed that way until after sundown. Men frequently dozed off while lying motionless
on the longer ambushes, and the patrol leader might later
yell at them but he would do nothing more. Sometimes a
man could stay awake no longer.

On top of that, O'Rourke had insisted that two Marines
remain on sentry duty nightly at the fort, despite its protection being a Vietnamese responsibility. O'Rourke's
easygoing manner had been deceptive, for he had trusted
no one and supervised constantly, tolerating no laxity in

combat matters. He had insisted on an edge of readiness which was hard to maintain night after night, especially since the combined unit had successfully carried the fight back to the enemy after their initial series of setbacks.

Sullivan had clearly favored an adjustment of the patrolling and sentry pace to a less hectic level; O'Rourke had not. With September bringing an ease to the combat and with O'Rourke gone, the sergeant decided to give his men a break. This seemed reasonable in view of an official assessment prepared at the end of a summer by a battalion inspection team which called the fort "a virtually impregnable fortress." So instead of two Marines awake at all times inside the fort, Sullivan cut the requirement back to one. Averaged out over the long term, this meant each man would be able to sleep an extra forty-five minutes each night.

The patrols continued unabated, but during the first week in September the enemy seemed to have given up the fight altogether. For several days in a row there were no firefights, Thanh's informants picked up no rumors, and the families of the PFs heard nothing from their neighbors about nocturnal guerrilla visits. The combined unit threw its small night ambushes out farther, venturing into the My Hué hamlets, where in June daylight raids had required at least a platoon. Still nothing.

The Marine battalion left the district to conduct an operation against an NVA unit back in the hills and its outposts were temporarily guarded by elements from another battalion. Charlie Company of the 7th Marine Regiment had a base on a hill in the middle of the sand dunes one mile northeast of the fort and a headquarters and service platoon occupied that position, while another platoon moved onto a steep knoll called PF Hill, a half-mile west of the fort. These were the regular units nearest the village, and although they had been ordered to "continue patrolling and effect liaison with the Combined Action Platoon at Binh Yen Noi," no officer from the temporary units visited the fort.

There followed during the second week of September a series of disquieting events, the rationale for which became known only after the capture of several prisoners a year later. The first of the events occurred on the night of September 10, when Charlie Company's perimeter—the top of a sand hill in an open desert—came under attack from six Viet Cong. The battle was predictably lopsided and no American was injured. Nor, it seemed, were any of the enemy, who, after firing at a few bunkers, fled in the direction of PF Hill. Three hours later that hill, even steeper than Charlie Company's sand dune, took harassing fire from the paddies below. For the next few nights, both neighbors of Fort Page were more concerned with protecting their own perimeters than patrolling in a strange area.

On the night of September 11, the eve of the GVN elections, the 409th North Vietnamese Battalion blew up the bridge on Highway One which linked Binh Son district town with Marine division headquarters at Chulai. The 409th, composed of some of the most skillful demolition and commando experts in I Corps, had come to the district in response to the repeated requests of Le Quan Viet, the one-armed VC district chief. In keeping with its elite status, the battalion was ordinarily reserved for use only at province level, and it was a mark of Quan Viet's political influence and urgent need that his request was filled. The battalion had come not just to destroy a bridge; it had another task as well.

On September 12, Riley, leading a tired patrol back in at three in the morning, stopped a hundred yards short of the fort to fire a green hand flare signaling his approach.

He was on the open section of the trail with paddies on either side, and as he knelt to pop the flare, his eye caught a slight movement behind a paddy dike to his right.

"Hey," he said, speaking aloud in his disbelief, "we got company."

Realizing they had been seen, two Viet Cong leaped up and ran toward the hamlet treeline. It took the startled patrollers over three seconds to react, and that was too long. They lost sight of the enemy, although they could hear them splashing through the paddies. The Marines were tempted to sweep the area with automatic-weapons fire, but the PFs refused to allow it, arguing that the bullets would rip into the houses in the hamlet unnecessarily. So, instead, they plunked a dozen M-79 grenade rounds into the paddies, more as a gesture and an alibi lest those at the fort accuse them of laxity, knowing the chances of hitting the sprinting enemy were remote. But the precaution proved unnecessary, as neither Thanh, Suong nor Sullivan questioned them closely or paid more than casual attention to the incident, although it was the closest the enemy had been to the fort in two months.

On September 13, Sullivan sent the patrols out over two kilometers from the fort, one ambush to be set in each of the three My Hué hamlets. And as had become his habit during the past few weeks, he let the PFs patrol the safer hamlets of Binh Yen Noi by themselves. The Marines joked that the PFs so assigned spent more time flirting with their girl friends than patrolling, so it came as a mild surprise when around midnight rounds started cracking over the fort, coming from a treeline bordering Binh Yen Noi, not two hundred yards away. Sullivan did not have his men return the fire for fear of hitting some sleeping villagers, and the Marines were a bit annoyed at losing a little sleep but were otherwise unconcerned over the incident.

The next morning the patrols from My Hué reported no contact at all to the north. The PFs who wandered in from Binh Yen Noi, on the other hand, were visibly upset, reporting contacts with numerous probers close to the fort. In response to requests for exact numbers, they would only insistently repeat, "Beaucoup VC, beaucoup VC." That could mean anywhere from two to twenty, however, for the PFs often exaggerated the size and intensity of encounters. Moreover, none of the PFs had been injured and the Marines had heard no sounds to indicate any large firefight during the previous night.

So Sullivan made no changes in the daily routine on September 14. Nor did the PFs attach any special significance to their scare. What finally quelled any lingering uneasiness Sullivan might have harbored was the afternoon arrival of Phuoc, who had traveled by sampan up from Binh Son to announce that the final tally was in and that he had been elected to the National Assembly. The district chief had asked him to warn the fort that intelligence sources indicated an attack was imminent, but in his excitement Phuoc forgot to relay the message. He did voice considerable concern, however, about information at Binh Son which pointed to the presence of an informer among the PFs at the fort.

Sullivan greeted Phuoc with affection. Suong acted as if he were Sullivan's equal, or superior, in military matters, a fact which Sullivan resented. Phuoc, the diplomat, did not pretend to expertise in tactics and in the past had smoothed over rifts between Sullivan and Suong, whom O'Rourke had admired. Sullivan had frequently sought Phuoc's advice and considered the man his friend.

The Marines were pleased at Phuoc's election, and in the growing dusk he sat down to supper as their guest, saying that he planned to spend the night with them and bicycle through the village the next day. As the PFs strolled in from the hamlets, Sullivan read the roster of the night's guard detail and patrols. Faircloth was to lead an eight-man ambush into My Hué, while Fleming was to take just one other Marine and a few PFs and move a half-mile into Binh Yen Noi. Fleming chose his friend, PFC Kenneth Learch, a small, cocky young man. Both patrols left before full dark. Night came thick and drizzling, with rain clouds obscuring a quarter-moon. Neither of the patrols saw or heard anything unusual on its way out. Each settled down to pass a dull, uncomfortable night.

At the fort, Sueter had drawn first guard and busied himself arranging his medical supplies before going out in the rain. Brannon was boisterously presiding over a three-cornered game of hearts with Glasser, the new supply man who had developed a vast admiration for him, and PFC Robert Theilepape, who was trading good-natured insults with Brannon on an even basis. Fielder had gone off to a corner to read his wife's letters in peace. Sullivan, Suong and Thanh were listening to Phuoc brag of his election victory.

Around ten, Sullivan said it was time for lights out. No one argued. The weather was ideal for sleeping and the Marines wandered into their unusually cool tent and stretched out on their cots. Thuoc accepted Sullivan's invitation to sleep in his private quarters, a small alcove off the central meeting room which served as the village office by day and in bad weather was filled with PFs at night. Only twelve were sleeping there on September 14, for in addition to supplying six men for the combined patrols, Suong had dispatched a seven-man unit into Binh Yen Noi to guard the rear of the fort against a recurrence of the harassing fire of the previous night.

It proved to be a sound idea poorly executed. The PFs

sent into Binh Yen Noi needed to knock on only a few doors to satisfy themselves that the Viet Cong were not in the hamlet, yet they were expected to hunker down in the cold drizzle less than a hundred yards from the fort with the supper smells of steaming rice and roast chicken in their nostrils and the inviting lights of warm houses blinking all around them. The temptation was too high; the danger too remote. The seven split up to pass the night with their families or friends, none suggesting a rendezvous point in case an emergency arose.

The first watch at the fort proved to be three hours of unrelieved boredom for Sueter, and shortly before midnight he quickly tramped through the mud across the courtyard to the squad tent and shook Theilepape.

"Huh?" Theilepape groaned, coming awake slowly. "What time is it?"

"Ten minutes to twelve," Sueter replied.

"How're things?" Theilepape asked as he pulled on his boots.

"Quiet."

"Who has the duty after me?"

"Fielder. And how about reminding him to wake me when he gets off watch. I'm holding sick call in the market first thing in the morning."

"O.K."

Sueter was undressed and already lying on his cot by the time Theilepape had slipped on a poncho and stepped out into the rain. Thin and self-effacing, Theilepape got along well with the villagers. His blond hair had on several occasions provoked admiring remarks from the bolder of the hard-working old women in the village and the PFs teased him that he would get "much boom-boom" once his Vietnamese improved. Before going to his post, Theilepape walked into the village office to check with the

PF radio operator, who said he had received no messages from district. Not wishing to awaken any of the PFs sleeping in the room, Theilepape did not linger in conversation. He stepped outside, walked hurriedly across the courtyard. He had not seen the Vietnamese who had the walking post but thought nothing of that. It was not his business to inspect the guard. In pulling a Marine off the walking post, Sullivan had passed full responsibility to the PFs for protection of the rear of the fort. The PF with that sentry duty was in the rear—sitting in a chair with his throat slit.

At the front of the fort, Theilepape ducked into the low bunker containing the Americans' only radio and machine gun. He called PF Hill to make sure the radio was working, then leaned back against the sandbags and looked out across the stake-studded moat through the slatted bamboo fence into the wet, flat black. The beaters at the outer gate were tapping the all-clear signal, the beat being picked up and repeated at other posts throughout the hamlet, the sounds reaching Theilepape like distant echoes, as familiar and reassuring to him as bell buoys to a ship's pilot.

What Theilepape did not know was that the Viet Cong were directing the beat. They had come across from Thuong Hoa village, deep in the Phu Longs, where they had rehearsed and planned the attack for two weeks. Nguyen Son, the quick-tempered leader of the local forces in the Phu Longs, had been reinforced for the attack by the 5th Company of the 409th NVA Battalion. Son had eighty men; the North Vietnamese added sixty more. At the fort, there were six Americans and twelve PFs.

Guided by the hamlet guerrillas from the My Hués and the Binh Yen Nois, the long enemy column crossed the river in a series of sampans, drifting below the village before paddling ashore and wading through the swamps and saw grass south of the fort, thus avoiding the usual river crossings to the north opposite the My Hués, where Faircloth and the others lay in fruitless wait. They came up to the small stream in front of the fort where Lummis had once set in and veered west, passing directly beneath PF Hill, knowing no combined patrol would set an ambush just outside the wire of their neighbor's outpost. Once in the paddies in front of the fort, the unit split up.

The main body moved east in the paddies parallel with the road running from PF Hill to the fort while the special platoon of NVA commando sappers and volunteers from the P31st struck due north, entering the Binh Yen Noi treeline several hundreds of yards to the west of the fort. They picked up a side trail and in single file bore down on the rear of the fort, the guides well out in front, hoping they would not bump into a PF patrol as they had the previous night. If they did, their orders this time were to stand and fight and perhaps distract those guarding the fort so that the main body could breach the front defenses. But that was only the alternate plan. Ideally, the sappers would already be in the fort when the main body assaulted.

The sappers flowed through the hamlet as silent as death, a long line of barefoot men dressed in black shorts and black T-shirts slipping along a mud path in the rain and in the dark. Silent but seen, thirty men in a column snaked through a labyrinth of tight houses from which patches of light fell, in the doorways of which men stood to urinate, from the windows of which children not yet tired peeked out at the raindrops. Behind the sappers lights winked out as the whisper passed from wall to wall and the farmers or the mothers gathered their families, lit their candles, took their thin blankets and climbed down into their deep, solid bunkers.

And the PFs who were supposed to be on patrol in the hamlet saw or were told about the enemy but hid in their separate bedrooms or by the cozy hearths and, when the moment of immediate danger had passed, fled to the bunkers. Frightened and alone, each man, not knowing what to do, did nothing and left it up to somebody else to do something. No man tried a mad dash through the mud to the fort. The risks three or four PFs might have taken together not one would run singly. They were the witnesses who did not want to get involved. That night the hamlet held no heroes.

With fear granting them immunity from exposure, the sappers sneaked into the backyard of the house directly behind the fort and crawled forward. In North Vietnam the men from the 5th Sapper Company had received training for five months in the silent penetration of heavy defenses, and for them the perimeter of Fort Page was about as difficult as would be a two-dollar lock to a master burglar. The single strand of coiled barbed wire was parted and tied back with strips of bamboo, one coil against another, eliminating the need for wire cutters and for the distinctive snap-twang sound of severed steel. Then they were at the shallow, stagnant moat, looking at the thousands of sharp punji stakes which had so impressed Marine inspection parties. The stakes might have discouraged a charging water buffalo, but against men they were useless unless covered by an alert man with a rifle. No one shot at the sappers as they plucked out the stakes with little more effort than is needed to pick flowers.

With them they had carried three boards, one of which they placed down the outer side of the moat, another across the water and the third against the inner side. They paused to put on their sneakers, which they had tied together by the shoelaces and looped around their necks, then climbed up the inner board, which reached within five feet of the back door to Sullivan's room. While some spread out along the sandbagged trench in the rear of the adobe building, most crawled to the right along the trench line to get closer to the Marines' tent, which stood catty-cornered to the building. They were ready. They waited for the signal to attack.

Outside, the main body with the heavy breaching weapons had had no difficulty sneaking up to the beaters at the outer gate and convincing them to continue with the all-clear signal while they set their rocket launchers and rifle grenade crews in position along the ditch to fire at the machine-gun bunker. Behind the heavy weapons a two-platoon assault party crouched, near enough to the fort to see the narrow trail across the moat, knowing that it was blocked by a barbed-wire gate and covered by the machine gun. Once the gun was knocked out either by the sappers inside the fort or by the heavy weapons outside, the assault platoons would rush the gate.

# 13

Inside the fort, Theilepape had snuggled deep into the comfortable sandbags, his poncho wrapped tightly about him, his back to the courtyard. Boots, a small, black mongrel with white legs, waddled over to be petted. Sullivan had found her as a starving, trembling pup, and she had grown plump and playful with the overattention of the Marines. Glad of the company, Theilepape picked her up and sat stroking her softly.

As he relaxed, death stalked him. The enemy's first attempt to kill him came at one in the morning in a fusillade of rifle grenades and a roar of rockets which ripped through the flimsy fence and slammed against the mud bank of the moat, the concussions jarring him but the misses wide enough of their mark to leave him uninjured. Unthinking, acting only from instinct, Theilepape reached forward and pulled back on the machine gun's trigger, loosing a stream of bullets from the gun, which was well seated in the sandbags. He could see the flashes of weapons less than one hundred yards in front of him and presumed the enemy was firing from the ditch along the main trail. So using the gun's red tracers as a gauge, he laid a sheet of fire along the road, pivoting the weapon back and forth on its tripod like a man trying to water the edge of his lawn with a hose that won't quite reach. Theilepape loosed six hundred bullets in a thirty-second burst which forced the rocket firers to go flat in the ditch and wait for a better opportunity.

Following his long initial burst Theilepape was dimly aware of explosions in the courtyard behind him. He thought they were from mortars or possibly more rifle grenades sailing over his head. Then he heard a shout in English and turned to see the squad tent pitching under the impact of grenades. Figures were dashing to and fro. The enemy were in the fort. As Theilepape watched, a corner of the tent burst into flames and he could see the Marines tumbling out. He started to go to them, then stopped, knowing he should not leave the radio and machine gun. Uncertain what to do, he whirled and peered desperately at the dark paddies to his front, momentarily panicking that he might see a screaming horde charging the main gate. Seeing instead nothing, he jerked the machine gun from its tripod and pivoted around to face the courtyard, hoping somehow to help his comrades in their confused fight. But too many figures were darting too quickly in too many directions in the poor light for him to start shooting a machine gun madly, so he became the agonized witness to the fate of his friends.

Fielder. Steady, quiet Paul Fielder pushed the others out of the tent ahead of him and then followed, pausing in the doorway to fire back into the tent, turning, starting to take a step, behind him the tent unfolding and flapping upward like a small rug being shaken out, the force and the shrapnel from the blast catching the Marine and hurling him into the mud. Fielder crying "Doc! Doc!" and dying.

Sueter. The corpsman was well away from the tent, beyond range of the explosion, running behind the big, shielding bulk of Brannon like a flanker back following a pulling guard, when he heard Fielder call to him. He pulled up short and Theilepape saw him stand statue still for about two seconds while the shooting and the shouting went on all around him. Then he made his decision and turned and ran back to Fielder. He reached down and was dragging his friend away from the burning tent when the bullets reached him. Sueter died a corpsman.

From twenty yards away, Theilepape watched that tableau in the jumping light of the flames and bursting grenades. He vaulted the sandbagged parapet of his bunker and was running to the aid of his fallen friends when four figures stepped from the trench line and converged on the bodies and stood gazing down at them. Thinking the figures were PFs, Theilepape yelled, "Get in that trench and get firing."

Startled, the four Viet Cong looked at him for a moment before moving to kill him. Their indecision gave Theilepape time to slide to a stop, reverse direction and race back to his bunker with the bullets zipping about him. Frantically he grabbed his machine gun, spun and fired from the waist, loosing a five-second burst at the attackers, who were firing wildly at him from fifty feet away. The impact of the machine-gun bullets drove one of the four backward for several feet in grotesque, jerking movements, and the others ducked back into the trench.

Theilepape hopped back into his bunker, grabbed the radio and screamed into the handset.

"Get us some goddamn illumination, we're getting murdered down here."

Then he called for help over the phone which connected him by wire to PF Hill.

"Get some people down here. Fast. We need them now."

"We're coming," came the reply.

Putting down the radio, Theilepape peered about, seeking the other Americans.

Glasser. The Marine whom O'Rourke had instructed in the delicate art of shooting rocks had been first out of the tent but had forgotten his rifle. Unarmed, he had dashed toward the front of the courtyard, opposite the machine-gun bunker. There he had hidden for a few minutes before making a dash back toward the tent, perhaps to snatch up a weapon. But the sappers had by then advanced up the trench line and they caught him in the open, a half-dozen rifles firing at him from a few feet away. He died instantly.

Brannon. The Marine who liked to laugh had barged out of the tent on the attack, continuing across the courtyard after Sueter had turned back, pausing to get his bearings, seeing the weapons winking at him from the trench line. Crouching, firing, moving, shifting and snap-shooting, oblivious to the drama of Fielder and Sueter behind him, intent only on the sappers in the trench, it seemed for a moment that he might make it. Then Glasser went down in front of him and Theilepape heard a roar, not a curse, not an intelligible word, just the primordial sound of rage from a dangerous, wounded animal, and Brannon was staggering toward the trench line, the fast sound of his M-14 mingling with the slower sounds of what seemed to Theilepape like a dozen enemy weapons. Then it was over and Brannon fell, having lost his duel and leaving Ho Chi no one to joke with and Luong no one to share point with. He was dead.

"Jesus," said Theilepape, more in prayer than in curse. He was on the verge of panic. Every Marine he had seen had been shot. Directly behind him, he could see that the PFs had swarmed out of the main hall and were clustered in the back corner of the trench. Desperately, he wanted to jump over the sandbags and run to them, but the part of him which controlled his legs would not let him leave the radio. He could hear Suong shouting to his men, his commands followed by an uncertain rattle of PF fire which soon swelled into a deafening volume. Momentarily, Theilepape was in the backwash of the fight. He could think only of getting help, and from the ammunition box he pulled out a dozen red-star hand flares, their light an emergency signal for the patrols to fall back on the fort. Frantically, he sent up one after another.

A few miles away, Faircloth and his men heard the firing but thought it came from Fleming's patrol. It did not occur to them that the fort might be in trouble. They never saw the flares, which were obscured by the rain and low clouds. They had no radio. The estimated the firing went on for over thirty minutes, but that did not worry them since they had listened to scores of firefights in the months they had been at the fort. So Faircloth and his seven men held their position and returned on schedule at dawn, unprepared for the scene which greeted them.

Learch and Fleming, manning the ambush close to the fort, saw the flares and headed back, automatically taking the main trail. They bumped head on into the enemy main assault party, still gathered outside the front gate waiting for the right moment to swarm in. Hearing the running men, the Viet Cong started shooting just before Fleming, who was at point, reached the beaters' perch at the outer gate. The enemy's burst of fire was so enormous and sudden that as one man the two Marines and two PFs dove headlong into a paddy and crawled, splashed and almost swam their way from the trail out to the nearest mud dike, behind which they lay.

"God," gasped Fleming, "there must be a battalion of them."

"What'll we do?" Learch asked. "From where we are, if we fire, we'll hit the fort."

"Let's not piss them off," Fleming replied.

"Well, I'm not moving again," Learch said. "If the Cong want us, they can come and get us."

The PFs agreed, so they held their fire and their position and waited for the attack which they considered inevitable, unaware that they were a worrisome distraction to the Viet Cong and not a main target.

Inside the fort, Teilepape's repeated shouts had finally raised a response from Sullivan, who had barricaded himself in his small room and, with Phuoc, was fending off the sappers who were darting about like hounds around a bear. The small adobe room had just two outside entrances, a set of wooden doors locked from the inside which opened to the moat in the rear and an open entrance facing the rear flap of the squad tent. The Viet Cong first tried to rush this open front, but Sullivan and Phuoc drove them back with their pistols. To Theilepape the reports of the .45s sounded like cap pistols. There was a heavy burst of firing which ended with the punctuation of a single .45 round. Sullivan had shot one of the enemy at close range and the impact of the .45 slug flung the man backward against the burning tent. This caused the other Viet Cong to retreat momentarily, and the sergeant took advantage of the respite to holler at Theilepape.

"What's it look like?" Sullivan yelled.

"I don't know," Theilepape yelled back. "They're all over the place."

"You hold them off up there," Sullivan replied. "We'll handle it back here."

A pause, then more shooting, then Sullivan yelling again.

"Where's that goddamn illumination?"

"I don't know. I don't know."

Sullivan didn't have a chance to say anything further. A satchel charge plopped inside the room and went off, the force of the blast blowing the rear doors outward off their hinges and setting fire to the woodwork in the room. Phuoc wandered dazedly out the rear into the waiting guns, while Sullivan, badly wounded, stumbled into the courtyard.

Theilepape was back on the radio, crouching behind the sandbags while rounds whined and smacked around him. He could hear the metallic clink of a round leaving a mortar five hundred meters away on PF Hill and hollered over the radio, "Where's my illumination?"

"We don't have any," came the reply. "It's a batch of duds."

"Listen," Theilepape yelled, "I don't give a goddamn if you have to shit some, I want some rounds—and some people."

"O.K. O.K."

The Americans on PF Hill called the nearest artillery battalion and within three minutes flares were bursting over the fort. But no relief forces were on the way.

On paper, there was a reaction-force plan under which reinforcements for Fort Page should have been moving within two minutes and arriving within five minutes after the distress call had been received by PF Hill. But the commander of the substitute squad on that hill, a second lieutenant, had listened to the fight erupt, heard Theilepape's first call and elected to proceed with caution.

"Let's wait and see what happens," he had said uncertainly.

One man, Sergeant Brown, thought the lieutenant showed poor judgment. A wiry black man with ten years' service, Brown knew from the intensity of the firing that a full-scale attack was being launched against the fort. It was not the time to wait. His two crews of 106-mm recoilless rifles had been attached to Charlie Company for several months and never once used. When the battalion had moved out, he was left behind because his large weapons, designed to shatter tanks, were not necessary. Now on his own initiative, he told his men to load the guns and aim their long muzzles into the dark paddies fronting the fort.

"Shall I fire, sir?" Brown asked his vacillating lieutenant.

"I don't know," the lieutenant replied.

"Fire," Brown yelled to his men.

With cotton stuffed in their ears, the gunners tapped the large firing buttons and with a sound like a thunderclap the guns spat flame and the shells roared through the air like express trains and exploded in the paddies, missing the Viet Cong, missing Fleming's patrol, but shocking the battlefield into silence.

Theilepape took advantage of the moment to sprint toward Sullivan's room, hoping to reach a rack of LAWs stored in a small gear closet. But inside the entire room was blazing and neither Sullivan nor Phuoc was to be seen. Cradling the machine gun in his arms, Theilepape stumbled backward to his bunker again.

Sullivan. Back at his post, Theilepape had just decided that Sullivan must have joined the PFs in the rear of the fort when he heard the sergeant yell from the front of the courtyard just opposite his machine-gun bunker. There followed a strong burst of automatic-weapons fire, punctuated by the feeble pop of a pistol. Another long burst. A pop. Another long burst. No reply from the pistol. Sullivan was dead.

Theilepape was the only American left alive, and his machine gun was blocking the hundred-odd men waiting to storm through the main gate, annihilate the PFs and raise the Viet Cong flag. So the sappers held a huddled conference near the burnt-out tent and then they came at Theilepape again.

From the way they started moving, Theilepape was sure he would soon die. No sapper again exposed himself by venturing into the open courtyard. Instead, they crept up the trench line past Sullivan's body to the front of the fort, and once there they entered the section of trench which ran straight to the machine-gun bunker. While several skirmishers peppered the bunker's sandbags with rifle bullets, a group of grenadiers with sackfuls of grenades bellied forward.

The first grenade was short and blew off harmlessly outside the bunker. Theilepape quickly grasped their simple plan but didn't know what to do about it. Each time he raised his head to loose a burst, he could hear the rounds crack and smack about him. To get at the grenadiers he would have to lean far out over the sandbags and he guessed he would be riddled the instant he did so. Believing the end had come, he spent his last few minutes in the bunker yelling over the radio to PF Hill. Between the booms of the recoilless rifles, he could dimly hear what he correctly thought was Fleming's voice from somewhere in the paddies.

"Turn it off! Turn it off!" Fleming kept shouting over and over, assuming the fort was in friendly hands and worried about being hit by the blind cannons blasting from PF Hill.

There were other shouts. Suong was trying to get his attention, calling something about PFs in the paddies, and Theilepape was aware that Vietnamese voices up the road closer to PF Hill were shouting Marine names and nicknames too. It turned out later that the voices belonged to the PFs who had hidden in Binh Yen Noi and who, after the firing began, had gotten together and moved to help the fort, driven either by shame or fear of what Suong might do to them later.

"Cease fire! Tell Brown to cease fire!" Theilepape screamed above the din into his radio. "There are Marines and PFs out there."

Then, sensing the closeness of his death, pleading, almost crying with the voice on the phone which for half an hour had been assuring him a Marine squad was on the way: "Where are they, man, where are they? Where are they?"

His eyes were watering with tears of rage and grief and fear when the enemy found the range and the first grenade bounced in and dribbled around his feet. Unable in the dark to see to pick it up, Theilepape tried to get out. He had almost made it when the blast caught him in his legs and buttocks and picked him up and hurled him from the bunker. Badly shaken and bleeding profusely, he staggered to his feet and rolled over the parapet back into the bunker. Another grenade sailed in and he dove out into the trench, only to land on a third grenade, the force of which lifted his body right off the ground. In a state of severe shock, unable to focus his eyes, with lacerations of the foot, wrist, shoulders and head, Theilepape reeled backward into the courtyard and collapsed.

The Marines' fight had bought time for the PFs to organize a defense outside the main hall at the rear of the fort. Suong had only ten armed men, plus Thanh and his two policemen, with which to work. There were about a dozen other Vietnamese sleeping in the fort that night, but they were village officials and elders, mostly old, all unarmed and none a military man. Suong lost three PFs in the first five seconds of the attack. Two died when a satchel charge was pitched into the main hall, and the PF walking post had disappeared. In the first few minutes while the Marines were battling the bulk of the sapper platoon on the opposite side of the courtyard, the PFs were kept on the defensive by a smaller group of enemy who were sniping at them from the rear trench line. Assuming they, too, like the Marines, were under full assault, the PFs had blazed away with their weapons on full automatic, doing little damage to the enemy using the cover of the trench.

It was only in the full lull before the enemy's final assault on the machine gun that Suong was able to sort out the pattern of the attack and calm his men down. Suong could clearly hear the enemy yelling back and forth from the paddies to the fort.

"Now?"

"No, not yet."

"Well, hurry up."

Suong told his men that when the machine gun went out, the enemy outside was coming in. He tried calling to Theilepape to tell him to get out of the bunker and join them, but Theilepape hadn't understood, and even if he had, his actions indicated that he was determined to stay there until the end. The PFs saw the bunker buckle under explosions. They saw Theilepape reel, stumble and finally sprawl face down in the mud.

Bac Si Khoi went after him. Khoi, the older brother of the PF who had been killed in June, was the self-taught medic for the Vietnamese. He looked fifteen years old and he usually had a shy smile on his face when he talked. Leaving his carbine behind, Khoi moved swiftly. He was out of the small PF perimeter at a full run, into the courtyard bright under the harsh, colorless light of artillery flares, and beside the fallen Theilepape before the enemy reacted. As the bullets started to whip about him, Suong called on his men to use what was practically the last of their ammunition to discourage the aim of the sappers. Under cover of the PF fire, Khoi dragged Theilepape behind the fort to the garbage pit, which was piled high with empty C-ration cartons and cans. In the belief that he and the other PFs could not hold out, Khoi rolled the unconscious Theilepape into the pit and heaped litter over the body, hoping the enemy would not find him.

The efforts of the PFs to protect Khoi and Theilepape displayed a surprising pocket of strength and checked the momentum the enemy had gained from silencing the machine gun. The sappers fell back to their stronghold, that portion of the trench directly behind the still flickering tent. They had been on the attack for half an hour, more often crawling than moving erect. They, too, were low on ammunition, short of breath, sweat-soaked, uncertain whether reinforcements for the defenders might arrive before their own did. Once forced back, the pressure and the excitement abated, and the sappers collapsed. Suong could hear their leaders exhorting them to get out of the trench and to keep firing at the PFs. But when only a few desultory rounds followed, the PF commander assumed he would have the respite of a few minutes while the sappers rested before resuming the attack.

In the lull, Suong set out to find more ammunition. But as Theilepape had been, he, too, was driven back from the storeroom by the flames licking at that side of the building. He went around to try the rear and encountered flames there also, so he was heading back down the rear trench when he saw Phuoc's body draped over a loose mound of sandbags. A man was kneeling beside the body and with a short knife was hacking the head away from the trunk. The man was absorbed in his task and Suong was standing above him before he looked up, just in time to see the blow which killed him. Suong swung his carbine like a baseball bat, smashing the man full in his upturned face, the man jerking backward over his own heels and Suong stepping forward, striking with the butt of his carbine again and again.

Suong dragged the mutilated corpse of Phuoc back to the PF position, where the PFs were watching the sappers scurrying up the trench line opposite them. It was apparent that the enemy, rather than charging across the open courtyard, would crawl around by the front of the fort past the machine-gun bunker and attack down the trench line toward them, using the grenading tactic which had worked against Theilepape. Luong scrambled up onto the sloping roof of the adobe building and lay facing the front of the fort. There was only one break in the square trench line around the fort, and that was at the front gate. In getting across, each enemy soldier would have to expose himself to the bright flares for at least two seconds. Luong waited for someone to try.

Behind him Theilepape had regained consciousness and pawed his way from the garbage pit. Hiding in a cor-

ner, Minh, the village chief clerk, saw him and called to
Khoi. Theilepape could hear yelling in Vietnamese but no
shooting, and with his mind not clear, his only thought
was to rejoin the Marines. He stumbled around the back of
the building, past the Viet Cong with the crushed skull, up
the west side of the fort to the smoldering tent, to the bodies of Sueter and Fielder. He knelt by his fallen friends for
a moment, remembrance coming back, then on his hands
and knees he crawled forward to where Brannon lay.

That was where Khoi caught up to him. He grabbed
Theilepape by the shoulder and shook him.

"VC. VC," he said, pointing to the front trench line, a
dozen yards in front of them.

Theilepape looked at him dully, reached out and picked
up Brannon's automatic rifle, and followed Khoi back
around the rear of the fort.

Luong watched them crawl from the courtyard. If the
Viet Cong had seen them, they gave no sign of it, so Luong
assumed the enemy's attention was riveted on the open
spot in front of them.

The first sapper to emerge from the dark trench into the
light by the front gate did not dash across. Once fully erect
and exposed, he hesitated, uncertain, reluctant, like a
bather at the edge of frigid waters. With one shot at a distance of less than twenty yards, Luong dropped the enemy
soldier, his shot spinning him back into the trench. The
other sappers quickly fired at the building, their rounds
ricocheting harmlessly off slate roof. Luong had dropped
out of sight on the back side of the roof and the next sapper could have scurried safely across the opening, but
none tried.

Instead, the enemy set up a great clamor, shouting at
the assault party still waiting in the paddies, yelling for
them to come in. And the PFs took up the shouting, jeering

at their enemies, cursing, daring them to come on. All were speaking the same language, all except the North Vietnamese having the same accent and using identical slang expressions and invectives, their voices drowning each other out. From the paddies farther from the fort the PFs from the Binh Yen Noi patrol were yelling to Suong while Fleming and Learch were bellowing in English. In the midst of this bedlam the leader of the enemy assault party was screaming for clarification, for just one voice to speak, obviously too confused or too reluctant to commit his men, knowing that the recoilless rifles on the nearby hill were loaded and looking for a target now that the flares had come, and believing that somewhere some Marines were moving, raising the specter that he might get into the fort but not back out again. Finally, he decided and yelled for the sappers to pull out and that he would cover them while they did.

Suong and Luong and Khoi and the other PFs and the village officials heard the shouted orders at the same time as did the sappers and set up a cheer. The sappers responded with curses and threats but few bullets, both sides being almost out of ammunition, Luong having fired the last of his clips to demonstrate to the sappers that the PFs were well stocked. As the sappers withdrew, a Viet Cong and an overly enthusiastic PF, darting forward too close, collided. Neither had a bullet left and they settled for an exchange of kicks before each fled back to his own ranks. The sappers, carrying their wounded and five dead, went out the same way they had come in, in plain and slow view as they crossed the moat, but in no danger from the PFs, who were throwing rocks. In the hands of an unsteady Theilepape who refused to lie down, Brannon's rifle supplied the last six shots at the enemy.

*          *          *

An hour after it had begun, the fight was over. By two in the morning the enemy was clear of the fort. They split into three groups when leaving. The main body cut south across the rice paddies to the Tra Bong River, where boats were drawn up to carry them to the Phu Longs. Once there, they would disperse and be in their wooded base camps before dawn. To protect the boats, a small group lingered behind on the edge of the mangroves and kept up a desultory fire on the fort and on Fleming and Learch. The third unit, a propaganda squad, scattered dozens of leaflets, some in English and some in Vietnamese, before leaving the fort. The English message ran: "Stop raping our women and butchering our babies, leave our country, refuse to fight, protest the war." The names of two U.S. senators to whom the Marines should write were given. The Vietnamese message stressed that the GVN was going to lose the war, so it would be better for the people to join the victors—the Viet Cong—while they still could. Distribution of the leaflets was not limited to the fort. The propaganda team left the area by passing through Binh Yen Noi, where they dropped leaflets on the main trail and laughed loudly to ensure that the villagers, huddled in their bomb shelters, heard the sounds of their unchallenged passage.

After the Viet Cong had left the fort and the firing had died away, the Marine squad from PF Hill entered the fort, claiming they had been held up by a sniper hiding in the schoolhouse at the foot of their hill. It was nearly three in the morning. The battle was over. Occasional rounds still sang through the night, but nobody paid them much notice. Six wounded PFs were bandaged, defensive positions were assigned the new troops, and Theilepape waited for the helicopter which would fly him out. The Marine radio operator from the reaction squad was nervous and unsure of his location, so Theilepape grabbed the radio and called in his own medical evacuation, as well as that of the wounded PFs. At three-thirty, the wounded were lifted out by helicopter. Theilepape's last impression of the fort was glimpsing the little dog, Boots, sitting by Sullivan's body, whimpering.

# BOOK IV

# "WORK VERY HARD—NEVER LOOK TIRED"

# 14

Theilepape would recover from his wounds, but five Americans—Brannon, Glasser, Sueter, Fielder and Sullivan—were dead, as were six Vietnamese defenders, including Phuoc. At first light, General Lowell English, commander of the 1st Marine Division, entered the smoldering fort and called aside the six surviving Marines who had been out on patrol during the night. Speaking softly, he said they had a choice. They could stay or they could go. Perhaps what was needed was a full Marine platoon operating as Marine platoons regularly did. The combined platoon might be too light for the job, and too exposed. They may have been overmatched from the start. Delicately, the general was telling them that he was considering pulling them out.

The survivors couldn't understand that.

"The general was a nice guy," Fleming said in an interview a month later. "He was trying to give us an out. But we couldn't leave. What would we have said to the PFs after the way we pushed them to fight the Cong? We had to stay. There wasn't one of us who wanted to leave.

"The only people we wanted out was that worthless reaction squad that didn't get to the fort until after it was overrun."

With a small smile and a firm handshake for each of them, General English left, promising that the six replacements for the combined unit would be first-class volunteers and that the strange Marines and other Americans milling around the fort would be gone by the next day.

As the general flew out, a helicopter from corps headquarters carrying a special police interrogation team
landed, having been called by Thanh, who suspected that
the PF walking post had been killed by an inside agent.
The interrogation team worked all day, with Thanh assist-
ing, and questioned every Vietnamese who had had extensive dealings at the fort. One PF was questioned closely,
but only for purposes of regular military intelligence. He
had identified by voice his brother as being among the
sappers. But no one suggested any collusion between the
two; his efforts to kill his brother had been too genuine.

The investigators, however, brought back for re-exami-
nation a second and then a third time a wealthy village
official who slept at the fort but was not there the night of
the attack. The Americans could not cope with the quick-
flowing dialogue, but the third time the man was questioned, a group of PFs were called on to listen. When they
vigorously denied what he was saying, the special police
took him away.

Later that week Thanh learned that the man bribed
some of his captors and was set free without further questioning. He never came back to the village; instead, he
moved to Saigon. There was talk for a while about taking
up a collection to send an assassin to Saigon to track the
man down, but it came to nothing because Thanh, the only
person among the parochial village militia capable of finding the man in the sprawling city, did not think he could
get away with it.

The American investigation team with General English
attributed the success of the Viet Cong and North
Vietnamese commandos to the work of "a fifth columnist"
and recommended Sergeant Sullivan for the Silver Star,
the only medal for courage ever to be given to a Marine at
Fort Page. But the Marines in the combined unit never

believed conspiracy had caused their defeat; complacency had. A summer of growing success had spoiled them. They had been too cocky, too sure. Once they had learned how to patrol, they had not thought of how the enemy might be forced to change. They had let down for the sake of sleep. And every new member of the combined unit, be he Vietnamese or American, was told the tale of that night before he was posted to guard duty.

On the afternoon of September 15, 1966, funeral services were held for the six Vietnamese and the five Americans in the small pagoda next to the marketplace in the hamlet of Binh Yen Noi. The Buddhist monks came to the fort and asked the combined-unit Marines to come with them, and the Vietnamese and the Americans walked side by side through the village in the massive funeral procession, with the cymbals clanging and the women wailing and the sky heavy with rain. When the prayers were said to Buddha, the monks mentioned the fallen Americans by name. The Marines thanked the villagers for their sorrow and for their prayers. In the drizzle of evening, they walked slowly back to the fort, where they found Sergeant James White waiting for them.

From the horse-riding region of Pennsylvania, White several years earlier had chosen not to follow his father and his older brother to the Hill School and to Yale. Instead, with a boy's dream of a military career, he had attended the lesser-known Manlius Military Academy, graduating as the class president and cadet commander. His marks were not sufficient for Yale, however, and college seemed dull, while the Vietnam war was receiving favorable publicity in 1965. So he enlisted in the Marines to fight, sure of himself and sure of his military prep school training. It was also sure that no Marine drill instructor would share that attitude, and White spent his first seven months in the service as a short-tempered and harassed private. Then came Vietnam and a rice paddy, with his platoon squashed down by machine-gun fire and White still able to think, shoot, encourage and direct. Five months and fifteen operations later, he was a sergeant and the most experienced squad leader in the battalion.

In early September his squad drew shotgun duty for a truck convoy driving the sixty miles north from Chulai to Da Nang. They had barely started when they ran into a nest of snipers firing at them from a distant treeline. White's squad debarked and, accepting the snipers as a routine irritant, followed a standard procedure. Covering each other, two fire teams advanced on the treeline while White stayed back with his third team to keep contact with the drivers. He was leaning against a truck hood talking on a radio when a few stray rounds zipped by. More from habit than any sense of danger, he dropped flat and continued talking. The movement proved to be his undoing. In a moment of panic, the inexperienced driver put the truck in gear and slammed his foot on the accelerator. One of the front wheels ran over both White's legs. Nothing was broken, but his legs were badly bruised. Sent back to the battalion medical ward, he had been recuperating in bed when he heard of the attack against Fort Page. White asked to see the doctor.

"Sir, I knew Sullivan and I know that gang at the fort," he said. "They're going to need someone. I can walk. I'd like to go down."

The doctor agreed, so White grabbed his rifle, limped to the medevac pad and hitched a helicopter ride to the fort. He was waiting when the combined-unit Marines returned from the funeral. He looked at them carefully and they stared flatly back, not accepting but not rejecting him, an acknowledgment that he might fit in, knowing who he was and what he had done.

"We'll take the watches in the fort tonight," White said, noting their red eyes and slack faces. "The reaction platoon can take the patrols tonight."

"This is our village," Fleming replied, "not theirs."

"Now listen," White said, with an edge on his voice, "starting tomorrow it's back to business as usual and you're going to be working your asses off patrolling all over the ville. Smarten up. That platoon's pulling out tomorrow so we might as well get some work out of them tonight and get a good night's sleep ourselves."

The following day, as soon as he was off guard, Combat Culver walked alone to the marketplace, bought a bottle of Vietnamese moonshine, and sat outside the house of a PF friend, drinking himself into oblivion in the morning sun. He had been friends with Larry Page and had been on patrol with him that calm June night when he was killed. And he had been closer to Sullivan than anyone else in the fort, acting as a confidant and staunchly defending the sergeant's actions. Shortly before noon some women passing by the fort told Faircloth that the American called Culver was crazy drunk in the marketplace. Faircloth went after him and returned to the fort with Culver, alternately bellowing and screaming, slung over his shoulder.

"Something's wrong in the ville," Faircloth said after he had placed Culver on a cot. "I'm not part Indian for nothing. I can sense it. I can almost smell it."

To better gauge what Faircloth meant, White sent his Marines to stroll around the hamlets while he stayed at the fort to assist in the departure of the reaction-force platoon, who were already climbing into the waiting trucks. The Marines walked nonchalantly down the paths, as they had on a hundred other afternoons. Only this time the villagers avoided them, walking off the trail when they saw them coming or shuffling rapidly by with downcast eyes. If a Marine shouted a greeting to a farmer he knew well, the man would reply in a low voice or with a furtive gesture, as if embarrassed or frightened to be recognized. Even Lance Corporal Larry Wingrove, a husky, smiling young man whose popularity with the children was magnetic, walked alone.

At twilight only the PFs gathered at the fort; the hamlet elders and the village officials had left to spend the night at district headquarters, as they had done before the Marines had come to the village. At the fort, Thanh told the Marines that when the patrols went out, they would be forced to fight. The Viet Cong had talked to the people and said they were coming back, like in the old days. Following the attack on the fort, they had said the Marines would leave and the villagers had seen the trucks leave that afternoon. Nervous neighbors had been urging the families of PFs to flee, lest they be denounced and punished when the Front held their first public meeting. In each hamlet secret cadres were organizing for the return of the Viet Cong, and some were openly giving instructions to the people. Thanh thought the northernmost hamlet of My Hué would be the site of the Liberation Front return rally, and White was eager to take a patrol and accompany the police chief there.

Suong did not object, so White took responsibility for the My Hués, leaving Wingrove, Fleming and Culver to work under Suong in the seemingly safer Binh Yen Noi hamlets. Suong did not say anything until White and Thanh had left, then he put Luong in charge of a five-man patrol which included Wingrove and Fleming. As he walked out the gate, Fleming noticed that the PFs who were staying behind were putting on their cartridge belts and that Suong was shaking awake a badly hung-over PFC Culver. Suong seemed to suspect that Binh Yen Noi might not be as quiet as Thanh and White thought.

It was not fully dark when Lin Thuc, a stocky PF with hard eyes and a quiet manner, took point and led the five patrollers down the main trail into Binh Yen Noi. Moving quietly through the hamlet, the patrol had almost reached the marketplace when Wingrove sensed a strange tempo to the place. As they were supposed to, the villagers had their lights out and were indoors. The hamlet was hushed—too much so. The Marines had argued long with the more stubborn of the villagers to tamp down fires, lower the pitch of conversations and not pile brambles on trails to enclose animals. Feeling that the way was too clear and the stillness too pervasive, Wingrove dragged the pace while trying to decide on a course of action. Several yards ahead, Thuc, having seen Wingrove's hesitation, drew up and stepped into the shadows.

Wingrove at that point was abreast of the house of Missy Tinh, a pretty girl with a coy manner and a warm smile who competed with Missy Top for the Marine laundry concession. Unlike Top, Tinh had not slept with any American. But she said no in a way which left hope for the future and she had several ardent suitors.

As Wingrove walked by her house, he saw her father standing in the shadows.

"Chao," Tinh said.

"Chao, ong," Wingrove replied automatically, inquiring after his health. "Mann gioi khong?"

Wingrove knew Tinh rather well. On several occasions he had eaten at his house, attracted there by his pretty daughter. Wingrove had a relaxed way about him and a guitar with one bad string on which he could pluck a few stanzas of two Vietnamese songs and fake his way in

English through several rock-and-roll numbers, a talent which had prompted his rivals to quip that Missy Tinh invited the guitar to dinner and let Wingrove tag along. Wingrove laughed tolerantly at the jibes of his American friends. While he was genuinely attracted to the demure Missy Tinh, with her composed manner and graceful style, he knew that the morals of the Vietnamese village society were strict and that Tinh's father kept a close watch on his daughter. But that didn't bother him. He liked visiting with the family, strumming his guitar near the hearth while Mr. Tinh sipped a beer and his wife busied herself in the kitchen and Missy Tinh helped her mother and smiled each time she walked by.

So when Wingrove saw Mr. Tinh out after curfew, he at first thought nothing of it and walked on after saying good evening. But after a hundred patrols in the village, part of Wingrove operated in accord with a delicate sense of self-preservation. As he started to walk on, Thuc, the point man, stepped out of the shadows and looked at him with a strange, puzzled expression, as if he wanted to communicate an unease he vaguely felt yet couldn't express in the pidgin language they used. Wingrove stopped and stood looking at the ground while the rest of the patrol moved up. Then, acting on an impulse he didn't understand himself, he doubled back and circled around Tinh's house. So quietly did he move that he was standing next to Mr. Tinh, who was whispering to a crouching figure, before either of the men saw or heard him. Mr. Tinh never tried to run. He just looked at Wingrove, first in shock, then in resignation.

The other man let out a stifled yelp and darted away. He ran right by Thuc, who took one look at him and yelled, "VC, VC!" The man swerved off the trail into a paddy. At a distance of twenty feet, Thuc shot him dead. Wingrove collared Tinh while Thuc splashed forward and stripped a

French submachine gun from the body. As Thuc waded out of the paddy, bullets snapped at him from several directions.

The patrollers flopped down and returned the fire, covering Thuc's dash to the dark of the bushes. But still the enemy fire did not abate; instead, it swelled and Wingrove counted flashes from over twenty weapons. Then the enemy started moving toward them, slipping along the sides of the main trail, firing and bounding forward by groups of three and four.

"Get help!" Fleming yelled, his M-14 slamming out short bursts across sixty meters of paddy at a winking treeline.

On his back Wingrove was carrying a radio loaned by the reaction platoon so they could be quickly contacted back at PF Hill.

"You get it," Wingrove replied. "Take that thing off me and call in. I don't know how to use it."

Fleming crawled next to Wingrove, tugged the radio from his shoulders and turned it on.

"We're really in it out here," he radioed. "It's either a reinforced platoon or a company. They're on the trail south of the market."

The enemy was trying to outflank the patrol, creeping between the houses and yelling to each other as they came on. Behind the Marines Luong's M-1 was cracking steadily while Thuc preferred to stay at Wingrove's elbow and direct his shots, since he had a grenade launcher. Thuc had remarkable eyesight. He would catch a movement in the bush and excitedly point out the location to Wingrove, who would then pump in shell after shell. Within two minutes, artillery flares were opening over them. Fleming was back at work with his automatic rifle and his tracers ignited two thatched houses, further lighting the scene and preventing the Viet Cong from entering the paddy to retrieve the body.

Inside ten minutes they could hear reaction forces thundering down the trail and crashing through the bush, their shouts and skyward rifle blasts adding to the melee in a signal to both the patrol and the enemy that help was coming. The enemy firing died abruptly and Wingrove relaxed, thinking it was over.

But Thuc and Luong would have none of that, insisting they attack the enemy immediately. They swore they heard the Viet Cong yelling to one another, "Get across the river. Get across the river." Wingrove told Luong he was out of his mind, that there might be a VC company out there. Then Suong arrived at the head of a PF squad from the fort, and right behind him came a Marine squad from PF Hill.

"You guys got here pretty quick," Wingrove complimented the Marines grudgingly. "You must have run all the way."

Thuc and Luong were busy talking to Suong, who merely glanced at the patrollers to make sure none of them had been injured before wheeling his ten PFs and heading for the river, leaving one PF behind to hold the hapless Tinh. Thuc urged Wingrove and Fleming to convince the other Marines to move. Wingrove feared an ambush, but he feared even more being upstaged by the PFs, so with Thuc in the lead, they were off for the river, taking a path parallel to that of Suong.

Occasional rounds snipped through the trees after them, but the snipers did not succeed in diverting the attention of the teams. Wingrove's group reached the river bank at the spot where Sullivan's rented coconut tree grew. The lady who owned it and with whom Sullivan had had his picture taken by O'Rourke darted out from her house as Wingrove passed by.

"VC, VC," she said, pointing to a small hut near the tree.

Wingrove and Thuc crept up as close as they dared on either side of the door. Thuc called to the occupants to come out.

"Hang oi," Thuc shouted. "Lai oay. Gio tay len."

Wingrove heard the enemy inside the hut whispering, then they shouted something to Thuc. Thuc shook his head.

"No come out. Hold here," he said to Wingrove, gesturing toward the clearing and the river beyond, making it plain that the first Marine or PF to expose himself along the bank would be shot.

There was a commotion behind them, and from the whispers Wingrove gathered that Suong's men had joined the Marines lying in the shadows out of the line of fire. Thuc held up a grenade. Wingrove held up two. Thuc nodded. They each pitched a grenade at the door. The explosions were sharp and violent, and what was left of the hut was still hidden in a cloud of dust and dirt when they threw their second grenades. When the dust rose a bit, they cautiously advanced into the rubble, finding two mangled and well-armed bodies.

Suong moved by the hut, leading the main body, which, now combined, numbered about twenty. In front of them on the river they saw the dark outlines of several small sampans and round wicker-basket boats disappearing into the night. Farther out in the blackness pricks of light, the hooded signal lanterns of the VC guide boats, danced and bobbed like fireflies under the mad, chopping strokes of rowers pulling to put as much water as possible between them and the bank. Suong had to issue no orders. The firing began as a ragged crackling and soon swelled to a roar as, incredibly, the crews of the guide boats kept their lanterns lighted while the red tracers went flicking by. LAWs were pulled open and the rockets sent banging forth to join the thousands of bullets skimming across the waters.

"Shift that illumination," Fleming was yelling into the radio. "Get it out on the river."

"That's out of range," a voice from the artillery battery replied. "We're firing at maximum range."

"Nuts," Fleming said, turning to the PF leader. "No more light, Mr. Suong, no more light."

And Suong shouted for them all to fire and fire and fire and to hell with worrying about ammunition. The Marines with their automatic M-14s were lying in an even line as though they were on a target range, firing, changing magazines and firing as swiftly as they could. The PFs in various positions with their puny carbines were doing the same, and the noise of the weapons reverberated from the packed earth like a thousand hammers beating on a thousand frying pans. The din ended only when some Viet Cong leader managed to scream some sense at the guides and those lanterns not yet hit were puffed out.

Thuc led the way back to the main trail, where Suong paused for several seconds to look at the man Thuc had killed at the start of the fight. Across the paddy a small group of villagers were fighting the flames from the two thatched houses ignited earlier by Fleming's tracers. They needed help to keep the flames from spreading, but most of the villagers were hiding in their bunkers, unaware of the danger to their homes. After posting a small outguard, Suong led his force to the fire, where he organized the soldiers into bucket brigades and used the paddy water that was a few feet from the houses. Soon the fire fizzled out. The families who had owned the two houses had huddled off to one side, trembling and sobbing, several of them burned or bruised. Fleming gathered them up, the Marines carrying the two smallest children, and followed Suong back the half-mile to the fort. The flares had stopped and the hamlet was dark and still as the long line of armed men moved quietly in the dirt of the trail, the loudest sounds of their passage being the frightened whimpering of the children, who had lost their homes, and the gagging cough of Mr. Tinh, who was pulled along with a rope around his neck.

At the fort, Bac Si Khoi and a Marine corpsman put salve on the wounds of the dispossessed families and set up bunks in the side room for them to sleep. In the main room, the interrogation of Mr. Tinh began. They beat the man until he could not stand, and then they beat him some more, yet he told them only what they already knew or what was obvious: that he had been a Party member since 1963; that he had told the villagers the Marines were not coming to the hamlet; that the Viet Cong were and that there would be a large public rally at the marketplace. He had been talking with Ba Bao, the assistant commander of the P31st Company and a native of Binh Yen Noi, when Wingrove walked up to him. Tinh would not say anything about the plans for the attack on the fort and he did not reveal the names of any other agents in the village.

At about three in the morning, Mr. Tinh was hanged from the flagpole in the courtyard of Fort Page.

Thanh wanted to go out immediately and pick up Tinh's daughter, arguing that her father had wanted her to sleep with the Americans so that she could gather intelligence. Wingrove refused to believe the police chief and told him to leave the girl alone. Missy Tinh was never again to speak to Wingrove, holding him responsible for the death of her father, yet were it not for Wingrove, Thanh would have killed her that night. The PFs agreed with

Thanh: Missy Tinh had to know who her father was and had been aiding him. But after that night they left her alone, because they feared what Wingrove would do if they did not.

At four that morning, Suong led his PFs and Americans from the fort, back into the still hamlet, back to the corpse of Ba Bao, whom Thuc had shot. By twos and threes, the Americans and the Vietnamese picked their positions, near the marketplace, near Tinh's house, near the body. They waited, as do hunters who have staked out a Judas goat for a tiger, hoping the Viet Cong would return to claim their fallen leader. It would not be until a year later that they would learn from a prisoner that the P31st District Force Company—the same men who had attacked the fort and killed the five Americans and six PFs—had lost fifteen men shot or drowned on the river that night. Unaware how extensive was the damage they had wrought, they waited while an hour passed and the dim light before dawn came. It was time for the fishermen to be stirring and for their wives to be starting the fires in the chill of the predawn. But the hamlet remained hushed as the villagers stayed in the candlelit dark of their thick shelters and listened for some normal village sounds to tell them the fight was over and who had won and who had lost. Dawn came, coloring the sky and the land, removing the chance that the enemy would venture back.

Still Suong waited, gesturing at his soldiers to be still—Suong, standing in his hamlet in his village, treating American and Vietnamese alike, claiming by his actions to be leader of them all; the Marines accepting that because it was his PFs who had held the fort after the Americans had been killed. The Marines were not racist, but they had had too much military pride; it had taken a bad defeat to humble them. Now they waited and let Suong run the patrol.

Finally with full light a villager cautiously emerged from his bunker, followed by another and another, and soon smoke from cooking fires hung like a haze over the hamlet and the toilers for the fields bustled outside, hurrying to their chores, anxious to make up time on this day which had started too late. That was how the villagers saw them and that was how Suong wanted the PFs and the Marines to be seen—Thuc and Wingrove sitting motionless back to back at the edge of the paddy, Fleming lying alongside a house, Culver leaning against a tree, Luong squatting next to an empty buffalo pen—strong, silent sentinels scattered through the hamlet like boulders along a shore. And in the paddy the body of Ba Bao, who had grown up in Binh Yen Noi and was known, and who said he was coming back after his unit had smashed into the fort and who had come back.

It was time. Suong signaled and they left their stands and no PF slipped off for a filling breakfast of thick, hot soup. They grouped on the main trail and the villagers had to edge around them to get by and Suong put them in two columns, Marine or PF making no difference. He timed it right, for White and the patrollers from the My Hués, where it had been quiet, were ambling down the trail, and White took his cue from Suong and his Marines and PFs fell in. Including the reaction force from PF Hill, the band numbered over thirty. They took the long way through the hamlet back to the fort, while the word spread before them and the villagers left their houses to watch. There was no music; nobody was in step; the rifles were carried at the various casual, careful angles of professionals.

But the Vietnamese militia and the American soldiers were marching, and the villagers knew it.

# 15

Escalation of the village war to the large-unit level had not succeeded in driving the combined unit from the hamlet, and the price the Viet Cong had paid in their district forces was too high to support repetition. After the 409th NVA Battalion went back to the hills, the local enemy forces in and around Binh Nghia tried to avoid pitched battles. The P31st District Force Company had lost too many men; replacements were not easily gathered. Still, during the next month the combined unit engaged in sixteen fire-fights—all sharp, quick clashes at night, one seeming to merge into the next, duly fought and duly recorded but hazy and scarcely remembered the next day.

There was one fight that was remembered, even though only one Marine participated. Corporal Lummis, Brannon's friend with the black mustache and the steady nerves, was working with a small group of PFs to build an outpost just north of the My Hués when they were hit at three in the morning by a Viet Cong platoon. The enemy broke through the hasty defense and captured the post's machine gun, which sat on a sandy knoll. As the Viet Cong turned the weapon on the defenders below them, Lummis left his safe foxhole and charged alone up the slope. The bullets struck him full in the chest. He went down, yet refused to die, kept trying to claw his way up the hill while the enemy kept firing at him until the PFs sneaked behind the gunners and killed them. They recaptured the gun and carried the body of Franklin Lummis back to the fort. Lummis was the seventh Marine to die in the village.

\*     \*     \*

A few days later the combined unit gained a member who perked up everyone's spirits. Wingrove was taking an afternoon walk by himself through the smallest and bleakest of the village's seven hamlets, at the northern edge of the My Hué area, an uneven line of one-room huts and parched vegetable patches strung out along the sand dunes. Wingrove had wanted to be alone, away from the other Americans and the clamor of the fort, and My Hué was the hamlet least visited by the Marines or the PFs. He was walking along absorbed in his own thoughts when he heard the shrill voice of an angry old woman interspersed with the sobbing pleas of a young boy and the harsh whacking of a bamboo cane. Wingrove winced and walked on, the loud cries following him to the next house, where a housewife stood, joggling an infant on her hip and mumbling insults at her invisible neighbor. Seizing upon Wingrove as the first person to whom she could talk, she continued her diatribe against her shrieking neighbor, only small snatches of which the Marine could understand. When Wingrove did not reply, the housewife repeated her story twice more, each time in simpler Vietnamese terms. Wingrove lingered because he was flattered that a villager thought he spoke her language well. After the third recitation, he had gathered that the boy being whipped was frequently so punished and that he was an orphan kept to tend cows and buffaloes. Since he was big and rich, the woman asked, why didn't he do something about it? It was not good for her children to see a boy treated like that.

Wingrove was trying to explain why he could not when the boy shuffled by, hair disheveled, cheeks wet with tears, thin shoulders sobbing beneath a filthy and torn shirt. His head came up to Wingrove's waist and he looked about six years old. Wingrove smiled and spoke softly to him. The boy sniffled and walked on as though he had not heard. Then he stopped and shyly turned to peek back. Wingrove winked. The boy took a few more steps, stopped and turned again. Wingrove knelt down, smiled and offered a piece of gum. Slowly the boy walked back.

An hour later Wingrove returned to the fort with the boy perched on his shoulders. White sensed that this was not just another youngster from the marketplace who had tagged along to watch Wingrove make one more funny face before scampering back to rejoin his shopping mother.

"He followed me home, Sergeant," Wingrove cracked. "Can I keep him?"

Before the sergeant could ask any questions, Wingrove was pleading his case to the other Marines who had gathered around, describing the conditions under which he had found the boy. He concluded by mentioning that the boy's "aunt" wanted a case of C-rations in exchange.

The boy stayed. The only English he knew were the words "Hi, Joe!" so he was dubbed Joe. The Marines gave him a cot in their new squad tent, but it was some time before Joe used it. Instead, he would wait until the others had gone to sleep and then scamper with his blanket over to Wingrove and curl up contentedly on the end of the Marine's cot. If Wingrove was gone overnight on patrol, Joe would pick the cot of some other Marine, who would always act startled and yell at Joe to get the hell back to his own bed, but somehow the discovery always came in the morning. The slightest rebuke caused Joe to burst into tears. Telling him to stop only made it worse, and the Marines were forever injuring the boy's feelings and being too lavish in their efforts to make amends. The attention and special position would have spoiled many boys, but not Joe. He was polite to everybody.

His days as a lonely buffalo boy were over. Ho Chi, the schoolteacher, tutored him at night, in addition to school during the day, to make up for the years he had lost. The PFs corrected his Vietnamese grammar, as best they could, and he picked up English at an amazing rate. Especially adept at mathematics, he loved the game of Monopoly and any card game. His concentration was ferocious and he liked to gamble, providing it was against the Marines, whom he could beat. He was wary of a few of the PFs, who treated him as an equal at a poker table. By selecting his opponents carefully, Joe could often double or triple his weekly allowance of one dollar. He kept his money in a large tin can and said he was saving it to go to high school.

His routine was that of the Marines. He rose at dawn, washed, scrubbed his teeth and took his turn setting the breakfast table and doing the dishes. Then he trotted down the road to school, returning at noon. If none of the Marines were doing anything special, such as going to the PX, Joe would wander out to play with his new friends. He quickly found out that his position at the fort enhanced his popularity, so he soon was conducting tours of the fort, selecting times when there were few PFs present, since they tended to be less tolerant than the Marines.

But Joe had given the Marines reason to be tolerant. For the privilege of eating a strange and enormous breakfast, the schoolboys would leave their hamlets at dawn, run to the fort, set the table, eat with the Marines, clear the table, do the dishes and dart off to school to tell their envious classmates of their adventure. With a politician's instinct, Joe rotated the breakfast privilege so that all the boys got a chance to eat at the fort.

The Marines held no illusions that they might reap significant military benefits from the goodwill they were gaining in the village when the schoolboys told their parents about their eating adventure. The Americans were not trying to win the hearts and minds of the villagers so that they would rise up and drive out the Viet Cong. They did not expect the average farmer or housewife to provoke retaliation by providing them information simply because they acted as decent human beings. So could the Viet Cong. Through their breakfast guests, the Americans anticipated only one benefit: escape from washing dishes.

The dozen Americans felt that the five thousand villagers accepted them. They ate in their houses, went to their parties, and to their funerals. Psychologically, this made the Marines' job easier; they probably would not have stayed in the village otherwise. In light of Binh Nghia's history of Viet Cong influence, this acceptance was puzzling. To the north and south there were villages in which the Viet Cong had assumed control later than they had in Binh Nghia but where there was staunch opposition to the government and to the American presence.

Luong offered a partial explanation for Binh Nghia's lukewarm attitude toward the Viet Cong. The local Communist movement, he said, had originated across the river in the Phu Longs, and the hostility between the Phu Longs and Binh Nghia was generations old, focused on a feud over fishing rights. It was natural that the Phu Longs assumed economic as well as political power when the Viet Cong were on the rise and this was done at the direct expense of fishermen from Binh Nghia. So later when the Viet Cong came across the river to spread the gospel, there were many in Binh Nghia who resented them and any cause they represented.

The police chiefs—first Lam and then Thanh—had fed this resentment with money and had built up a spy network. Thanh was proud of this information web and scorned as petty gossip the rumors the PFs heard in the hamlets. But it was higher headquarters which, one day in November, warned Thanh that a three-man assassination team, supposedly trained in North Vietnam and carrying a telescopic rifle, was reported to be in the district. The government presence in Binh Nghia was said to be their special target.

The Marines tended to shrug the warning off, saying that a man with a gun was a man with a gun and that if there were only three assassins, they would take them on in a firefight any day. Thanh was more nervous. He asked for a Marine guard whenever he left the fort and he told the PFs and village officials not to go off alone, not even to visit their wives. It was obvious not all the listeners took Thanh seriously, and the police chief was resigned to the inevitability of some deaths.

One morning the man who ran the village rice-polishing machine and his wife set out in their sampan for the district town of Binh Son. The next afternoon fishermen retrieved their bodies from the mouth of the river. Their arms had been bound behind them and their throats had been cut. A childless couple, they were buried without great ceremony in the cemetery of Binh Yen Noi. Thanh had lost two undercover agents. He would have recruiting problems in replacing them.

Next it was a pretty nineteen-year-old girl who lived in the barren hamlet of My Hué Number 3. The resupply truck for Charlie Company took a road through the dunes which cut close to her house, and she had sometimes smiled at the whistling, waving Marines, not inviting bedding offers but just being friendly. So when one day the company gunnery sergeant stopped and asked if she had time to wash some of their laundry, she leaped at the offer, which meant wealth for her family. Thanh did not know her; she spoke no English; she gave the Marines of the regular unit clean clothes and a bright smile and nothing more. The assassination squad entered her house late at night, accused her of aiding the Americans and told her she was going to the mountains to be a Viet Cong nurse. When she denied working against the Viet Cong and refused to go, the Viet Cong leader took out his pistol and shot her in the temple in front of her mother and her father.

About a week later, Xu Bui, the senior hamlet chief in Binh Nghia, a man in his mid-fifties, received a message from his family to return alone at night to his house in the My Hués. There the assassins were waiting. After capturing him without a struggle, they blindfolded and dragged him to a nearby house, where with knifes they began to pry from him information concerning the routes commonly used by the Marine patrols in the area.

At the same time a small patrol from the fort moving through the hamlet saw the light in the house where Bui was being tortured. Luong was at point and he started forward to tell the occupants to turn out the light. Thinking they were being attacked, the startled Viet Cong opened fire. The fight was brief and furious, with the Viet Cong pouring out a high volume of fire to pin down the patrollers, then ducking out the rear of the hut.

The firing was over in less than a minute, and as soon as it was quiet a woman came running from a nearby house, screaming hysterically and holding an infant, who had been shot in the stomach. The Marine in charge of the patrol dropped his rifle and took the baby in his arms.

"I shot her," he said. "I shot her."

The others tried to tell him there was no way of knowing whether it was a Marine, a PF or a Viet Cong bullet that had hit the baby, but the Marine was in shock and all he would repeat was "I shot her. I shot her."

With tears in his eyes, he grabbed the handset to the radio and called the fort.

"You people call a medevac," he sobbed. "I have a baby here who's been shot in the stomach. I'm coming in, and I'm coming in fast. You better have that chopper there when I get there. Out."

Taking a pistol in one hand and cradling the baby in his other arm, he set out on the dead run alone down the dark trails which led through five hamlets back two dangerous miles to the fort. The others let him try it. He had threatened to shoot them if they tried to stop him. They believed him. The Marine had been at the fort several months. He was capable. He had performed coolly in several touchy firefights.

From the fort, White sent out a patrol to clear the trail as far as they could, and then step aside when they heard him coming and stay out of his way. The patrol had scarcely reached the treeline of Binh Yen Noi when they heard the clumping feet and the hoarse breathing and ducked into the bushes. The Marine ran by with the baby, lengthening his stride and pushing for home with what was left of his strength when he came out of the treeline and saw the fort and the helicopter with its red lights blinking, blades turning and engine roaring.

At the helicopter door a corpsman was waiting with his medical kit open while the crew chief and White stood on either side of him with powerful flashlights. When the corpsman reached out and took the baby from the exhausted Marine, the crew chief started to wave his hand at the pilot in the takeoff gesture. But then the corpsman spoke.

"Hold it," he yelled. "We're too late. The baby's dead."

A PF stepped forward and took the infant from the corpsman as the Marine who had made the run sank gasping and sobbing to his knees. The corpsman reached forward and patted him on the head and the crew chief clapped him on the shoulder and gave the takeoff signal. The pilot looked out at White and turned his gloved hands palms upward. White nodded glumly in response. The helicopter rose and whirled away. The Marines and the PF reentered the fort. They left the Marine on his knees in the paddy, crying. From the fort they could keep watch on him.

The Marine remained at the fort for several more months, but after that night he was not much good on patrol. White, who never forgot the incident, did not report it. He didn't know how to express it.

Later that night Luong brought the patrol back from My Hué, with two prisoners carrying the mutilated body of Xu Bui, the hamlet chief who made a mistake. The prisoners, a middle-aged couple, had run a "safe" house where the three assassins had hidden. The next morning the villagers carried in a body and a carbine found in the mangrove swamp. The prisoners identified the corpse as one of the assassins, who had been wounded in the fight the previous night. That afternoon a squad from Charlie Company brought in another assassin and his rifle, which was fitted with a four-power telescopic sight. He had been spotted wandering on the dunes and had been chased down, surrendering when he saw escape was not possible.

The man was tough and Thanh was tired. Few questions were asked and none were answered. After one hour Thanh ordered the three prisoners roped together and led to the boat landing. He had them placed in a sampan and then climbed in himself. Supposedly he was going to the district jail, a trip which would take at least two hours. He was back within half an hour, alone.

Around noon the parents came to take their dead baby home. The Marines asked if there was anything they could do. The mother said it would be a great help if she had ten dollars and a small wood box. Ten dollars and a small wood box.

That afternoon there was a large funeral for Xu Bui, and Father Cappadola, the regimental chaplain, who was to die saving a Marine up at the DMZ, drove down and spoke to the Buddhist monks. Together the priest and the monks offered a quiet prayer at the fort for the powerful hamlet chief and the little baby girl.

# 16

In early November, White had to relieve one of the few surviving original members of the combined unit. It was Riley, whose nerves were rubbed raw and who constantly volunteered for patrol, only to fire at the slightest wrong sound. In one week he triggered four ambushes by false alarm. Finally White told him he was finished.

"I'm sorry, Riley," White said, "but I have to send you back to the battalion. You're a good man, but you're too jumpy."

"Bull," Riley replied. "I volunteer all the time, right? I have the best eyes of anybody. Lieutenant O'Rourke knew that. I was his point a lot of times."

"That's the trouble, Riley, you're seeing ghosts. You're trying too hard to avoid a repeat of Page or Sullivan. You're shooting at thin air, man, and you're screwing people up. Go back to company. When you unwind a little and take the edge off those memories, then you can come back down."

The unit also never regained Theilepape. When he recovered from his wounds, he rejoined Charlie Company and talked quite a bit about going back to the combined unit. He was all right when he was awake and keen on patrols, but he couldn't sleep. He would wake up screaming and reaching for his rifle, and White was convinced that the man would be an insomniac if sent to the fort. Under those circumstances, the battalion doctor refused to allow Theilepape's transfer back to the combined unit.

About the time Riley left the fort, back came the Revolutionary Development troops, two teams of sixty men each. The assassinations had lowered the pacification ratings of Binh Nghia's hamlets and the RDs were to rectify that slippage. According to the script written for them in Saigon, the RDs, as grass-roots representatives of the Saigon government, were to convince the villagers as a massive and homogeneous whole to fight against the Viet Cong. The RDs were supposed to demonstrate their sincerity and their promise of a better economic life by working with the people in the fields and on the river. The Marines never saw an RD bending his back in a paddy, while the teenaged RDs themselves laughed when the old farmers sarcastically asked their advice on planting. Only one RD worked steadily. A man with extraordinarily nimble fingers, he moved about the hamlets showing the women new knots for weaving and repairing fishnets.

Since the youths of the village found them pleasant fellows, the RDs had no trouble recruiting a hundred young men for a People's Self-Defense Force (PSDF). Three afternoons a week for a month the RDs drilled their recruits, giving them bamboo sticks for rifles and showing them how to walk in step and how to sing the RD marching songs. In late November there were graduation exercises, attended by officials from province headquarters.

The courtyard of the fort, 1966

The fort's entrance; Missy Tinh at right

Author *(left)* and
Lieutenant O'Rourke,
1966

Trao (drowned) and Suong (KIA), 1966

Sergeant Sullivan (KIA), 1966

The rear of the fort, 1966

The fort's defenses, 1966

Paddies at the fort's entrance

The combined unit, September 1966. Standing (*left to right*): Glasser—killed in action; Culver—wounded; Garcia; Theilepape—wounded; Sueter—killed; Fleming—killed; Learch—wounded; Carlson; Wingrove; Brannon—killed; Sullivan—killed. Kneeling (*left to right*): PF "Eleven-Fingers" Pham—killed; PF Trong—killed; PF "Rabbit" Hoai—killed; Melton; Swinford; Fielder—killed. (Courtesy of Captain G. G. Pendas, Jr., USMC)

Bac Si Khoi,
Suong (KIA),
and author,
1969

Author and Joe (KIA) at the
market, 1968

Foster's adopted son

Fishing boats at My Hué, 1969

Foster (KIA) prepares charge
to dynamite fish, 1969

Sergeant White, 1966

Sergeant White visits
Missy Tinh, 1966

Sergeant
McGowan
with Joe, 1967

McGowan with PFs, 1967

The village, 2001

Author in the village, 2001

Memorial to fallen Marines, 2001

For the big parade, each new defender had a clean carbine. But just for the parade. The next day the RDs collected the carbines again and the PSDF went back to their sticks.

The RDs were lucky the Viet Cong did not choose to test them, with the weather contributing to that luck. November had ushered in the monsoon season, with the river spilling over into the paddies at each high tide. This made patrolling easier, because it limited the mobility of intruders. So the Marines moved farther afield and, because it was different, they took to patrolling in sampans which they paddled everywhere—across swollen paddies, up tiny streamlets, in and out of the mangroves, even across the river to the edge of the Phu Longs. The PFs refused to step foot in the boats, calling the Marines fools for inviting ambush and saying they were lucky the Viet Cong were sensible and disliked moving in the cold rain. White finally was forced to abandon the boat patrols when Suong threatened to tell Major Braun, the district adviser, and the Marines returned to slogging through the paddies at three in the morning with their teeth chattering, mumbling to each other about the bone-chilling winter nights.

Following the disruption of the assassination squad and the onslaught of bad weather, clashes with the Viet Cong dropped to less than one a week. In the first two weeks of December there was only one significant contact. That occurred when a patrol engaged an enemy squad in a running firefight in Binh Yen Noi at two in the morning. Having captured one Viet Cong, the Marines bound his arms behind his back, shoved a gag into his mouth, put him in front of the point man and continued after the others. When the enemy fired a few rounds to discourage pursuit, the prisoner bolted loose and plunged into the mangrove swamp. He ran through the heavy swamp grass and, unable to evade his pursuers, finally dove headfirst into the deep waters of the river, never resurfacing. To the Americans, the incident indicated that the enemy was as tough as ever; he was just less willing to engage than had previously been the case.

With combat at a low ebb, the RDs felt it was safe to hold a five-day fair, stressing the themes of village unity and solidarity against the Communists. The last public political gathering had been held by the Viet Cong in 1964. The first day was to be a twenty-four-hour session, followed by four days at a less hectic pace. All teenagers were forced to participate; such mandatory attendance absolved the participants from later retribution by the Viet Cong.

The fair began at noon on Christmas Day and the people came in droves, using the RD coercion as an excuse to gather and gossip, to gamble and to be entertained. The day was dismal, with a steady drizzle and a sharp wind which left a man shivering and longing for a stiff drink. So the village officials, the RDs, the PFs, the farmers and the fishermen drifted from the marketplace in little groups to various homes to drink beer and rice wine and cheap liquor. The women who stayed in the market claimed the large tents which had been set up for the youth groups and settled down to gossip. Dispossessed and not caring to sit in tents anyway, the youths drifted around in tight knots of boys or girls, the boys strutting, the girls giggling, all freshly scrubbed and dressed in clean, pressed clothes, enjoying each other and their holiday from work.

Not on duty until sundown, the Marines had scattered throughout the village. Garcia and Corporal Paul Swinford had holed up with the village officials, telling each other that they were there to improve their Vietnamese, refusing the rice wine but drinking beer, eventually slurring their words so badly one wasn't sure when the other was speaking English or Vietnamese. Convinced that Wingrove's charm was his guitar, his friend Corporal Larry Melton had bought one also and they spent the afternoon with PF Thinh Muy and Corporal Robert Clements practicing quartet numbers. Along with some other Marines, White had been invited by one of the village's few Catholic families to a Christmas lunch. The leisurely and filling meal took two hours, and White was sure that by himself he had eaten one whole roast duck, a salad bowlful of steamed rice, three small ocean perch and a head of lettuce.

At the end of the day the villagers began to drift toward the torchlit warmth of the marketplace. The RD leader had planned on an attendance figure of one thousand from a total population of five thousand. By full dark there were four thousand people, lured by the promise of songs and skits, jammed into the marketplace. The bedlam of the crowd drowned out the opening speech of the RD leader, who was standing on the wooden stage. Thanh, in visible contempt of the RD leader's futile efforts, stepped out from the shadows.

"Dung noi," he said in a flat voice, walking through the thick of the crowd with the people pressing back to get out of his way, even the children choking off their giggles. "Ngoi xuong. Dung noi."

The people quietly sat down on the benches or wrapped ponchos around themselves and sat on the ground. With a casual wave of his hand, Thanh gestured to the RDs that the show was theirs and turned aside. Immediately the villagers broke out chatting and laughing and the RD leader couldn't be heard. Again Thanh stepped forward. Silence. He turned away. Bedlam. He stepped forward. Silence. He turned away. Bedlam.

Even Thanh had to laugh. The RD leader gave up trying to speak and signaled to his assembled troops, who broke out singing the RD marching song. The people liked the tune and quieted down to listen, and the RDs swung through a few more martial numbers, encouraging the people to join in. The PFs watched silently until the RDs sang a refrain which went:

How splendid is our country!
Brave people, let's go forward for the sake of
   Happiness, Liberty, Justice and Charity.
Brave men, a happy future is before you—
As cadres, you must motivate everyone to back up
   the Government.

Such sentimental self-esteem was too much for Luong, who was more than a little drunk, so he shouted: "That's buffalo shit!" The audience howled, while the RDs gamely kept trying to sing and other PFs joined in with catcalls and Suong started yelling at them to shut up, fearing a brawl. The villagers thought it was great fun. The RD leader waved to Wingrove, who bounced onto the stage with his guitar-carrying quartet, and the PFs and RDs forgot their differences with a common target to hoot and hiss. The quartet disappointed no one. Their efforts at both Vietnamese and American songs failed so badly that they made excellent parodies. Their appreciative audience kept them on stage for an hour, calling them back for encore after encore.

They were followed by a series of skits, each of which had a political message but which were well received because the village actors had laced them with ribald humor. There was a story about a cuckolded Viet Cong guerrilla hero who was given frequent medals and overnight assignments from the village committee chairman who was bedding his wife. There was a mock speech by a VC leader explaining that the Americans had come to Vietnam for capitalistic expansion. As all could now see, it was obvious the Americans needed rice and wanted to steal their water buffalo. From the way the villagers laughed and clapped, it appeared that a VC political officer had seriously made such a speech to them before the Marines' arrival. The actor concluded on an unexpected note. Pointing toward the bench where the Americans sat, several balancing two or three youngsters on their knees, he asked them to stand up and for Sergeant White to say a few words. The Marines tried to duck and White didn't know what to say but the villagers gave them no choice. They clapped and shouted at them until White walked on the stage.

"Thank you," he said. "I am glad you are happy here tonight. I and my men are glad. Thank you."

At midnight the fair was still packed and the outguard patrols of the PFs and Marines had reported all was quiet. White was changing the guard.

"Bevan," he said to one of his senior corporals, "take a patrol up to the My Hués. Take a couple of RDs with you."

It was flood tide and near the market a section of the trail was under water. Bevan collected four men, and before he left, he turned to White.

"Hell, we're going to get wet anyways," he said, "so we might as well wade straight through the paddies."

White stood at the edge of the crowd to watch the patrol leave. Barely were all five in the paddy when the sergeant heard a soft splat in the water, as if someone had thrown a large rock. White flinched. The patrollers momentarily froze. Then they waded a few feet farther before they heard a tiny, dull thunk from across the river. All knelt down, none willing to dive completely under water, and ducked their heads to their chests. White stood on the edge of the oblivious, laughing crowd and thought of yelling "Mortar!" He knew he had a good ten seconds, but what was the use of a panic and of people standing up, offering more of their bodies to the shrapnel? So he kept his mouth closed and willed himself not to crouch down. He stood waiting for the explosion, growing old and thinking of Christmas in the snow. Then there was another splat and White breathed again and the patrol splashed back to him.

"Two duds in the water," Bevan said. "What are we going to do if they drop one into the crowd?"

"A whole lot of people are going to die," White replied. "But they're firing blind. They don't know whether they're short or over. Give me the phone."

"Charlie Six, this is Fat Boy Six Actual. We are getting mortared at the market from somewhere across the river. We got thousands of people here. Get them off us or it's going to be a slaughter. Over."

White listened for a moment, then said to the crowd of Marines, PFs and RDs which had gathered: "Illumination's on its way. They're going to get some choppers up."

Even as he was speaking there came a subdued crumping sound from farther out in the paddy as a mortar shell struck and went off under water. Those on the edge of the crowd clearly heard the muffled explosion and turned in that direction. Seeing the Marines milling about between them and the sound, they lost interest and turned back to the RDs singing on stage.

"They've traversed wrong," White said. "That was farther away than the duds."

Before anyone could reply an illumination flare burst overhead, followed within seconds by another and another and another. The crowd stirred uneasily. For the next few minutes in an unbroken chain, the flares kept popping, with as many as eight burning at the same time. The villagers had become plainly frightened, knowing something was awry, while the children accepted the flares as part of the show and jabbered excitedly. Then came a loud roar and two helicopters passed over the marketplace at treetop level and swooped down on the mangrove swamp across the river.

"The U.S. cavalry," Garcia cracked.

"Well, I'll give those zoomies their due," White said. "They got here in one hell of a hurry. No mortar crew is going to be firing from across there again tonight."

The villagers also knew that whatever the crisis had been, it had passed with the arrival of the helicopters. Gradually, they drifted away from the fair, until only the teenagers were left, giggling and laughing in their large tents. Several Marines and PFs stayed with the RDs to protect them, while the others walked back to the fort. Suong was unusually talkative at four in the morning as he and White checked the sentries at the market one last time before plodding back in. He said the story that the Viet Cong had tried to kill the villagers would be known in every hamlet the next day. That they had tried and failed was the worst possible combination for them. The villagers had been given the most powerful reason not to like them while not being made to fear them more. Suong believed the mortar attempt was a stupid, desperate act.

Faircloth was on the front post when the two leaders walked into the fort.

"You're going to have to sack out on sandbags, Sarge," Faircloth called out. "All the cots are taken."

"Why? We have six guys still out on patrol."

"Yeh, but all the village honchos are here. They've been straggling in by ones and twos for the last two hours. You're too late."

It had been over three months since the village officials had dared to sleep in the fort.

"I felt good about that," White said later. "It had taken us a long time to work back and we had lost Lummis along the way. But we kept hanging in there and finally the village officials had enough trust in what we and the PFs could do to stay overnight. I had to move in some extra cots, but it was worth it. It was sort of like a Christmas present and a good-bye present all wrapped up as one."

White was due for relief in December, but he did not want to leave until the unit had a new leader. He had chosen nobody from within it. The men had lived together too long to accept the sudden elevation of one of their own to the position of final authority. They could all fight well; what was needed was someone who could think in a crisis without giving way to gang consensus. White had discussed the situation at length with Charlie Company's new commander, Captain Dave Walker, a veteran leader with a scar across his neck from a 30-caliber bullet.

Walker said he was watching a twenty-year-old sergeant named McGowan. In November he had sent the sergeant to the besieged Special Forces camp at Ba To to take over a squad. The sergeant had fought in the hills for a month. He had made dozens of patrols and lost nobody from his squad. Unlike many other NCOs, he had not sold the weapons his squad captured to the Vietnamese for personal profit, despite pressure from some salty squad members.

White went back to the fort and discussed the candidate with his men. Two of the Marines, Swinford and Corporal Ed Gallagher, had served with McGowan a year earlier on board a Navy cruiser. Gallagher, a new replacement at the fort, liked him. Swinford, a rugged youth who had been in the combined unit for several months, did not. Before they were corporals, McGowan had became a sergeant. Both agreed he deserved his promotions but differed on whether he was right for the unit.

"He won't screw you," Gallagher said. "He's a tough bastard. He'd throw hands with you, but he wouldn't go running to the CO."

"Man, he just got over here," Swinford objected. "They were fighting by regiments at Ba To. What good is that going to do him here? He's green. We don't need a green man in charge."

A tall, husky, black-headed Irishman, Vincent McGowan had fought in the Golden Gloves and tended bar in his father's tavern in New York City. Calm under pressure and confidently self-reliant, he had an easy smile and an outgoing manner. Since Christmas, Captain Walker had been sending him out on patrols to gain familiarity with the terrain and the style of small-unit fighting in Binh Son district. Knowing he was competing for command of a unit with a large reputation, McGowan had been trying unsuccessfully for a solid night contact to impress Walker. On the night of January 7 he took an eight-man patrol out from the company perimeter and across the dunes, in order to set up an ambush well to the north of Binh Nghia. The route was new to him and the patrol was being guided by a corporal scout who had been with Charlie Company several months. After a three-hour trek, McGowan was convinced that the scout was lost and that the patrol was moving in a wide circle. But then the scout insisted that they had arrived at the right ambush site, so they burrowed in along the crest of a scrub-covered dune, with eight automatic rifles pointing down on a path twenty feet below.

Half an hour later they heard voices and the jangling of equipment.

The ambushers crawled closer together and slipped off their safeties.

"Fire when I do," McGowan hissed.

On the path below a line of eight figures appeared, men walking haphazardly, with little space between them, their rifles dangling loosely. The scout strained forward to shoot.

McGowan grabbed his arm and shook his head fiercely. The figures on the path trudged on and out of sight.

"What's the matter with you?" the scout whispered. "You chicken?"

"Shut up and give me the radio," McGowan replied.

The sergeant called the company and asked if there were any friendly patrols slated for his map grid square that night. Told no, he asked for a check on the nearest patrol. The reply came back that one mile south the Fort Page unit had a patrol out. McGowan asked if it was eight men strong. The company checked. It was. And Swinford was the patrol leader.

The next morning White and Swinford went to Charlie Company to see McGowan.

"You almost killed me last night. You know that, don't you?" Swinford demanded. "You were just plain lost and screwed up."

"Our guide got us lost, Swinford, but we weren't screwed up. If we had been, you'd be dead," McGowan said. "Have a beer, they're cold."

"Why didn't you shoot?" White asked.

"No Cong would dope along the way those guys did. They're too smart to do that."

The two sergeants talked for three hours, after which White dropped by to see Walker. He recommended McGowan as his relief.

White's departure was low-key. The night before he

left he took out a patrol and on the day of his relief he rose early and walked to the marketplace, accepting quick, warm good-byes from several people and scores of children. When he returned to the fort, he shook hands all around, climbed into a waiting jeep and drove to company, where he had one last talk with McGowan, passing on information he did not want anyone else to hear.

"Thanh's definitely mean," he said. "He hates. He lives only to kill VC. The people are afraid to death of crossing him. I keep the Marines out of that room when he starts to thump. He's the only problem you might have among the Vietnamese, but there are a couple of Marines you better watch. —— is a crazy drunk. Don't let him near booze. He could kill somebody. —— is into the Viet merchants for $300. I've cut off his credit in the village and in Nuoc Man and I've been collecting his pay for him. He lost most of his dough playing cards with ——, who's damn fine on patrol but I wouldn't have him at my house for dinner. He's a wild man in a firefight, but in the fort he looks out only for himself.

"Those are your three problem children. The others are squared away. They know their way around this village and you don't have to worry about guard duty. Everybody stays awake. Suong has a penalty for a PF who dozes off. He says he's going to give the guy one grenade and drop him off alone the next morning across the river at the Phu Longs. I believe Suong would do it. So do the PFs. Any Marine who goes to sleep on duty in the fort is out of the unit.

"There's only one other thing. The latrine should be burned off twice a week—and everybody tries to duck out of that detail."

On January 9, 1967, Sergeant James D. White left the

village of Binh Nghia. Before he reached home, his
mother had received two letters. The first was written by
Trao, the acting village chief of Binh Nghia. It read:

To Sgt. J. D. White Family

Today I write this letter to you. I hope when him
leaving here you still remember me allways.

My name is "trao," second village chief working
with Sgt. White and Sq. about 4 months ago. Our
people thank him very much, because he is very
good man. Evry day he is a few to sleep he works to
much.

All my cadre very happy. Sgt. White and his Sq.
evry days evry night go to empust with P.F.

My village no more V.C. Stay evry one here at
Fort Page is very sad because of his departure, but at
the same time is very happy for him, because here be
able to go home to see his family.

Sgt. White and Sq. work to hard at this duty sta-
tion. They work very hard never look tired. If one of
my people get seck or wtunded by V.C. Sgt. White
makes it to a radio and calls a helicopter for help. A
helicopter is very forte for removing the sick and
wounded.

My people are very poor and when to see a
marine they are very happy. When V.C. come to people, people come and talk to Sgt. White so Sgt.
White can talk to P.F. and marine to fight V.C.
Maybe die.

It's a late letter but I'll say a Happy New Year to
you. Jod bless you all.

Your friend always,
HO YAN TRAO

The second letter was written by Brannon's friend, Ho Chi, the schoolteacher. It read:

To SGT. WHITE FAMILY

I'm friend of Sgt. White. My name is Ho Chi. I want to show my sympathy toward Sgt. White. He is a good friend a lot of people like very much. He had done a number one job. For our people I want to thank you for having a number one son.

About 3 months ago my village was having trouble with Viet Cong and Sgt. J. D. White and Sq. help protect my people and land. I want to thank him very much for helping have peace in my village.

I'm very happy that Sgt. White is going to home.

I wish in my heart that every man was like him.

I hope in my heart that Sgt. White does come back when my country is at peace. Many of my American friends have died. I'm very sorry at has happen to your people.

I hope some day we will all have peace and Charity.

I wish that you are very happy when your son has return home to saftey and peace.

Your friend always,
HO CHI

# BOOK V

# THE CHALLENGE

# 17

Mainly due to the monsoon flood conditions, January and February of 1967 were quiet months in the village of Binh Nghia, and in the absence of violence the Americans and Vietnamese grew to know each other better. But March brought both good weather and village elections, which the Viet Cong had promised to disrupt. In response, district headquarters ordered the combined unit to throw out as many night patrols as possible. To do so, McGowan wanted to use RDs as well as PFs. Although resentful of the RDs' higher pay and lazy manners, the PFs agreed to patrol with them because they owed McGowan a favor. In February the district chief had tried to transfer the PFs to another village, leaving the RDs and Americans to protect Binh Nghia. But the district chief changed his mind after McGowan threatened that the Marines would leave with the PFs. So when McGowan asked for cooperation, Suong agreed that the RDs could patrol with the PFs and Americans—provided they could keep up.

By forcing the RDs and PFs to work together, McGowan was able to send out seven patrols a night and the village was quiet until a few nights before the election. That night he scheduled the first patrol out to move to the northern tip of the village. Just two Marines were going, accompanied by three RDs. McGowan chose Colucci to lead the patrol, and gave him Brown as his backup man. Soft-spoken, thoughtful and quick-moving, Corporal "Chip" Colucci was a natural leader among both the Vietnamese and the Americans. And PFC William

Brown—Brown was just tough. In a firefight he was as emotionless as Faircloth, and almost as accurate with a LAW.

Colucci chose as point man Hiep Trung, an RD with whom he had spent long hours practicing his Vietnamese, but when the patrol left the fort, Colucci decided to take point himself. For an hour, he led the way through a maze of black bypasses. When he reached the My Hués, he turned off by a narrow side path to check an inlet for boat traffic. After circling around the backs of a few houses, he lost direction and Trung stepped forward, kidding Colucci for his befuddlement. Trung led the patrol back to the main trail. Once again on the right track, the patrol proceeded northward, Trung holding point.

The path was wide, the way clear and the stars bright when a burst of bullets slammed into Trung and flung him backward against Colucci. The Marine was knocked off his feet before he knew what had happened. Then the grenades were bursting around him and he was rolling free of Trung, his hands drumming the earth for his dropped rifle, like a blind man groping for his cane. Behind him Brown was ripping off a magazine from his M-16, the red of his tracers all jumbled with the flashes of the enemy weapons, the effect like that of a can of red paint splashed against a wall. Colucci found his rifle, tore through twenty rounds in three seconds, flipped out the empty magazine, palmed in a full one and fired again, his movements as instinctive as a housewife turning on and off a faucet. His ears still echoing from the sting of the first fusillade, he was unable to hear Brown yelling at him. He only knew that within a few feet of him there were a dozen enemy and he had to keep firing. But Brown was tugging at him, trying to pull him back.

"No," Colucci yelled. "Trung."

He had to say nothing more. Brown understood. They both took to pouring out fire, emptying five magazines apiece before there was a lull, one of those frequent, momentary pauses in heavy firefights when both sides in the same interval of three to six seconds are between magazines, shifting positions, talking it over or taking time to breathe.

Brown and Colucci crawled over to help Trung.

"He's dead," Brown whispered.

"Get his carbine and ammo sack," Colucci whispered. "Let's get out of here."

Together the two scuttled into a low drainage ditch which ran alongside the trail. That was as far as they got when the lull broke and the bullets started whipping around them. But now they were about a foot lower than their ambushers and the trail was between them.

"Are the others hit?" Colucci asked.

"Bugged out," Brown replied.

"We better get up some flares," Colucci said.

Handicapped by a lack of radios for patrol work, the combined unit relied heavily on its flare warning system. Brown and Colucci started shooting up signal flares—a green, a red, a green and a red. Knowing what the signals meant, the enemy came on again, seeking to overwhelm the two men before reinforcements arrived. But Brown and Colucci also had taped to their web gear several white parachute flares and these they sent up one after another. The short spells of glare kept the enemy from closing.

At the fort, the flares were seen and McGowan rolled out as many men as could be spared from guard duty— three Marines and one PF. He led them on the dead run straight across the dunes toward the My Hué area, a trek of two miles through loose sand. He moved at the steady, searing pace of a cross-country runner, exhorting, cursing and pushing his men to keep up. At first, the five men ran as a pack, scrambling up the dunes by digging in their feet, lifting their thighs and holding their rifles chest high as though they were splashing through the surf; churning down the dunes by letting their legs run out from under them and then pitching their upper bodies forward to catch up, using the momentum to hurl them forward several yards onto the flat sands at a sprinter's pace before physics and fatigue slowed them down. At the end of the first mile, the pack had strung out, with Bac Si Khoi, surging steadily ahead. Vainly striving to keep up with him came the Marines, gasping for breath, their arms aching, their high strides reduced to steady clops, like draft horses plodding up a steep hill. McGowan was still trying to talk, but the men had to know beforehand what he was trying to say in order to understand him. The unit's new communicator, Corporal John Kokla, had a thirty-pound radio strapped to his back and tripped face forward three times, each time pushing himself back up and stumbling on.

They made it as far as the fence around My Hué before collapsing, two men vomiting while the others knelt or lay down, gulping air. The firing sounded close. McGowan waited until everyone could stand. He was about to advance when another patrol, led by Faircloth, came panting up. Faircloth had two Marines and three RDs with him.

But when McGowan swept his force into the hamlet, it consisted of seven Marines and one PF. The RDs hung back. The reaction force bore down quickly on the sound of the firing, keeping well spread and whooping and firing as they advanced. The Viet Cong pulled off, and Brown and Colucci stood up without drawing fire, tired and happy.

"Got any ammo?" Brown asked.

"How many are there?" McGowan asked.

"Ten," Brown replied promptly.

"Colucci?"

"Brown has it about right. One squad of them, more or less. We can take them."

"Where are they?"

"They faded back into the ville, probably trying to make a hat for the river. We go?"

"We go."

The enemy now had the bad position. The fence hadn't kept the Viet Cong out of the hamlet, but it stood a fair chance of locking them in. McGowan took point and the Marines swept slowly through the dark hamlet. Not a light shone anywhere. The villagers were in their bunkers. In file so they would not shoot each other, the patrollers moved among the houses, McGowan taking most of the shots because he was in front. Neither he nor any of his men saw a clear target, but on over half a dozen occasions there was a blur of shadows or a rustling of bushes and the M-16s would chatter. Twice a few hurried shots cracked back at them. The patrol made a circuit of the hamlet without bringing the enemy to bay.

"Think we got any?" Brown asked.

"Who knows?" McGowan replied.

"Better round up some villagers to carry Trung back."

"I think Khoi's doing that now, Sarge," Colucci said. "He just ducked out."

"Uh-uh," came a voice from the rear of the line, "he's gone hunting those two RD dudes who were with Colucci. He'll kill them dead if he finds them, Sarge."

"Oh, my God. You guys stay here with Colucci," McGowan said. "Brown, do you know where the RDs are hiding?"

"About."

"Let's get back there."

Moving quickly, Brown and McGowan ducked back to the main trail, passed Trung's body and came to a section of the path bordered by a dense bamboo thicket. And there was Khoi, poking the bushes with his rifle like a gardener trimming shrubbery and softly, gently calling for the RDs to come out.

"Bac Si, quay lai," McGowan yelled harshly. "Get out of here."

Reluctantly, Khoi turned toward the Marines, raised his carbine muzzle in the air and followed Brown back down the trail. When he had gone, the sergeant had to wait only a few seconds before two frightened and dejected RDs came out of the undergrowth.

With four women carrying Trung's body, the dozen patrollers returned to the fort, where Khoi bitterly denounced those who had run away. The Marines laughed tolerantly at the anger of the PFs, remembering how unreliable at times they had been ten months before and knowing that the RDs, with their jaunty airs and urban backgrounds, were admired by the girl friends of several of the PFs. McGowan found the prejudice of the PFs toward a less professional unit rather ironic; it reminded him of the way Marines in line companies looked on the PFs.

The next morning Thanh led a patrol back to My Hué, and arrived as a funeral procession was disbanding. The villagers talked freely, saying that four Viet Cong had been killed in the action. Two had families in the hamlet and so had been buried there. The others were strangers and their bodies were carried back to the fort, where they lay unclaimed all day and at dusk were buried in a potter's field.

When Thanh had returned to the fort, he also had in tow a farmer and his wife from near whose house the Viet

Cong had sprung their ambush. Under the lashings of thin bamboo whips, the couple cried out that they had had no choice. The VC had come in and threatened to shoot them if they did not tell how often the patrols came by. The VC had come back each of three nights before their ambush was successful.

For wanting no part of the war, the farmer and his wife received no sympathy or absolution from those who had chosen a side and who risked death. To keep their farm the couple had helped the Viet Cong to kill. The PFs whipped them until their screams turned to sobs and their minds seemed to have drifted beyond the pain. Then they carried them to district and dumped them in the common jail, where they languished for three weeks, after which they were released and returned to their farm.

Also, on the morning after Trung's death, the RDs were back in form, tromping through the marketplace holding aloft a Thompson submachine gun found when they had searched the shootout site at first light. After parading about the village, the RDs caught a boat to the district town of Binh Son, where they presented the captured weapon to their senior cadres. The district officials looked on approvingly—until McGowan arrived to tell the PF version of the previous night's fight. Suong, deferential and timid toward those of higher rank, was afraid to confront the RD leaders, lest they make a report which would lead to his transfer from the village. McGowan, on the other hand, accused the RDs of cowardice, thievery and boastfulness. He didn't care about the weapon, except that it had become a symbol. The PFs and Marines had fought for it; the RDs had run away. He wanted the RD district cadres to give the gun back. The PFs needed proof to squash the rumors that were buzzing in the marketplace.

The district officials tried to soothe the sergeant,

explaining that the RDs were more than just fighters; they were organized and directed by a powerful faction of the VNQDD, or Nationalist Party, and provincial politics were involved. McGowan was unmoved.

For four days he appeared daily at the district headquarters. On the fifth day the district RD leader handed him the submachine gun. McGowan gave it to Suong and for a week Khoi carried it ostentatiously as a demonstrable rebuke to the RD claims of superior fighting prowess.

Soon afterward a gaunt Marine corporal in torn utilities stopped by the fort on his way back to base after an operation. He brought word that the combined unit had lost its eighth Marine. It was Fleming, who had gone off on the operation as a special scout and immediately attracted attention with his black beret, black utilities, wispy mustache and flamboyant manner. He was happiest at lead point, far in front of the hundreds of infantrymen moving through the rice paddies over a wide front. That way, the corporal explained, Fleming avoided the growls and scowls of staff and gunnery sergeants who were astounded at his costume. On the third day of the operation, reacting to some sudden information, they were helilifted into an abandoned paddy. Before them loomed a low, canopied hill mass, reputedly hiding an NVA regimental headquarters. The intelligence proved correct. Fleming was among the very first struck by a 50-caliber machine gun. The men talked about him after the fight, the corporal said. They talked about the Marine with the black beret who was hit in the chest and went to his knees and who wouldn't die until he had fired his rifle.

"We thought you'd like to know how he died," the tired corporal said to the Marines and PFs gathered around him, "so the captain sent me down to tell you."

\*          \*          \*

There were other visitors during election time. Four university students had returned home and they were greeted warmly by the village officials, who were proud of their academic status. Bright and fluent in English, the students were surprised to see a dozen Americans wandering about the hamlets and eating in several homes. The first afternoon they were back, the students came to the fort, together with Suong and a cluster of villagers. They had been asking critical questions of the villagers about the conduct of the Marines, and Suong had warned McGowan that they disliked Americans.

Arriving at the fort, the students stood outside in the courtyard, and when McGowan came forward to meet them, one began in English to denounce the U.S. presence in Vietnam, while another translated for the crowd. Pointing to PFC Richard Williams, the chief spokesman asked how a black man could fight in a war denounced by Martin Luther King.

McGowan had not read a news magazine in six months, and Williams was no better informed. It was the first time they had heard the charge. The student followed up his lead with a half-dozen more questions: Why did the Marines not help the Vietnamese people in their moral uprising in 1966? Why did Westmoreland prop up the tyrant Ky? Why did President Johnson not listen to Senator Fulbright?

McGowan was at a loss.

"Look," he said, "you want to know what we're doing here? Ask Suong. Ask Khoi. Ask anyone. Ask the VC. We're here to fight VC. We're here to help people who seem to be friends of yours. If you don't like what I've done here, or what my men are doing, O.K., let's have it. But don't yell at me about General Westmoreland or

Senator Fulbright. My job is in this village. I'm not a general, and I'm not a politician."

A student translated the remarks, referring to McGowan by the pronoun "it." The sergeant was growing angry and embarrassed. Suong came forward and whispered to the student leader, who listened intently. Then the student turned to McGowan and suggested they continue the conversation some other time. When the villagers left the fort, Suong lingered behind.

"What did you say to him, Suong?" McGowan asked.

"I said many Marines have died here with us," Suong replied. "And that you were a violent man. Even in the Phu Longs they are afraid of the Marines. It was not good to provoke you."

"Well, you keep them away from here, and I'll keep the Marines out of the village until they leave. I don't want anyone else put down like I was."

"They are only students. They have the attitude of Hué."

"Maybe that's because they've never had to fight."

"But they are most smart."

"You mean, smarter than me," McGowan laughed. "Well, it looks like you're right."

Out of respect for Suong, or because of what the villagers said, or both, the students were more friendly toward the Marines their second day in the village. They were staying only a few days to campaign for Ho Yan Trao, who the PFs asserted would be elected village chief.

Trao did not look like a leader. He was a tall, thin young man who wore old clothes, owned one buffalo and a few scrawny cows, and farmed a half-acre of land. Although he had little formal education, in six months he had learned how to speak and even how to write enough English to send a letter to Sergeant White's family. Trao was the elected chief of one of the Binh Yen Noi hamlets, and the PFs had urged him to run for village chief. Known for his honesty and humility, he seemed sure to win.

His opponent was a man named Buu, who owned a large fishing fleet in My Hué, a villa in Saigon, a house near the district headquarters and another home in Binh Yen Noi. An impeccable dresser with an aloof manner and extraordinarily long fingernails, Buu visited Binh Nghia only a few times a week. He had been appointed village chief through political influence but was content to let the village council, of which Trao was the elected chief, handle the daily administrative matters.

Trao and Buu were enemies, thanks to the Americans. In January an American captain had several times driven to the marketplace and indiscriminately tossed out food and clothing to the villagers. Trao had complained to McGowan that, although the captain had good motives, his handouts had disrupted the assistance projects of the village council, undercut the authority of the hamlet chiefs and eroded the discipline of parents. Those who lounged around the market drinking and who gathered the scraps others dropped had organized into gangs. They were the ones who clung to the captain's jeep and smiled and pawed at him while pushing other villagers aside.

McGowan had brought the matter to the attention of the commander of the 7th Marine Regiment, who called a staff meeting at which he forbade all his Marines to enter the village and ordered that all aid be channeled through the combined unit. The colonel's command was at first enforced a little too strictly, and a shipment of cement, which had been requested for the village through Vietnamese channels by Mr. Buu, was delivered to the fort. By the time Buu collected the cement, McGowan had counted the bags and told his men to keep track of how they were used. The sergeant had acted as much from his old habits as a bartender as from suspicion, since neither Trao nor the PFs would discuss Buu.

But when Buu used the cement to build a well in front of his house, McGowan complained to the district advisers, who agreed to send future aid materials to the village council and not to Buu. When he heard of the new arrangement, Buu was certain Trao had supplied the Americans with their information.

Buu struck back by declaring Trao's home hamlet of Binh Yen Noi Number 3 ineligible to vote in the village elections due to procedural irregularities. Trao did not wish to contest the ruling because he lacked the political power. He and the PFs were organizational orphans. Although they were fighting for their village and their homes, their political ties stopped at the village gate. While they hated the Viet Cong, they also strongly disliked both factions of the VNQDD. Their only source of political leverage lay in the presence of their American allies, since they could not rely upon the government of South Vietnam to treat them fairly, as should have been the case if all South Vietnamese elements opposed to the Viet Cong had shared the same ideological frame of reference. They were not judged according to their competence to ward off the Viet Cong and to govern the village justly.

As a VNQDD, Buu had little to fear in manipulating the election, which he easily won. The outcome infuriated McGowan, who, over the protests of Trao, rushed to district to lodge a complaint. Captain Nguyen Dang, the aggressive district chief, told the irate sergeant to let it go. There were good reasons why Trao was not protesting; he had never served in the Army and, therefore, could be jailed as a draft dodger if Buu turned him in.

McGowan showed Dang his notes on the disposition of the cement which had gone to the village. After reading the notes carefully, Dang hopped into his jeep and drove to Binh Nghia, explaining to McGowan en route that it was best for everyone if the sergeant were Buu's accuser. Buu's influence did not include retribution against Americans.

Buu was in the village office when they arrived at the fort. Dang strode in, ordered everyone else to leave, and in a voice which carried into the courtyard upbraided the village chief for his conduct in a shrill monologue which lasted half an hour. When he left, Dang shook hands with McGowan and publicly thanked him for bringing certain matters to his attention.

Shortly thereafter the village chief reported McGowan to district. Thanh had been receiving persistent rumors that the VC across the river were bartering woven mats for rice. Supposedly the wives of the richer farmers in Binh Nghia were quite willing to trade surplus rice to avoid the tedious task of weaving. My Hué was the trading spot. To put a stop to the traffic, Suong ordered all boats pulled out of the water each night, since it was hard to distinguish between three dozen moored boats and one moving. Two nights after the order had been passed, McGowan took a night patrol to My Hué and discovered a large boat moored offshore. It was destroyed with three LAWs.

The next day the village chief came screaming into the fort demanding the Americans pay for his sunken boat. After a heated argument, he came away convinced the sergeant intended to destroy his entire fleet. So he went to district and complained to Captain Dang, who was vaguely sympathetic but who said he could do nothing about the Americans.

After that Buu went to the village less than once a

month. His financial affairs were competently handled by his relatives, and Trao assumed chief responsibility for village affairs.

# 18

Contrary to what Dang told Buu, the Americans in Binh Nghia would do what he ordered. Corporal Gene Foster, one of the combined-unit soldiers, referred to the district chief by saying: "I'm not exactly afraid of Dang, but I treat him like I would blasting caps—with a hell of a lot of respect."

A short, stocky man with a crew cut and fierce black eyes, Dang had served the Viet Minh as a battalion commander before breaking with the Communists over policy matters. Although he had a fanatic's belief in the injustice of the Communist cause, he believed their organizational and propaganda tactics were superb, so he copied them. In an indoctrination center, he lectured those villagers who had aided the Viet Cong and he held pep rallies for his district officials.

He was more than just a showman. He organized special three-man assassination teams to seek out the Viet Cong while they rested in their homes. Gracious in victory, he held no resentment against any Viet Cong who rallied to the government side, while he would summarily execute any dedicated enemy leader who, after capture, appeared to be slipping through the lax legal system of the government. He called the dozen Americans at Binh Nghia "his" Marines and everyone understood what he meant. He was their commanding officer, as well as the commander of the PFs. When there were problems no one else could solve, Dang stepped in.

Once an American had a hundred-dollar watch stolen. Thievery of military items such as compasses or grenades occurred from time to time and was tolerated by the Marines, as they in turn would steal from any unit richer than themselves. It was part of the Marine code of "scrounging." But personal items were different, and when no PF would admit to the theft, Captain Dang came to the fort. While the PFs stood apprehensively straight, he talked to them for an hour, pacing back and forth, the soldier-patriot in simple black pajamas, the ex–Viet Minh battalion commander, the man who wouldn't bend and whom Saigon would not promote.

We are Vietnamese, he told them, and what have we done? We have stolen, and we have stolen not from some rich American who flies a helicopter or who can give away a jeep. No. We have stolen from our brothers—from one of those who came and lived with us and ate our food and went up to My Hué and never took anything from us. What are we, he asked them, if we do such things? Perhaps we should take the rice of each other, and teach our children how to steal schoolbooks, and have our wives become prostitutes. Beggars and thieves, is that what we are?

There was more, some of it appeals to manhood, some of it threats. There was one thing all the PFs knew: Dang was not bluffing. If the thief did not admit his guilt then and there, Dang would kill him if he was discovered later.

Whether from fear or guilt, or both, the thief stepped forward.

"Take down your pants," Dang said, "and bend over."

There in front of the PFs and Americans, Dang whipped the thief with a thin bamboo cane which bit the flesh and left long, red welts on the man's bare buttocks and left a searing memory of pain and shame in the mind of every PF who stood as witness.

Dang then told the thief to retrieve the watch from wherever it was hidden and return it to its rightful owner, who accepted it gingerly, as though uncertain he could prove it was truly his, and frightened about what might happen if he couldn't.

It was not just the PFs who stole. When an American battalion commander came to inspect the fort one day, he saw some U.S. AID material stored in the courtyard. Among the various items was a bolt of oilcloth.

"Who's that for?" the lieutenant colonel asked.

"The villagers, sir," McGowan replied. "The district advisers left it for Mr. Trao to distribute."

"I could use that for backing for my mapboards. Put it in the jeep."

"Sir, it's for the villagers."

"You heard me, Sergeant—put it in the jeep."

McGowan looked away and refused to acknowledge the order.

The colonel's driver, sensing a major blow-up was coming, darted forward, loaded the bolt of oilcloth in the jeep and said, "All ready to go, sir."

Knowing he was in the wrong, and given an out, the colonel left. It was a little thing, materially speaking, just a bolt of cloth. But the Marines had seen the show, and so had Trao and Suong and some of the PFs. In the weeks that followed, many of the PFs helped themselves before doling out materials to the villagers. It was always little things, like soap and candy and other items of which the PFs, in justice, probably deserved a share. But to McGowan the oilcloth was a major setback, and he felt like a hypocrite for running around with his little notebook jotting down what materials the village chief used while an American officer flouted the rules.

The colonel also insisted upon his troops' wearing flak jackets and helmets at all times and had limited ammunition to one hundred rounds per man. Sergeant White had considered both orders absurd. To wear flak jackets while the children went to school and the women to market would have made his men a laughingstock. To limit a four-man patrol to four hundred rounds was foolhardy. In a fire-fight one man would fire four hundred shots. White had not obeyed the orders; neither had he flaunted his disobedience. He had hidden the extra ammunition supply beneath the floorboards of the squad tent and stockpiled flak jackets and helmets near the marketplace. He had asked the villagers to warn the Marines whenever the colonel visited. Then any Marine out of the fort would don his armor before venturing near the colonel.

McGowan was content to follow White's system until the oilcloth was stolen. After that his men openly disobeyed the order, walking into the company area without helmets and with more than a maximum five magazines. Captain Walker might have been able to reason with McGowan, but Walker had gone home and his executive officer had taken over the company. Exasperated by the CAP (Combined Action Platoon) Marines' swagger and lack of discipline, the exec radioed McGowan to report to him. In defiance, McGowan strolled into the company perimeter bareheaded and in a T-shirt and shorts, carrying his rifle and a sackful of magazines. The exec blew up.

"McGowan," he yelled, "you are not some Chinese warlord. You are a United States Marine Corps sergeant. And that band of bandits of yours look like they've gone native—with you setting the example."

"Sir," McGowan said. "That colonel—"

"McGowan, that colonel happens to be your superior officer. You have been given a direct order. Helmets, flak jackets and ammo. Now I'm giving you that order to your face. I don't care how many generals visit you. You're not God Almighty. You obey or I'm going to relieve you."

McGowan went back to the fort and hid the extra ammunition under the floorboards and reverted to White's tactic of unobtrusive disobedience. News of his putdown became common gossip throughout the battalion and the district. McGowan stayed in command at Fort Page because to remove him would have risked the wrath of General Walt.

Some of the men wanted to remove the colonel. One Marine, whom McGowan relied upon for his rifle but distrusted for his willingness to use it, approached McGowan with a plan.

"Sarge," he said, "you remember how the grunts got rid of that platoon commander?"

McGowan remembered. After O'Rourke had left Charlie Company, another lieutenant had moved up to executive officer, and in turn his platoon was given to a new second lieutenant who persisted in donning shiny black gloves before each operation, and carried a walking stick instead of a rifle. The platoon would have forgiven him for his foibles had he proved competent. But he repeatedly blundered into sticky situations and then insisted upon striding straight ahead, ignoring both bullets and common sense. One afternoon the lieutenant set out with a squad on an armored reconnaissance. They ran into some light sniper fire and somehow the lieutenant ended up with a hole in the back of his leg. He was medevaced out with a Purple Heart, and the company never heard of him again.

"We could do the same thing with the colonel," the

Marine argued. "I can borrow a carbine from the PFs and hide in the bushes near the road. The next time the colonel comes by, I ding him and hat it out. It's simple."

"No. We weren't sent down here to shoot colonels. Besides, you can't blow a guy away just because he's an asshole."

"I'll just hit him in the leg. Hell, with his helmet and flak vest all buttoned I couldn't kill him if I wanted to."

"No, man, I'm telling you no. We'll wait him out. We'll be here after he's gone."

McGowan's strained relations with higher headquarters showed in other ways as well. The combined unit was accustomed to receiving only first-class volunteers as replacements for any casualties or for men who rotated home. Late one afternoon in mid-March a supply truck jounced down the narrow track to the fort. As it pulled into the courtyard, Corporal Ed Gallagher looked closely at five Marines sitting on their duffel bags in the open bed.

"These guys are going to stay with you," the driver called out.

While the truck was slowly turning around, Gallagher ran to the tiny messhall.

"Sarge," he burst in, "I know three of those guys. They were shitcanned from Charlie Company after the last op."

"I know the other two from battalion headquarters," Swinford added. "They're supply pogues. They've never been outside of camp."

McGowan walked outside. The others followed.

"You people hold it right there," he said. "Don't even bother getting off the truck, because you're going right back wherever you came from."

The radio yelps from battalion came in as soon as the truck had driven back. By then McGowan had down a pat story: there was not enough room for more Americans.

District would not allow it, and the fort was a PF outpost. When queried, Captain Dang confirmed the story.

Had the replacements seemed halfway decent, McGowan would have accepted them, since messages were coming in at a furious rate warning of an attack upon the fort. Like White, however, McGowan refused to allow squads from the line units to enter the boundaries of Binh Nghia. Yet one night it happened.

A squad left Charlie Company to rendezvous with two amtracs which were to ferry them to an ambush site far upriver. Dusk had fallen by the time the ambushers reached the river, where they found no amtracs waiting. The corporal in charge radioed headquarters for instructions. For some reason never fathomed, a voice without a brain told him to set up an ambush for a few hours in the nearest hamlet rather than return to the company position.

The ambushers were then at the edge of the Binh Yen Noi hamlet complex, and the squad members argued with the corporal, telling him the men from Fort Page covered the Binh Yen Nois like a blanket and that it was suicide to obey. The corporal called headquarters back and said he was concerned about friendly patrols. Headquarters assumed the ambush team was across the river and gave the coordinates of the nearest known friendly ambush—on the other side of the river.

"See?" said the corporal. "It's all clear in there. We can go in."

He convinced nobody. The members of his team wanted no part of the trespass, headquarters or no headquarters. Finally, the corporal gave them a direct order.

"I'm not going to lose my stripes over this," he said. "We've been told what to do, and we're going in there. I'll take point myself."

And so he died. Among the houses beside a black section of the trail, two Marines and two PFs from Fort Page lay in wait. Their leader heard movement, saw a figure loom up in front of him on the trail and fired. The corporal from Charlie Company died instantly, and the curses in English from the other ambushers told the combined-unit Marine of his tragic mistake.

"Cease fire! Cease fire!" he screamed. "It's us from Page. Who are you?"

"Charlie Company."

"Oh, God Almighty."

He stood up, walked the few feet to the fallen corporal, looked down, and slowly sobbing, shot himself in the foot. It was reported that he was wounded in a fight with the Viet Cong, during which another Marine was killed, and so he was evacuated to the United States and would never again have to carry a rifle.

Shortly afterward the combined unit lost another American, when he tried to murder the villagers. Proficient at patrolling, a member of the unit from the beginning, hand-picked by Beebe for his expert weaponry, the man was hard on everybody—himself, the other Americans, the PFs and the villagers. He rarely smiled and seldom relaxed. He was most content when out on patrol and savored those special moments when he could demonstrate his remarkable accuracy with a LAW. Once in October he had consumed half a bottle of the local rice wine and had torn about the fort like some demon fiend. It had taken five Marines to subdue and tie him up, and the next day when he was sober, White told him he was through at the fort if he touched hard liquor again. White had warned McGowan about the man and his drunken rages.

Still, when it happened again, there were no warning signs. The man quietly left the fort one morning alone and was gone for several hours. In the afternoon he suddenly appeared, reeling through the gate, saying nothing, turning and stumbling toward the machine-gun bunker, manned only at night. The few PFs and Marines who had seen him enter the fort had smiled that tolerant, pitying smile reasonable people reserve for drunks and had gone about their business. Suddenly it hit them as they watched him grope his way behind the handles of the long, sinister, black 50-caliber machine gun: he was intent on murder. As he fumbled to cock the weapon, startled cries in English and Vietnamese filled the fort and floated out to the paddies.

"——'s on the gun! He's drunk out of his mind! Get down! Get down!"

Scattered in the paddies were a dozen women and several buffalo boys, and the PFs were calling to them.

"Nam xuong! Nam xuong! Get down! Get down!"

The drunken soldier was set now, having leaned his body over the rear of the gun and swung the heavy barrel upward. It wavered around the fort and then slowly swung out toward the paddies, like a compass needle coming to rest. There came the solid, belting jackhammer sound of the weapon firing and the thick incendiary slugs, big as cigars, burned over the paddies. In red arcs the shells lazed out, almost casually reaching for the people who lay among the rice stalks, as if shells designed to stop planes and armor thought it humdrum to squash mere skin and bones.

Before Thanh could decide to use his unholstered pistol, while Colucci was agonizingly lifting his M-16, McGowan broke from the village hall. In a few strides he was across the tiny courtyard and up over the sandbag parapet, his fist hitting the drunk behind the ear, once, twice and a third time.

No one had been struck by the twenty or thirty wild

shells which had been fired, and Trao called a quick meeting to instruct all in the fort to tell their families and neighbors that the shooting was the result of a runaway gun being test-fired. But, of course, the story did not hold up.

They kept the man under guard at the fort until the next day, when McGowan told him to pack his seabag. He was through. He was sent back to Charlie Company, where he was immediately made a squad leader because of his tactical knowledge and hard reputation.

Had the incident happened in June of 1966, it might have been brushed over, for the Marine was an able tactician. But nine months later the Americans at Fort Page were unwilling to excuse a man who tried to murder a villager. None of the Marines asked McGowan to reconsider. The man was finished. They no longer wanted him with them and the PFs in the village.

The Americans were beginning to feel at home in the village, with its guerrillas and PFs, fishermen and farmers, women and children. Many of the Marines let months go by without writing a letter or reading a newspaper. The radius of their world was two miles.

At least, that was how it was for most of them. Their corpsman was their most diligent letter writer, a fact attributed to his being married. The man had served in the unit for four months, performing his chores well and getting along without friction with both the villagers and the Marines. He was a Navy enlisted man, for all Marines must qualify as riflemen and rely upon the Navy for noncombatant support, such as chaplains, doctors and nurses. He liked the village.

But one afternoon McGowan entered the squad tent to find him alone at his cot in the corner, crying. McGowan backed out and told the other Marines and PFs to stay away for a while. Still, in such close quarters, a man cannot hide his distress for long and by evening all the Marines knew that his wife was living with a sailor and had written to ask for a divorce. Then, in confusion, she had written a second letter saying she did not want to leave him and what should she do?

The advice of young bachelors was predictably unsettling. Most blithely urged that he divorce her and celebrate his freedom by going to Taiwan or Hong Kong, where, if he worked at it, he could sleep with a dozen girls during a week's pass, and return refreshed and content. This struck everyone but the corpsman as a splendid idea, and several offered to go with him. A few suggested they could write some friends in San Diego who owed them favors for help in past firefights. These returned veterans could work over the wife's boyfriend. The corpsman perked up at that, but became glum again when McGowan suggested it would probably ensure a divorce.

Next, the corpsman sought the advice of Lieutenant Carlson, a district adviser. Carlson was a mustang, a first sergeant who had been commissioned to the officer ranks at the age of forty. Salty and understanding, he offered simple advice to the corpsman: go home, see his wife, talk to her and to his parents or a priest or someone with a level, older head, make a decision, stick to it and come back. The corpsman agreed.

The personnel department at headquarters did not. In comparison with the justifications for emergency leaves usually granted, such as the death of a parent or terminal illness at home, the love life of one corpsman seemed insignificant. His request refused, the man could not concentrate on his work. The PF corpsman, Bac Si Khoi, filled in, taking care of the Americans, the PFs and the villagers. Since he had saved Theilepape's life, the Marines had complete trust in him.

McGowan told the corpsman to take a week off. He could go anywhere in the province he pleased. Military police treated Marines from combined units as they did Army Special Forces and Navy Seal commandos: with a mixture of respect and wariness. It was better to stay out of their way, and if they were drunk, just return them to their units. Arresting them did no corrective good; and there was always that awkward moment of seizure when they might choose not to be arrested.

The corpsman took the time off but didn't leave the village. McGowan kept four quarts of whiskey under his cot so that anyone could take a drink, provided others knew. A private bottle or a pouch of pot spelled automatic expulsion from the CAP since slack reflexes on patrol could not be tolerated. Drinking steadily, the corpsman consumed all four quarts in six days. He rarely spoke, rarely ate, just sat on top of the trench line sipping at his bottle, broiling in the sun, and frequently vomiting into the stagnant moat.

McGowan knew something was coming, and when the man did flip out, he did so with flair, ensuring that even bored processing clerks would read his case twice. By the seventh day of his drunk he was dehydrated, beet-colored, scrub-bearded, stinking and red-eyed. He lolled around the fort until ten in the morning. By then the market was full, the PFs had gone home and most of the Marines were napping or sitting in some cool thatched house teasing the girls or whiling away the time somewhere with the PFs and the old men.

No one was watching the corpsman. He walked slowly out of the fort and took a side trail into a treeline. A few moments later he emerged onto the main trail, and ran full tilt into the marketplace, shrieking at the top of his lungs, stark-naked.

Three days later, on orders signed by a doctor who

examined psychiatric cases, he flew to San Diego on
emergency leave. He stayed married to the girl and
returned to Vietnam one month later. There he had to join
a rifle company. The bureaucracy was not about to send
him back to Binh Nghia. Besides, Binh Nghia had been
sent a new corpsman, named John Blunk.

Faced with the draft after scholastic difficulties in his
junior year of college, Blunk had chosen to enlist in the
Navy as a corpsman in order to further his premedical
training. Bright and bouncy, he strode into Binh Nghia
with the attitude of a young doctor hanging out his shingle
for the first time. Like a conscientious doctor with a
wealthy clientele, Blunk looked upon the chronic ailments
of the Marines as trivial. Although he was assigned to the
fort in order to be available for emergencies, Blunk
decided his day-to-day patients should be the villagers.

In the past, CAP corpsmen had attended the villagers
on a Band-Aid and penicillin level and had called helicopter medevacs for serious cases. With a higher level of
skill and dedication, Blunk went beyond those rudiments.
He spent long hours with Khoi, who also said he wanted
to be a doctor, a claim some thought was influenced by
his admiration for Blunk. From Khoi the corpsman
learned of the sicknesses and hurts which went unre-
ported, because it took the fear of death to drive a villager
to the province hospital, what with the expense, the distance, the strangeness, the crowded sick and the harried
doctors. Most of the villagers who fell ill preferred to stay
at home and suffer steadily. So Blunk did not lack for real
patients. He started with those he could treat with the
tools and drugs the United States Navy provides each
combat corpsman: Terramycin, malaria pills, aspirin,
stitches and bandages. Both the local needs and his own
skill exceeded those basics, and Blunk dipped into the

medical slush fund Marine headquarters had set up for village care. There, too, he quickly exceeded his quota, since patients were starting to come from Binh Thuy Island and from the Phu Longs. Blunk told McGowan he had to have more and better supplies. He had pulled several teeth lately and infection was spreading in one farmer's jaw. Some of his minor-surgery cases needed similar follow-up attention and he did not have the proper drugs. If he got a bad reputation, so would the combined unit.

McGowan got the message. He sought out Lieutenant Carlson, who could only suggest sending any relapse cases to the Vietnamese hospital. The medication Blunk wanted required forms in triplicate and a doctor's signature.

"Oh hell," McGowan said. "If I have to go through the paper mill, we'll all be dead and buried before that stuff arrives."

He knew of a faster way. The head corpsman for a nearby rifle company, a chief petty officer who had been in the Navy for twenty years, was notorious for his thirst. Under General Walt's order, no bottles of hard liquor were officially sold anywhere in I Corps. The rifle companies received a weekly ration of beer, scarcely an acceptable substitute to the chief's discriminating tongue. McGowan's stockpile included a quart of Johnny Walker Red Label Scotch whisky. In return for the liquor, Blunk got his shopping list filled, including a credit voucher for drugs which needed refrigeration.

# 19

Although the Americans were gradually becoming involved in nonmilitary matters in the village, their primary effort and the focus of their attentions remained tactical. But after nine months of some of the hardest village fighting in Vietnam, Binh Nghia was still intact. There was never an air strike called in the war for that village. It was a battle fought with rifles and grenades at such close quarters that both sides used their senses of smell and hearing as much as their eyesight. The villagers did not stroll around at night, and in the firing at sounds, flashes and shadows, it was usually the participants on both sides, not the villagers, who died. There were exceptions, but they were exceptions.

March brought the warm sun back and, as the waters subsided and the muddy trails dried out, both the villagers and the Viet Cong moved about more frequently. One night McGowan was at point on an evening patrol moving slowly through the far reaches of Binh Yen Noi. It was a little after ten, a time when patrols rarely made contact, and the sergeant was not especially alert. But by habit he stopped every hundred yards or so to listen. It was during such a break that he heard someone moving rapidly toward him up the hard-packed trail. McGowan fired from the hip, spraying the trail from right to left.

A man went down groaning, then lay still. The patrol waited for two minutes before moving. They heard nothing further. Advancing cautiously, they switched on a flashlight and in its beam picked up the face of the dead man, whom a PF identified as one of his neighbors. He was not carrying a weapon or anything else which associated him with the Viet Cong.

The next day the PFs found out the story. The man had been having an affair with his wife's sister. Several evenings a week, on one pretext or another, he would visit her just before dark, then run back home shortly after curfew. Since he never was gone overnight, his wife suspected nothing. The evening of his death, he had stayed too long. The sister begged him to wait until dawn and give some excuse to his wife, but he said he could dash home safely and so not risk arousing suspicion. He was almost home when he was killed.

A few nights later another villager died as a result of poor judgment. On that night, a three-man patrol was prowling the outskirts of My Hué when the point man saw a group of men digging in the sand dunes. The patroller returned to the fort to gather a reaction squad, but when they arrived at the scene, the men were gone, having dug and camouflaged a trench line near the main trail for ambush purposes. The reaction force destroyed the trench line and the next night McGowan took a patrol back to the scene. He was at point nearing the edge of the hamlet when his head bumped a board. Without hesitation he dove flat, yelling "Grenade!" The other patrol members jumped off the trail and the booby trap exploded harmlessly.

Something about the setup bothered McGowan. Not quite what it was, he led another patrol the next night back to the same spot. As he moved through My Hué with his safety off, three rounds from a carbine cracked by his head. Their sound was still hanging in the air when he returned fire, hitting his assailant in the chest and killing him instantly.

The patrollers dragged the body from the bushes and turned on a flashlight. McGowan recognized the man immediately. Several times he had eaten at his house and once, on a week's stakeout in the hamlet, he had slept there. The man had been friends with several of the PFs.

The PFs roughly questioned the man's wife, who admitted that her husband had been a secret, in-place Viet Cong agent. A few nights earlier, some guerrillas had rowed across from the Phu Longs and set to work digging a fighting trench with the intention of ambushing a PF patrol. After the PFs destroyed the trench, a Viet Cong who knew her husband had sneaked back to talk. Her husband had laughed at the guerrilla for his poor plan and the guerrilla had replied that at least he had the courage to fight and not just hide. His pride stung, her husband had rigged a grenade as a booby trap, a safe, clever response which McGowan had sensed was the work of a local resident. When it failed, rather than lose face, her husband chose to use the carbine, despite her pleas to leave the patrols alone.

Although he thought the man foolish for allowing pride to goad him into a senseless act of defiance, Thanh was chagrined that in his dossiers there was nothing which had associated the man with the Viet Cong. He guessed that there were no more than a dozen secret enemy cadres in the seven hamlets, but he had little hope of finding them. This left the first move up to them, and it was only by a quirk that one such valuable agent had been exposed and eliminated.

For their part, the enemy appeared to have modified their strategy toward Binh Son district in general and toward Binh Nghia in particular. Where some months earlier they had eagerly sought contact, the guerrilla and small Viet Cong units were avoiding the patrols. Vietnamese military intelligence reported that in late January three hundred VC political cadres from the five lowland districts of Quang Ngai province had attended a conference in southern Binh Son, where it had been decided not to fight the spreading pacification efforts on a daily guerrilla basis. Instead, the guerrillas were to gather intelligence and act as guides and reinforcements for the main forces who would come down from the hills for strong attacks. The primary targets were to be the RD teams and combined units, of which there were then five in Binh Son.

Shortly afterward district informed Thanh that a commander of the 409th NVA Battalion, which had participated in the September attack upon the fort, had visited the village and stayed overnight. Then a farmer told the PFs that five VC had held him prisoner in My Hué for five days, seeking information about Fort Page. The warnings about enemy observers from the main forces coupled with McGowan's clash with the secret guerrilla disturbed Suong. He suggested that the nightly patrol to that hamlet take the PF radio, and the PFs at the fort would double up on the Marine radio. This sensible precaution was followed for several days without incident.

Then in the early morning of March 25, the My Hué patrol received a call from battalion ordering them to cross over to the Phu Longs. When an attempt was made to raise the fort for confirmation of the dangerous order, the caller from battalion cut in on the frequency and repeated the battalion commander's orders. The radio procedure was correct and the English unaccented, but the radio operators at the fort could not identify the voice, and they knew the battalion operators on a first-name basis. McGowan told the caller to go to hell, assuming the man was an American at one of the many Chulai bases. In response to McGowan's curses, the voice signed off by saying: "Auf Wiedersehen, Marines." The incident was reported to counterintelligence, who confirmed the next day that the enemy had moved a powerful radio onto the peninsula across the river, along with an English-speaking operator, whom they believed to be European.

The combined unit was warned that the main forces would not be monitoring their net without reason. Special reconnaissance teams were dispatched by Marine headquarters to scout the Binh Son peninsula. They sighted numerous enemy bands dressed not in the black garb of guerrillas but in the green and khaki utilities characteristic of main-force units. The pilots of spotter planes brought back similar observations. There was gossip about a large enemy band seeping into the Phu Longs. The women who went downriver to the district market were buzzing about it, and Mr. Lee, the district census taker and top intelligence agent, insisted it was true.

Then at ten in the warm morning of March 26 a combined unit on the other side of the Phu Longs sent out a patrol with rudimentary medical assistance to a hamlet with a reputation like that of My Hué: influenced by, but not fully organized or fanatically dedicated to, the Viet Cong. There were sixteen men in the patrol, and they walked straight into a main-force bivouac position. Within a half-hour ten Marines and five PFs were dead. One PF survived by hiding in some underbrush while the Viet Cong shot in the head each of the fifteen bodies. The news raced through the district, with the Viet Cong reinforcing their victory by declaring they would strike again. The question was where.

Intelligence indicated that at the Viet Cong district committee meeting in late January the Binh Nghia combined unit had been denounced more bitterly than any other U.S. or GVN program. The unit was a military impediment; its patrols and ambushes prevented easy use of the Tra Bong River and blocked one route toward the Chulai air base. Its presence also impeded rice collections, taxation, proselytizing and recruitment. Worse still, after destroying the fort in September, the district committee had expected to regain the Binh Yen Noi area and re-establish suzerainty over the entire village, an expectation calculated on the belief that fear rather than revenge would dictate the actions of the survivors. Six months later, rather than having gained Binh Yen Noi, the Viet Cong faced the loss of My Hué.

Three days later, the intelligence came in hard and specific. Charlie Company received from headquarters a report that "120 VC dressed in green utilities with unidentified patch, were at Phu Long Hamlet Number 5 and armed with 60mm mortar, one 30 caliber machinegun, nine BARs and small arms. VC to attack Fort Page from the south." That same day, Captain Dang called Suong with information from other sources, confirming that Fort Page was the target.

By midafternoon the people were leaving, first a trickle, then a steady flow of families heading to district or to spend the night with friends in other hamlets. By four o'clock the river was boatless and the trails empty. At the fort, Suong for once did not have to wait until it was dark before he knew how many PFs were going to show up for guard duty. All his men had come in early. So had Trao and Thanh and some of the other officials. Not all. Many had gone to Binh Son, rather than die like Mr. Phuoc. They were not fighters. The RDs stayed, their leader telling Suong that he had pulled his men back to Binh Yen Noi. While it was still light, the leaders of the PFs, RDs and Marines made up their common battle plan, liberally helped in their patrol decisions by the kibitzing of their men.

The plan was simple. If the attack came from the south, the scout patrols were to let the VC pass without firing, the hope being to draw the enemy into the open paddies. The 1st Marine Division had artillery illumination and helicopter gunships on alert. If the enemy entered the open, they were to finish him. If the attack came through the hamlet from the north, the VC could remain concealed and still slip up to within twenty meters of the wire. Trao and Suong insisted it would have to be a rifle fight. They did not want to destroy their own homes, and there were some families huddled in their household bunkers. The RDs were deployed along the northern edge of the hamlet, facing the sand dunes, to prevent the enemy unit from getting in among the houses. While limiting damage to the hamlet, this deployment might deprive the unit of the opportunity of delivering a hard blow, since the enemy would be unlikely to persist if discovered before they were in their assault position.

Each group was thoroughly briefed. Six of the Marines and eight PFs were to go out on two patrols to warn the fort when the enemy approached and to ambush the VC when they pulled back. Colucci was leading one patrol; Luong the other. The perimeter of the fort was manned from inside the trench, so Suong and McGowan could shift their forces as needed. By dusk they were ready. The Marines and PFs gathered in the courtyard for a final weapon check.

"All right," McGowan said, "I want—"

"Sarge," Gallagher yelled, "you got a call from company."

While the Marines and the PFs waited and listened, McGowan moved to the radio and picked it up.

"Lima Six Actual, this is Charlie Six," the radio crackled. "We have almost proof positive that you are going to be hit by a battalion. Repeat, by a battalion. You are to fall back to this position immediately. Over."

The Marines heard. So did the PFs, and those who knew enough English to understand were whispering the news to the others even as McGowan was replying.

"Ah, Charlie Six, you told us that already today. So did Captain Dang. I'm afraid I don't understand. Everything is set down here. We'll stay. Over."

"Lima Six Actual, this is Charlie Six Actual. This is an order from Serpent Six Actual, repeat, Serpent Six Actual."

The commander of Charlie Company had his orders from the battalion commander, who had to bear the final career responsibility for what happened at the fort. Fort Page had gone under once. The entire patrol from another combined unit had just been wiped out. If Page fell a second time, the lieutenant colonel would almost certainly be relieved and passed over for any future promotion.

"Charlie Six, this is Lima Six Actual," McGowan replied. "We're O.K. here. Over."

"Lima Six, hold on while I check with Serpent Six Actual."

McGowan changed the radio frequency and picked up the battalion net. The Charlie Company commander was catching hell from the battalion commander: either McGowan left the fort or faced a court-martial. McGowan turned the radio off.

"All Marines into the mess deck," he said.

He turned toward the waiting Vietnamese.

"The Marines must talk alone, Suong."

The twelve Americans gathered in the small room and sat on the floor and benches to hear McGowan.

"You all heard the man," the sergeant said. "We could get hit by three hundred Cong. Yet if we leave now, it's all over. We could never come back. At least I'd never come back. I can't order you to stay, and you have been ordered to leave. It's our choice: go or stay. So let's take a vote. Is anyone in favor of leaving?"

Swinford jumped up. He was close to tears.

"You can go to hell, McGowan," he shouted. "You can all go to hell. Screw your vote. I don't give a crap what any of you do. I've been waiting for them to come back ever since Sullivan. I'm not going to run from those little bastards. I'm going to stay here and blast them. They're not getting *this* fort. They're not getting *this* ville. I'm not leaving here no matter what. And you're not getting me out of here. I'll lock myself in the storeroom and I'll blast any mother who tries to come through the door. So help me God I will."

For several seconds no one spoke. Then Garcia said: "I'm with Paul. It was all for nothing if we leave now, I mean, what are we going to say to the PFs?"

"Yeh," Gallagher said. "There's no way I can see bugging out."

"We can hold," Colucci said.

"All right," McGowan replied. "Then it's settled. We stay."

"We'll visit you in the brig, Sarge," Gallagher said.

The Marines filed back out into the courtyard and approached the silent PFs.

"What are you staring at, Luong?" Wingrove asked. "Let's di-di on out of here. We're wasting time."

The PFs laughed and the patrols joined up and left the fort.

McGowan called back to company.

"Charlie Six, this is Lima Six. Cannot—repeat, not—

leave this position. We have two—repeat, two—patrols already out and the RDs are in the hamlet. No radio contact with these units. If we leave, we'd get ambushed by our own men. Over."

Company relayed the message to battalion, where no one was willing to accept responsibility for ordering a move under such circumstances. Instead, as a career hedge in case of a later disaster, Charlie Company was told to inform McGowan that battalion had wanted him to move while there was still time.

About ten in the evening the enemy scouts started slipping into Binh Yen Noi, a few men moving cautiously, dodging from shadow to shadow, hugging the sides of the houses, avoiding the paths and coming slowly, very slowly. Alerted by the stillness of the hamlet and the absence of lights and of people, as well as by contact with some of their secret cadres who told them the defenders were prepared, the scouts darted back and forth trying to reassure one another to go deeper into the hamlet and draw closer to the fort. At length, one man braver than the rest sneaked as far forward as the stalls at the marketplace while the others hung back and waited to see what would happen.

The scout knew his business. When he drew near to the bushes on the far side of the marketplace, he went down to one knee and bobbed his head back and forth, trying to catch any strange silhouette against the skyline. He was looking straight at a group of patrollers, and his suspicion was evidently so strong that at any second he might raise his rifle and fire.

Deciding one of the patrollers might be killed if that did happen, Luong shot the man in the chest. As he crumpled to earth, the other scouts scurried away and Luong knew it was over. They would signal the main body not to cross that night. The fort's defenses were too strong and poised. But throughout the rest of the night the Marines, PFs and RDs waited in their positions, while a reaction platoon at Charlie Company played cards, strummed guitars, loaded magazines and waited for the firing, and while the artillerymen and pilots at Chulai dozed fitfully, waiting for the call to help.

It was not for nothing. In a sense, it was the most important battle the Americans at Fort Page ever prepared to fight. They had chosen to stay; the PFs knew it, and soon so would the entire village.

# BOOK VI

# ACCEPTANCE

# 20

The next morning the villagers streamed back into the hamlets. Upon hearing about the repulse of the enemy battalion, they treated the PFs and RDs as heroes. For the next few days the PFs could not buy a drink, as they were invited from house to house to sip rice wine and boast of their defense of the village. In the retelling, the cautious retreat of the enemy was exaggerated until it became a full-fledged rout under fire. With the PFs absent from duty, the Americans were forced to do more patrolling, since they stayed away from the parties, both because some were not invited and those that were dared not risk expulsion from the CAP by getting drunk at night. Although the Americans were free to roam during the day, it was hard to interest a PF who had been drunk the night before in starting all over again at ten in the morning, with children scurrying about and women yelling at him to do some constructive work for a change.

The PFs were enjoying themselves hugely. The previous June their prestige had been so low even a child would not fetch water for them, and now they were local celebrities. But the Americans, most of whom could not speak the language and few of whom sensed the historical significance of the successful defense, seemed forgotten in the festivities, or just taken for granted. They continued their usual routine: linger at the fort, wander around the hamlets, and patrol, patrol, patrol.

Few of the Americans had been able to convince any girls in the village to sleep with them. The hamlet elders at

first had strongly disapproved, and any girl who bedded
down with an American risked a public beating. After several months, when the Americans in the combined unit
were accepted, that deterrent was lifted. But still the villagers had a strict moral code, and the physical environs
did not lend themselves to private lovers' trysts. A Marine
had to convince not only the girl but her parents, and, in
some cases, her brothers. That done, he had to find seclu-
sion without leaving the hamlet boundaries and then coax
the girl to bed during the daylight hours. To hurdle all
these impediments required language skill, facial charm,
diplomacy, long patience and much luck. In most cases, a
Marine's courting skill simply did not match his desire.
Most remained celibate while in the village, some taking
solace in their virtue, others making occasional trips to
whorehouses in the shack towns along Highway One. The
three Americans who were sleeping with girls in Binh
Nghia had to contend with Trao's scowls, and the knowledge that he was just waiting to be able to report to
McGowan a parental complaint.

So the Marines were momentarily stunned when, a
few days after the abortive attack, Trao drove up to the
fort in the ARVN truck, lifted the back canvas and
revealed two giggling, attractive young prostitutes, a pre-
paid twelve-hour gift from the village council. Although
most of the Marines were delighted, McGowan was
appalled.

"Trao, what are you trying to do?" he asked. "Get me
fired? If they're found here, I'm finished."

Trao laughed and told the sergeant not to worry; the
truck would be back to pick up the girls before dark. He
said he had planned carefully to avoid interference.
This explanation satisfied McGowan, but he had not
questioned closely enough. Trao meant that he had

Captain Dang's permission; McGowan assumed his Marine battalion commander had been called out of the district.

About an hour after the prostitutes had arrived, so did the battalion commander.

"Sarge," the guard at the gate hollered, "the colonel's jeep is coming."

"You've got to be shitting me."

"Take a look."

McGowan did.

"I've had it. We've had it. It's all over," he said. "Those girls—we've got to hide them."

He ran to the squad tent and burst in without knocking. Lying on one of the cots were a Marine and one of the prostitutes. Both were sweating and naked.

"McGowan," the startled Marine yelped, "who the hell do you think you are? Get out of here!"

"The CO's coming. We have to hide her. Now. Get her over to the supply room."

"Like this? What, are you putting me on? Is this a joke? Is everybody lined up outside?"

"——, I'm dead serious. Honest to God. It's my stripes if he walks in here. You gotta move. You gotta move right now."

Out the back of the tent and into the side door of the adobe building they scampered—a naked Marine and a naked girl. In the small side room used as a messhall a cot had been set up to accommodate the other prostitute, who had her blouse on but nothing else when McGowan and the first couple burst in. She looked up from her work with an expression of mild surprise, while her Marine partner was too flabbergasted to say anything.

"The battalion commander's right behind me," McGowan said, "so grab her trousers and your clothes and get in the storeroom, and keep these girls quiet or we'll all end up in the DMZ."

The jeep jounced up and the lieutenant colonel hopped out, returning McGowan's salute.

"I'm on my way to regiment, Sergeant," the colonel said. "I dropped by for a minute to see how you are making out."

"Yes, sir. Would you like to inspect the men's rifles?"

"Rifle inspection? Where do you think we are—on some parade ground? No, I just want to take a look around. Rifle inspection! Sometimes I wonder about you, McGowan. That's as crazy as your stunt the other night. If that VC battalion had attacked, you'd have been wiped out. You know that, don't you?"

"No, sir, I don't think so."

"Well, I'm not here to argue with you."

The colonel walked briskly to the squad tent and strode through with barely a glance at the inside. Then he entered the adobe building by the same side door McGowan and his naked companions had used only minutes before. He almost tripped over the cot in the messhall.

"What's that doing here?"

"These are my quarters at night, sir. I sleep apart from the men."

"That sounds sensible. But you should put your cot away when you're finished with it."

"Yes, sir."

To the colonel's left was the storeroom, a piece of canvas draped over its doorless entranceway. Directly in front of him was the doorway connecting the small messhall with the large village office. The door was open and a mob of PFs and village officials were peering in, those in the back rows jumping up and down to peek over the heads of those in front. They were all laughing and exchanging loud remarks and several were trying to catch McGowan's eye while pointing furtively toward the storeroom.

"What is all this, Sergeant?" the colonel shouted. "I can hardly hear myself think."

"It's nothing, sir. I'll take care of it," McGowan replied, glaring at the PFs. "Di oi, di oi. Dung noi. Quay lai, quay—"

"Never mind, McGowan. You don't have to impress me. I know you can speak some Vietnamese. I don't have the time for them anyway."

The colonel turned and walked back out the side door, McGowan lingering for a second to give the PFs the finger before running to catch up with him. The colonel climbed into his jeep, took McGowan's salute and drove off without saying another word.

The fort exploded. The Marines came running forward to clap McGowan on the back and the PFs tumbled out of the village office and joined the throng, one PF strutting around in imitation of the colonel while another, playing the role of the sergeant, flapped his arm up and down as though saluting constantly. The Marines who had hidden in the storeroom came forward to claim they had made love to the girls standing up while the colonel was in the messhall.

The story was all over the village by evening and the advisers at Binh Son heard it from the district chief the next day. Eventually it made its way to Combined Action headquarters in Da Nang and at least one general learned what had happened. But none of McGowan's superiors ever mentioned the incident to him, except by innuendo. On the other hand, McGowan asked Trao not to do him any more such favors.

Not that he had to worry about the battalion commander, for shortly afterward all Marine units left Chulai and moved farther north to fight the North Vietnamese. Their place was filled by an amalgam of separate Army brigades, called the Americal Division. The Marines at Fort Page, and those at the few other Combined Action Platoons scattered in the Chulai area, were staying. The Army had agreed to look after them and General Walt felt he would be reneging on a promise to the Vietnamese if he pulled them out. None of the combined-unit Marines volunteered to leave.

As the Marines pulled out, the Army moved in to the same prepared positions, thereby eliminating much construction work. On April 7, 1967, when Charlie Company moved by truck from their perimeter out on the sand dunes, an Army platoon took their place. The Americans at Fort Page assumed the platoon was there to stay and paid no attention to the transfer until the next day, when a group of villagers shuffled into the fort to excitedly claim that the company position was empty and that people were stealing ammunition.

While not quite believing the story, McGowan and Gallagher borrowed bicycles and pedaled the two miles to the position. They found the barbed-wire gates wide open, and not an American in sight. The ammunition bunkers had been partially rifled and gear lay strewn about. As they stood gazing at the scene in dumb surprise, they glimpsed a woman, already outside the wire, running down the back of the hill. She was clutching two white phosphorus rocket rounds.

"Dung lai! Dung lai!" McGowan hollered. "Lai-day. Lai-day."

The woman had almost reached the edge of a treeline. At McGowan's commands to stop, she ran faster. McGowan dropped to one knee, quickly sighted and squeezed the trigger. Hit in the arm, the woman fell. The

Marines walked down to her. McGowan poked with his toe at one of the rockets.

"If we tripped one of those things up at My Hué some night, it would really fry us," McGowan said. "Get her evacced and watch the hill. I'm going into Chulai."

The sergeant walked down the road to Highway One and stopped the first jeep he saw. Thirty minutes later he was at division headquarters, where a joint Army-Marine task force was overseeing the division shift. In bitter tones he reported the mixup to a concerned colonel, who ordered a replacement company flown in by helicopter. Believing it closed the incident, McGowan accepted a jeep ride back to the fort. On the way he asked the driver to swing by the company position to see if Gallagher had been relieved of guard duty.

As they drove through the small hamlet of Dong Binh, near the company perimeter, he noticed that no children were running about and that some people were peering at him from the entrances of the family bunkers. On the hamlet's outskirts he could see a group of Marines clustered, so he was more puzzled than worried. As the jeep drew nearer, he saw another group, a bit farther away, identifiable in their black outfits as RDs. The Americans and the Vietnamese stood with rifles pointed at each other. No one was talking.

"What the hell is this?" McGowan shouted as he jumped from the jeep. "Put those guns down."

"Talk to those assholes first, Sarge, they started it," Swinford replied.

"If that dude with the BAR keeps eyeballing me like that, I'm going to blow him away," another Marine said.

The RDs were equally close to killing, and in their anger and nervousness spoke too rapidly for McGowan to understand.

"How'd it start?" McGowan asked.

"All we did was take the grenades off them. They were strutting around Dong Binh with ammo from the hill," Swinford said. "They didn't want to cooperate, so I slapped their honcho around a little bit. You told us to get that stuff back."

"Yeh, but we're not playing Wyatt Earp. Where are the PFs?"

"They di-di'd out of here when those jerks drew down on us. They don't want anything to do with this."

The situation was beyond McGowan's authority and language ability. The RDs were ignoring him, and he feared a firefight even if he got the Marines to back off. He walked to the jeep radio and dialed the district frequency. In a loud voice he asked Captain Dang to come to Dong Binh immediately.

Dang, and his adviser, Lieutenant Colonel John Jarvis, arrived within fifteen minutes. The Marines said they were trying to recover stolen goods. The RDs said they did not consider it stealing to take grenades from an abandoned position. And in any event, the Marines had no right to push them around.

Dang berated the Marines for physically mauling the RDs. He berated the RDs for selfishly gathering loose grenades while ignoring the looting by villagers. The RDs responded that the villagers would hand in the explosive items in return for the rewards American units offered for ordnance found and reported. Dang did not accept the response as legitimate. Even if most villagers did take the explosives for profit rather than politics, the few who would pass on ammunition to the guerrillas could cause many deaths, including those of RDs. He ordered the RDs to help the Marines in searching the hamlet.

Before leaving, Jarvis drew McGowan aside.

"Don't let Dang's ass-chewing get to you," he said.

"Actually, he's sort of pleased with the RDs for standing up to you. So am I. I didn't think they had it in them."

"Well, sir," McGowan replied, "if you run across a good interpreter, I could sure use him. I don't want to end up with any of my men gut-shot just so some RD will feel more like a man."

As Jarvis had predicted, the RDs felt better about themselves for having stood up to the Marines, who hadn't shown much respect for them since the night Trung was killed and his two companions ran away. Because the RDs had been willing to take the Marines on in a gunfight despite the disparity in fighting skills, the Marines modified their harsh opinion. For the few remaining weeks the RDs were in the village, the Marines worked more closely with them.

When the RDs departed in mid-April, claiming they had once again pacified the Binh Yen Noi hamlet complex, they left behind little evidence of their stay. They had organized no village militia, and if they had infused the villagers with a hatred of the Viet Cong, it did not manifest itself in actions, or even in words spoken publicly. The RDs did leave behind two physical memorials. One was a truck garden, on the edge of which they had solemnly erected a plaque reading: "Anti-Communist Vegetable Garden." Unfortunately, the garden had not grown, and the pompous sign presided over a bunch of weeds.

The other memorial was the rickety bamboo fence they had insisted the villagers build around the My Hué hamlets. Shortly after the RDs left the village, a dozen Viet Cong paddled across the river, entered My Hué, rousted several villagers out of bed and had them tear down a section of the fence. Through the village gossip system, the PFs at the fort heard of the VC presence, but when a reaction force arrived, the VC had already gone, leaving behind a gap in the bamboo fence.

The PFs gathered some villagers and rebuilt the fence.

A week later the VC gathered some villagers and tore it down.

The PFs rebuilt it.

The Americans thought the struggle over the fence, which had little tactical value, was silly. Trao, who had opposed the original construction of the fence, recognized the absurdity of the contest yet insisted the PFs could not afford to lose since the Viet Cong had decided to make an issue out of it. The PFs had to fight back.

So late one night Trao and Suong slipped into My Hué and pulled up several sections of the fence. In the post holes they placed grenades with the spoon flush to the wood; by repacking the post with dirt, they made sure the grenades would not go off so long as the fence remained standing. But ripping up the fence would be Russian roulette. At dawn they gathered the residents of My Hué and told them what they had done. The message naturally got to the Viet Cong, who were then faced with the choice of forcing some villagers to commit suicide or of leaving the fence alone.

The RD fence received no more attention.

# 21

The newcomers of the U.S. Army had their own way of doing things, and the Marines at Fort Page were delighted to see the emphasis which was placed on expanding and improving facilities at nearby Chulai airfield. The Non-Commissioned Officers' Club was soon air-conditioned and stocked with an inexhaustible supply of chilled beer. By April six of the twelve Marines at the fort held the grade of sergeant. The rank did not affect the workings of the unit. Each man knew his job, and the dirty chores, like clearing out the two-holer, were rotated among all. Promotion basically meant more pay and cold drinks at the NCO Club. On slow and stifling afternoons, the sergeants liked to hitchhike dusty rides to the air base.

One evening Colucci and Sergeant Norwood returned to the village to report between burps that the Army had a new weapon, the XM-1332A, an M-16 underslung with a grenade launcher. Aggressive and quick-moving, Norwood was particularly keen to fire the weapon.

"My God," he said, "with one of those things, I'd be a walking tank. And would you believe it, they carry them in bags to keep the dust out—I kid you not. I don't think they've ever fired. Even chopper guards have them."

"What do the bags look like?" McGowan asked. "We might make a trade."

Based on Norwood's description, Missy Top sewed four bags in four days. The following Sunday Norwood and three other sergeants from Fort Page, their battered M-16s in the fresh new bags, strolled up to the large Chulai messhall a little late for the weekly steak dinner. Like skis at a mountain resort, hundreds of rifles rested against the messhall wall. Many were bagged. The sergeants split up and individually peeked and poked around until each found a bag containing one of the new weapons. Then each made his swap, one battered M-16 for one brand-new XM-1332A.

McGowan hoped to use the weapons to find the enemy and to keep a fine tactical edge on the combined unit. The pace of the fighting had slackened. No longer would one out of every two or three patrols engage the enemy; it was becoming more like one out of every thirty or forty.

Some of the older Marines, who had been in the village with Sullivan, were not adapting well to the slower pace of combat. For some, the shooting had made up for the sweat and the danger for the boredom. Flirting with death held an almost sexual excitement: the guerrilla grenade answered by the rifle, the lurking "Hello, Marine!" shouted from the darkness around the fort answered by a "Fuck you, Charlie!," the nightly blind man's game of hide-and-go-kill played against a skilled enemy whom they felt they knew, the villagers' open awe when they kept going out with prices on their heads and the P31st District Force Company trying for them and the North Vietnamese having come in.

But it was slowly changing. Even without the Americans, the PFs were patrolling frequently in small groups. The enemy did not choose to fight as often. The Marines weren't so special any more. Without a daily dose of danger, some resented the daily toil and drudgery, the night patrol passing through full paddies, then lying sopping wet in rough dirt at four in the morning, the stinging empty wait with the mosquitoes and ants, the diarrhea, the daily clean-up at the fort, filling sandbags, burning waste, standing guard. It was becoming too routine, the pay-off in a shootout occurring less and less. Suong and Thanh admitted the enemy was beginning to avoid the village, but they insisted some Viet Cong were still moving in and out, only they weren't as anxious to fight any more. Suong claimed that the combined patrols of six men were too big and too noisy and that the Marines smelled and so the Viet Cong could avoid them.

McGowan felt that action would pick up due to the new weapons. Their firepower meant that the size of patrols could safely be cut down. With less noise, the chances of encountering the enemy would be better. He decided to test the theory right away.

The evening after they had stolen the new weapons, Norwood and Colucci set out for My Hué as a two-man patrol. In addition to the over-and-under rifles, Colucci was packing two LAWs in case he saw some sampans, while Norwood carried a night-seeing Starlite scope.

"After all this, man," Norwood said, "we better get something."

They left at dusk and those at the fort settled down to wait and to monitor the radio. The hours went by dully. Two close-in patrols went out, sniffed around the marketplace and the school yard, and came back in by different routes, having seen or heard nothing unusual. Only the guards and radio operators were up at three when Norwood's excited call came in.

"We see them. We see them," he whispered. "Ten or twelve of them digging a trench line."

The Marines and PFs scrambled awake and clustered around the radio, jabbering among themselves.

"Knock it off. Will you guys shut up, dung noi—dung noi," McGowan shouted. "I can't hear a word he's saying."

Norwood was trying to describe his location.

"Out the back gate of My Hué 1. On the dunes. You know, near the place where the people take a crap."

"Norwood, people shit all over the place. You have to do better than that."

"I can't. What do you want me to do? Get out my map and turn on a light? Come out the back gate and I'll pick you up."

"O.K. We're on our way. Don't take them on alone."

Fifteen heavily armed Marines and PFs quickly left the fort, half-striding, half-trotting in their haste. Luong took point and coursed up the main trail. By the time he reached the front of My Hué Number 1, those behind him were strung out and breathing hard. Without slowing down, he jogged toward the back gate, the others coming on fast lest they miss out on the firefight. Fearing an ambush as the patrol was funneled through the gate, Luong veered off the trail and struck out across a paddy dike which connected with the dunes about three hundred yards away from the gate. This was a mix-up in Norwood's instructions, and McGowan, well back in the column, broke from the dike and splashed through the rice shoots in an effort to catch and stop Luong.

He was too late. Crouched behind a scrub-topped dune, Norwood and Colucci heard the splashing and turned to see a line of dark figures running at them. Norwood raised up, yelled "Look out!," jerked an off-balance burst in the direction of the line and followed Colucci over the top of the dune.

Directly in front of him, Luong had seen a man pop up and was already diving face first off the bank into the water when the rounds zipped by him. At the same time, with the instinct of practiced reaction, rifles all along the line were throwing full magazines against the empty dune. Colucci and Norwood thought they would soon be killed. Then they heard McGowan shouting orders.

"Hey, you dumb bastards, it's us. It's us," Norwood yelled.

The two forces met at the top of the dune.

"Are they still there?" McGowan asked.

Norwood was scoping out the trench.

"Yeh. Your burst must have pinned them down, too. They're staying in the trench. Let me try a LAW. Then we can mop them up."

Luong was opposed. So was Suong. They wanted to

pinch in on the trench from two sides and not fire until the enemy did so. McGowan agreed, so they split the force and moved on the trench by bounds. Luong, as usual, was out in front and first to reach the trench.

Even then he did not fire. Instead, he stood erect and started screaming at the occupants of the trench. Under his threats seven men and three women slowly climbed out and cowered together. Not one had a weapon. They were villagers, not Viet Cong.

They stammered out their story. Around dusk that evening a squad of Viet Cong had crossed the river and entered My Hué Number 1. They had come straight to the houses of these people at the rear of the hamlet and told them to take their picks and shovels and come with them. They had herded them out into the dunes and pointed to where they wanted the trench dug. They did not say why. Two guards had stayed with them. They had almost finished when suddenly firing started. The guards had run away and they had hidden in the trench.

Suong told the villagers to go home. The CAP force headed back to the fort, Luong and Norwood kidding each other, McGowan and Suong smiling in bemused relief.

Weapons and violence were part of these young men. Their hardened attitudes toward physical danger and death were reflected in their humor, sometimes tastelessly. To them, comedy could be tragedy avoided; it could also be danger faked.

One day a Marine took a grenade, removed the firing mechanism and screwed back on the pull pin and release lever. For a while he horsed around with the other Marines in the fort, throwing the defanged grenade back and forth like a baseball. McGowan watched them and said nothing.

Then the Marine saw Luong approaching. After winking at the others, he staggered out of the fort as if drunk. Weaving along, he threw his arms askew and Luong, grinning tolerantly, held him up. Then the Marine dangled the grenade. When Luong reached to take it away from him, he pulled the pin and threw it straight up in the air.

In an instant, Luong had dropped his rifle, thrown the Marine flat, spun around, caught the grenade and in the same motion flipped it underhand into the paddies while going flat himself. Five seconds went by and nothing happened. Then the Marine started laughing, followed tentatively by the Americans and the PFs in the fort. Luong stood up, looked at the Marine and hit him full in the mouth. The American went down and Luong stormed into a silent fort. He strode up to McGowan and just stood there looking at him as if to say: How can you call yourself a leader and let one of your men do something that stupid?

McGowan apologized.

But it might be that bad luck and bad judgment run in streaks, for McGowan shortly compounded his embarrassment by a more serious error. Frequently the unit did not report weapons captured during a firefight, a dodge started by O'Rourke in an effort to ensure that the men could keep deserved war trophies. Subsequently a change in regulations permitted soldiers to keep bolt-action rifles but not automatic weapons. Having captured several of the latter, the unit kept them hidden at the fort as backup weapons. A few days after the grenade incident, McGowan was sitting at the sturdy wooden dinner table cleaning an unloaded enemy submachine gun. Alfano was standing in front of the sergeant, chatting. In answer to a question, McGowan raised his head and brought up the barrel of the gun. As he did so, the bolt slammed home and the weapon fired.

The bullet just missed Alfano's right eye.

For a few seconds neither man moved. Then McGowan handed Alfano the gun.

"Here," he said, "you shoot me."

Short of an earthquake, McGowan did not think things could go any worse than they had for the past few weeks, so he allowed the two-man rover patrolling with the special rifles to continue, although only the best tacticians could participate. The patrol rotated among five Americans and five Vietnamese. Without action the novelty soon wore off and the rovers became just another type of patrol.

About two weeks after the rovers' initial misadventure, Norwood again drew the duty, with a PF named Nguyen Thi Tri as his partner. Again Norwood headed for the dunes behind My Hué, leaving the fort after midnight amid the kidding of the guard and radio operator. It took Norwood and Tri over two hours to cover two map kilometers, Norwood being edgy about the route and moving slowly. The back stretch of the village seemed quiet enough, however, and after lying in a likely ambush spot for an hour, the two headed home. They were stiff from the wait and their sweaty clothes were chilly, so coming in they moved along at a brisk pace, Norwood's uneasiness having been dispelled by the dull, familiar routine of another patrol without contact.

Despite their haste, the sand absorbed their footfalls, so they were midway across the dunes when a figure loomed up right in front of Norwood. Norwood fired in a frenzy. The figure fell, Norwood leaping on top of him with Tri a step behind. Five other men were lying in a row. Norwood pivoted to gun them.

"No shoot, no shoot," Tri yelled.

He had had a second to look while Norwood was moving. The ambushers were Americans.

"Man, you almost killed me," yelled the man whom Norwood had shot. "Look what you done to my rifle."

The man, an Army staff sergeant in charge of an ambush team from a nearby rifle company, held out an M-16 with a stock smashed by bullets. His team had been assigned an ambush position two miles to the north, but he had not felt like walking that far. When the patrol was halfway across the dunes, the sergeant had radioed his company that he was in the assigned position. Then he had his men flop down in the soft, empty sand, set out claymore mines to their front and rear, and go to sleep, rotating one man awake. At three, it was the sergeant's turn to guard the ambush and, to fight off drowsiness, he had stood up to stretch just as Norwood walked by.

On two rover patrols in less than a month Norwood had almost killed or been killed by his own, and he was too shaken to talk coherently. Tri used the ambushers' radio to call the fort. McGowan and Suong were awakened and ran to the spot, guided in by Tri's hand flare.

Upon seeing McGowan, the Army sergeant started to scream at Norwood, who was still in a state of shock.

"That asshole almost blew me away," he yelled. "What sort of kooks do you have in your outfit anyway?"

McGowan wasn't listening. He handed his M-16 to Suong, turned and hit the staff sergeant in his open mouth. For the second time that night the man was knocked down.

The next day McGowan was ordered to the Army battalion headquarters to report the incident. Upon hearing his story, the battalion commander ordered the sergeant relieved. Then, noticing McGowan's worn M-16, he commented that his unit had recently been issued a supply of the new over-and-under combination rifle and grenade launcher. He thought that the Marines at the fort might be more in need of them than his troops, so he would issue a dozen on indefinite loan.

"Sometimes," McGowan said to Colucci that evening, "I feel like an ass."

The next day he personally carried back to the Chulai provost marshal's office the four weapons he had stolen weeks earlier. He recited a lame story, which was accepted without questioning, and returned to the fort with the four battered M-16s. When he arrived, his men were wiping the packing grease from their XM-1332A special rifles.

# 22

Given the firepower of their new weapons, further retention for tactical purposes of the captured weapons was unnecessary, and the Marines had reluctantly concluded that it was idiotic, if not impossible, to smuggle automatic weapons into the United States as souvenirs. But no one suggested that they turn the weapons in legally; they represented too much hard work and commanded top black market prices among other U.S. units. The combined unit held a meeting and decided that the times of petty trades had passed. They would barter as one single package the captured weapons and other war booty, such as paper flags, holsters and belt buckles. The word went out, and from the Navy Seabees came back the most interesting proposal: a 100-volt generator in return for the entire collection, provided two pistols were added. A valued status symbol among Vietnamese leaders on both sides of the conflict, the pistol was the one weapon prized above all

others by the PFs and village officials. In a year of fighting, the combined unit had captured only three. They had
gone to Trao, Suong and Thanh. None offered to give his
up in the trade, and the Marines held little hope of capturing another.

"What do the Seabees expect us to do," Garcia said, "go
over to the Phu Longs and ask some VC company commander to give us his?"

But toward the end of April the Seabees trucked in the
generator in exchange for the enemy weapons on hand and
a promise that they would receive the next pistol captured.

The electricity resulted in a quantum jump in the quality of life at the fort. There were lamps by which to read
without squinting, and floodlights to guard the wire. From
the PX a Sony television set was bought, as well as a
record player and dozens of albums, and plans were made
to purchase a refrigerator. The villagers who lived nearby
started buying or stealing wire and stringing electricity
lines to their houses. Trao toyed with the idea of running a
main line through Binh Yen Noi.

The luxury of simple modernity had drawbacks. The
generator was a monster which gulped gas and snorted,
clanged, rattled and shook all through the night, forcing
conversations to be shouted and the men to sleep with
jackets wrapped around their ears. McGowan believed the
music and light lulled his men, dulled their fighting edge
and put them in the wrong mood for night patrols. The
men wanted to schedule their patrols so as not to miss
"Laugh-In" or any special with Joey Heatherton, their
favorite from the Bob Hope Christmas tour. Little Joe's
pals kept popping in at dusk to watch the TV show
"Combat"; then they would have to stay overnight, worrying their parents by their absence and annoying the
Marines and PFs by their giggles, or a patrol would have

to walk them home. Suong worried continuously about sappers cutting the wire unheard and slipping in. The anxieties of the two leaders grew, and they came to look on the generator as a symbol of complacency and an invitation to disaster. Four weeks after it arrived, they decided to get rid of it.

Again they sought trading bids, while asking their men what they might take in exchange. Doc Blunk and Bac Si Khoi knew what they wanted. Each morning, often in the gray predawn, their patients bustled into the fort, frequently barging right into the squad tent, tripping over rifles, scattering socks and boots, screeching "Bac Si! Bac Si!" and pawing over the squirming figures on the cots until they found Blunk. Rules and regulations did not work since many claimed that their particular cases were genuine emergencies, and the guards on the dawn watch spitefully enjoyed upsetting the sleep of their luckier comrades. Since the guard rotated, the disturbances forced a cycle of revenge, with each guard remembering the morning he had been awakened.

The corpsmen suggested a trade for timber. If they had their own dispensary, the squad tent would be much quieter; if McGowan was determined to take away the lights, the Marines might as well sleep soundly.

Hearing that lumber might be coming, old Mr. Minh, the timid chief clerk of the village, pestered McGowan, arguing that he and the other clerks needed a place of their own to work. It was impossible to keep records and request requisitions in the main room of the fort amidst the racket of the Marines eating and strumming guitars and the PFs screaming at each other over their playing cards and Khoi with his wailing babies and district headquarters sputtering over the radio each hour. Besides, how would it look to give Khoi, who was not even thirty, his own building, when the hamlet and village officials had no place where they could conduct private business?

As the rumor of an upcoming trade spread, Trao became the target for the invective of irate parents. Why should the officials demand a new office, they asked, while the children had to attend school in the grass? As the combined unit had furthered its combat control, more and more families from My Hué had sent their children down to the school at Binh Yen Noi. Even with two classes a day, all the children could not crowd under the one scraggly thatched roof. What would happen when the rains came in the fall, and they could not sit outside in rows along the side of the road? Trao suspected that Ho Chi was secretly urging the parents to complain, but as the chief official whose re-election depended upon popularity rather than influence, Trao was not about to back the professional clerks who were clamoring for the village office. So Trao tried to convince McGowan to trade for a schoolhouse.

Unable to decide, McGowan brought his problem to Lieutenant Carlson at district, who was firm in his advice. He said whatever McGowan decided was his own business, but he should not have to wheel and deal to provide the village with certain basics, such as a school. There were official Vietnamese channels for requesting that sort of help, and if Trao did not use them now, he would be completely at a loss when the Americans left.

Trao reluctantly agreed to send in the official requests for school building materials, while at the same time telling McGowan he would never get them.

With the village school supposedly a Vietnamese matter, McGowan put out the word that he needed only enough lumber and fly screening for a small dispensary and village office in return for the generator. A nearby

Army battalion responded to those trade terms immediately.

Within a week the villagers had both buildings up, and two days later a midwife came to the fort, escorting a woman on a stretcher who was expecting a difficult delivery and wanted Blunk's help. Blunk was flattered and excited. The other young Americans were nervous. That night at Fort Page a baby boy was born within ten feet of the spot where Brannon had died nine months earlier. McGowan's liquor supply went down that night.

The quick sprouting of the two wooden structures mocked the bureaucratic germination of the request for the schoolhouse. Although district had approved and forwarded the requests to province, province had not replied. Nothing. Not a word. Trao was embarrassed to use his new office while the children sat in the grass and dust.

Finally McGowan had had enough. He went back to district and called on Lieutenant Carlson.

"Sir," he said, "I cut Trao out of that generator trade because you said do it through channels. Well, now what do we do?"

"We'll still go through channels," Carlson replied. "Only we'll go, not a piece of paper."

In Carlson's jeep they drove the ten jolting miles to Quang Ngai City, arriving at the province headquarters at noon. Both the American and Vietnamese staffs were on their two-hour lunch break, habitually taken to avoid the sapping heat. Carlson asked directions to the home of the AID chief, and a few moments later they parked their jeep in front of a clean, attractive, whitewashed two-story colonial villa with a long patio, gardened shrubbery and a high fence topped by watchtowers and Vietnamese guards. Dust-caked, their green utilities baggy and soiled, McGowan lugging along his M-16 like a child attached to a rag doll, the two Marines walked onto the veranda and knocked on a closed door. An American in a clean white shirt and pressed trousers carrying a cold beer opened it.

"You fellows lost?" he asked.

When Carlson explained whom they wanted to see and why, they were invited into the air-conditioned room and offered beers, which they eagerly accepted. After the AID chief had heard their story, he promised the materials would be delivered through Vietnamese channels within a week.

"We'd invite you to lunch," he concluded, "but—"

"No, no," Carlson interrupted, "we've got to be going. But thanks for asking, sir."

"That's quite all right. Anytime I can help, you just give me a ring. The province chief's a good sort, really. The reason your district is so low on his list of priorities is that he thinks the Americal Division helps you out."

"Yes, sir," Carlson replied, looking at McGowan. "Thanks very much."

The two Marines walked back to their jeep.

"Well, Mac," Carlson said, "I guess that's the price of fame. You see what happens when the word gets out about your deals? Trao gets no help through channels."

They started the drive back.

"Hey, Lieutenant," McGowan mused, "there's something I don't understand. Why didn't we stay for lunch? That room was an iceberg. Man, that felt good. Why did we leave so sudden?"

"Just looking out for your interests, Mac. I don't want you to get spoiled."

"Come on."

"I don't think we were actually invited."

"Oh. It sure was nice, though."

Two weeks later the building supplies arrived in Binh

Son. McGowan borrowed a dump truck from the Americal Division and drove up to the district headquarters with a working party of Marines and PFs. He was directed to the warehouse, where a Vietnamese clerk met the truck. In Vietnamese, McGowan asked where he would pick up the timber and the fifty bags of cement. Grinning, the clerk said there were only forty. McGowan couldn't believe it. The clerk seemed to have no leverage for a shakedown. He told the man he was stupid.

The clerk shrugged and said, "All right, there's your cement."

He pointed to a heap of shredded bags which had been left out in a rain, soaked through and hardened into heaps.

"You are stupid, stupid," McGowan said. "Why should I give you ten bags, or take those useless lumps? People should not pay you. They should laugh at you."

With that McGowan told two PFs to watch the clerk, while he led the rest of the working party into the warehouse and took fifty bags of dry cement.

Shortly later, when McGowan drove the truck up to the site of the new school, he was greeted by Trao and a dozen armed PFs. Under guard nearby were twenty laborers, who set to unloading the cement. It reminded McGowan of a chain gang, and he asked Trao why.

"No PFs, all cement go. Everyone take," he said.

"But aren't those VC families?" McGowan asked, pointing at the laborers. "Why no one else?"

"Two years ago we work for Viet Cong," Trao replied. "In Phu Longs, Catholics still work for Viet Cong."

He would not discuss the matter further, but McGowan understood what he meant. It was another reminder to the Marines of the hatred, revenge and servitude which were major ingredients of the Binh Son war. In the Phu Longs the VC Village Committee forced the anti-VC families to do the menial communal tasks, which meant time lost from the fields and fishing. In Binh Nghia it was the families of the Viet Cong who were forced to lose time from work. Yet the children of Viet Cong families were free to attend the school after it was built, and they did so.

The PFs and the Viet Cong had certain rules to their war, understandings which were kept because, and only so long as, they were mutually advantageous. What often has been called accommodation frequently has been nothing more than a precarious balance of power, perceived as such by both sides. Deterrence is a better word than accommodation to describe a situation wherein each side is unwilling to undertake certain acts while the other side retains the capability to retaliate in kind.

The Viet Cong families would be forced to lose a day's wages because there was no way the Viet Cong could collect an equal amount from the PF families. Suong felt strong enough to put out the word that he would tax the Viet Cong families two dollars for each dollar taken from a PF family. The ultimate step in escalation—the murder or wholesale slaughter of PF families—was unlikely in Binh Nghia because the VC families acted as hostages. Suong had declared that he would kill ten of their children for each member of a PF family killed.

Vulnerability to retaliation set limits on the actions either the PFs or the Viet Cong were willing to take in the struggle for Binh Nghia. It was the elementary tribal system for keeping wars within tolerable bounds, practiced throughout history, and a cornerstone of the current theoretical strategy of nuclear warfare.

The Marines were hostages, too. They knew it and the villagers knew it. As long as they were there, the hamlets were safe from indiscriminate air and artillery attacks. Although until March of 1967 the My Hués were marked as VC on military operational maps, they were also hash-marked in red as out of bounds for harassment and inter-diction artillery fire because Americans patrolled there on the ground.

# 23

The Tra Bong River was the major commerce route for the residents of Binh Nghia and a dozen other villages, while for the island village of Binh Thuy, adjacent to Binh Yen Noi, boats were the only means for moving supplies. Starting at first light each day, the river was cluttered with traffic. The fishermen from the My Hués habitually rose at four, and when there was just enough light so none of the lurking patrollers would shoot them, they left their houses. Since the combined unit demanded that all boats be beached each evening, the day's first task for the fisher-men was to haul their boats to water. Most could be man-handled by four men, but some took thick log rollers and the strength of six or eight. The long nights ended for patrols with the scraping sounds of water-bound boats or the soft chug of the low-powered engines as the boats slipped downstream on the Tra Bong River to the sea two miles distant.

If the Viet Cong could control the river, they could undercut the growing prestige of the PFs and force the local officials to abandon the island of Binh Thuy. This had been done in 1964. With the VC holding the Phu Longs and Binh Thuy they would have direct access to Binh Nghia.

On the sixth of May the Viet Cong set out to ambush the PFs who were stationed on Binh Thuy Island. Leaving before dawn from their base in the Phu Longs, the enemy had sculled out on a waning tide. About three hundred yards out from Binh Yen Noi near midstream squatted a small mud bank dotted with a few scraggly bushes used as warning markers by helmsmen when high tide covered the flat. Digging there was easy, and before light the Viet Cong had scooped out three fighting holes. After two marksmen had scrunched down in each hole, other Viet Cong camouflaged the tops of the holes and rowed back to the Phu Longs.

By the time the fishermen were on the river the VC were waiting. They let the fishing boats pass by. The sun rose cloudless, and in Binh Nghia two patrols straggled away from their ambush sites, all the PFs and most of the Americans stopping off at one house or another for a breakfast of steaming broth crammed with the leftovers from the heavy evening meal. The children had left for school, and the women were setting out for the fields or the markets.

From the island of Binh Thuy three long boats jammed with villagers puttered slowly downstream to the sea-mouth hamlet of Son Tra to trade rice for fish. This haggling lasted long, and it was past noon before the trading boats started back up the crowded river. The VC watched them glide slowly by. The boats looked like long, rough, leaky canoes, each holding eight to ten people squatting single file among baskets of stinking fish. There were about a dozen PFs scattered among the women, old men and young girls. Four PFs were sitting bunched in the stern of the second boat.

From a distance of thirty feet, the VC popped up and unloaded on that target. The first burst was all theirs, and three PFs were riddled. The VC were using high-velocity automatic rifles, no low-powered carbines or submachine guns. The weapons prevented a slaughter. The bullets smashed through wood and flesh at high speed, so the bodies of the victims were not pushed from the boat, causing a capsize. After the initial fusillade the helmsmen chugged away as fast as their sputtering outboards would allow. But their boats were soft, wallowing targets, and the Viet Cong still had a chance to inflict a total wipe-out and gain province-wide publicity. Set on sinking at least one boat, they jumped up from their holes and ran to the edge of the mud bank to get a better line on the panicked boats. With ricochets skimming off the water at odd angles, the traffic on the placid river was scurrying to and fro like frantic water beetles.

Villagers along the Binh Yen Noi waterfront, seeing the action, yelled at a boy to run and fetch Luong, whose house was close by. Landless and poor, Luong and his family lived in a skimpy thatched hut on a flood-prone lot near the river's edge. He was at home asleep, after a night of rice wine. He came awake quickly and sent the boy to fetch two PFs who lived nearby while he grabbed his M-1 rifle and dashed to the water's edge.

Luong reached the river bank on the run, stopped a moment to catch his breath, sized up the enemy position and moved laterally until he found a high mound of dirt. He could clearly see the Viet Cong on the mud bank, who had their backs to him and were shooting at a boat farther out on the river. Luong lay stomach down, raised the sights on the receiver of his rifle, dug his elbows into the loose dirt, put the stock to his cheek and sighted in.

In a shooting contest in front of the fort, Luong had once shot a bird out of the air with his M-1. Some claimed it was luck, but Luong was thirty-six years old and had fought against the French as well as the Viet Cong. That he was still alive was not luck.

He sighted and squeezed the trigger.

On the mud bank, a Viet Cong pitched forward dead, shot in the back. Forgetting the boats, the others turned to engage the unexpected enemy. The range was long and an ineffectual exchange ensued, with two more PFs joining Luong. Now time was running against the Viet Cong. On Binh Thuy Island, Mr. Minh, the hamlet chief, had frantically called district for help.

At Fort Page, a few PFs were dozing in hammocks while two village clerks pecked away on typewriters at the endless papers. Most of the Marines were scattered about the village, and in the fort were only the few late sleepers who had had guard duty the previous night. McGowan was sitting near the clerks, filling out his weekly report sheet.

When he first heard the firing from the river, he did not even listen. It was common for the PFs and Marines to take target practice or to shoot fish or birds. He stopped writing only when the firing did not stop. The continual shooting also broke the sleep of the tired Marines and dozing PFs. They came awake reluctantly, uneasily.

"Hey, Sarge," Brown called out, "what's going on?"

At that moment McGowan was receiving a radio message from Lieutenant Colonel Jarvis at district.

"The VC are on the river, Mac," he said. "They've nailed some PFs."

"We're on our way," McGowan replied.

McGowan turned to Brown.

"How many men we got?"

"Five Marines, counting you, and three PFs."

"That's not much."

"There's always Mr. Minh and the other clerk. They have their typewriters."

"Funny man. Grab one more Marine and a PF. Tell Minh to spread the word to get the others back to the fort. And post somebody on the .50 in case we're getting faked out. I'll start ahead into Binh Yen Noi to grab a boat. Meet me there."

On the river bank Luong and the two other PFs were sniping at the Viet Cong on the island, who in turn were signaling and shouting at a passing boat. Faced with the threat of death, the helmsmen pulled over to the mud flat. McGowan reached Luong just as the five Viet Cong jumped up and ran toward the boat. Firing steadily, Luong dropped another enemy soldier as they climbed into the boat.

McGowan and Luong spent several minutes corralling a boat of their own, they too threatening a helmsman when cajolery did not move him. The fisherman did not want himself and his boat mixed up in any gunfight chase across the water, but he was given no choice. Brown had arrived with two others, and the seven armed men arranged themselves single file in the narrow boat and putted off in pursuit. They nosed up to the mud bank, with Brown hopping out to check the two men shot by Luong.

"Both dead, Sarge," he shouted. "They got two M-14s. Should I scoop them up?"

"God, no," McGowan shouted back. "We're overloaded now. Those Cong can't use them. Leave the rifles. Let's go."

Its freeboards less than three inches from the flat water, the boat plowed out into midstream with the helmsman nervously jabbering at Luong, who ignored him. On a straight line between the mud bank and the Phu Longs sat a small island, at most sixty yards long and shrub-grown. When the pursuers had left the mud bank, the Viet Cong had been pulling up to the island. Now rounds were zipping over the Marines and bouncing off the water. In the bow, Brown was firing back with his M-79 grenade launcher, plunking grenade after grenade into the bushes. The PFs were giggling nervously. The boatman had folded down behind Luong, who looked at McGowan.

"We're too close to turn back," McGowan yelled. "We're going in."

"Great," Brown muttered.

The boat hit the island bank at its flank speed of four knots, the bow cracking and the boat twisting. The seven men spilled out and scrambled toward the bushes, shouting, shooting, stumbling forward, knowing they might live if they could get close to the enemy. They crashed through the bushes quickly and were across the dot of an island before they realized they hadn't been shot at. They looked toward the Phu Longs.

There went the Viet Cong. The enemy had gotten off on the mud-bank side of the island, run across it and hailed a passing boat at rifle point. Then a few of them had scrambled back to send a desultory fire against their pursuers before the five set out for the Phu Longs.

Luong was the first to react. He turned and ran back to bring their boat around. It was not on shore. After the pursuers had clambered from it, the boatman had poled off the bank, restarted his outboard and headed back toward Binh Nghia. When Luong saw him, he was seventy-five yards out into the current, steering with one hand while bailing frantically with the other to stay ahead of the leak in the bow. Luong shouted, screamed, shot his rifle in the air, cursed, threatened, pleaded, reasoned and begged—all to no avail. The boatman hunched his back lower, looked fixedly toward Binh Nghia and pretended he heard not a word or a shot.

Brown and a PF had in the meanwhile trotted to the

upstream tip of the island and there were waving in a fisherman who, in steering a wide arc to skirt the boat with the
Viet Cong, had drifted within hailing distance of the
island. The pursuers ran to his boat.

"Dau?" the fisherman asked. "Binh Yen Noi?"

"Di Phu Longs Viet Cong," Brown replied.

"Xin ong noi di Binh Yen Noi!" the fisherman
screamed.

"Guess I sort of misled him," Brown said. "I saw Luong
wasn't having much luck his way so I told this guy we
wanted to go back home. What the hell. We'll pay him a
hundred piasters when we get back."

"Right. When we get back," another Marine echoed
sarcastically.

Having opened up a lead of two hundred yards, the Viet
Cong were almost to the other side of the river before the
fisherman started his engine. His outboard was new and
powerful, however, and the gap had closed to one hundred
yards before the enemy soldiers gained the shore and
splashed into the shelter of the mangrove swamp at the
edge of the Phu Longs. Their boatman, freed from his
impressed service, headed back toward mainstream, gesturing sympathetically to the fearful fisherman as the
boats passed.

The pursuers landed at the same spot, Luong leaving a
PF to hold the boat until their return. They advanced
slowly, not knowing whether the enemy had been reinforced. Rounds started cracking past them.

"They're trying to keep us off them," McGowan yelled,
guessing the enemy were still few.

"Or sucker us into the mangroves," replied Brown,
guessing the opposite.

The fire was coming mainly from an area two hundred
yards inland where the roots of several dead mangroves had

been smashed and thrown together by bombs or artillery shells. With rounds snapping closer, the pursuers sought tree cover and returned fire at the unseen enemy. This continued for several minutes, until a Viet Cong popped up from behind the deadfall, stood looking at the Marines for several seconds, then darted into a clump of bushes. Every few seconds he would poke his head up or wave.

"That very bad, trung si," Luong said to McGowan. "Viet Cong bay. Nghia Quan bi chet."

"Look, Sarge," Brown said, "if Luong thinks that guy's a decoy, this could be a messed-up show. Let me fix that cat and then let's hat out."

"He's yours," McGowan replied.

Brown put down his M-79 and tugged a LAW off his back. He pulled its pins and extended the tubing. Crouching behind a tree, he placed the rocket launcher on his shoulder, sighting in.

"Don't scare him off," he said.

The Marines and PFs stopped shooting. The enemy poked his head up. Brown squeezed. With a bang which clapped the ears of the pursuers, the rocket took off and burst against the roots which had protected the Viet Cong from bullets. His body pitched, then slumped broken among the broken roots.

The swamp fell silent, both sides momentarily stunned by the quick way in which life had left the man who tried to lure others to their deaths. Then the firing resumed, gradually growing in volume although harmless in effect. The long afternoon shadows were darkening the swamp, and no participant in the battle was indulging in any further display of bravado exposure. Unwilling to advance farther, the pursuers decided to get out of the Phu Longs before they were outflanked. McGowan radioed his decision to district, where Colonel Jarvis swiftly concurred.

The decision delighted the fisherman, and the packed boat was several hundred yards from shore before the fast enemy snipers had cautiously advanced to the bank. All the Viet Cong could do then was send a few resentful bullets across the water.

When McGowan arrived at Binh Nghia, he saw that Colucci, who had been left without a radio, had the entire unit assembled beside six boats. They had intended to go into the Phu Longs if the pursuers had not returned by dusk. The fisherman refused payment. He wanted to take his pay in the prestige his participation in the chase would win him among the villagers. So, too, did the boatman with the broken prow, who even came up and joked with Luong.

Mr. Minh, the hamlet chief of the island of Binh Thuy, sent a boat to Binh Yen Noi to pick up the pursuers. They were ferried to the island and in the waning twilight were taken to the marketplace, where Minh and hundreds of villagers were gathered. The bodies of the three militiamen killed in the trading boat had been removed in preparation for burial, but the bodies of the two Viet Cong killed on the mud bank by Luong lay on display with their rifles at their sides. They would await claiming by villagers from the Phu Longs the next day.

Minh gave a short public speech, thanking especially Luong for his actions. He told McGowan that the VC rarely attacked his PFs in force on land. It had been primarily by means of river ambushes that the Viet Cong in 1964 had forced him and the other hamlet officials off the island. The Viet Cong had not employed the ambush on a daily basis. They did not have to; instead, they had struck just often enough to instill a high level of uncertainty about death into the normal actions of normal people. They had set traps along the river, and killed the militia one and two at a time, until no one associated with the government could get into a boat with other villagers. The villagers did not want to be killed themselves or have their boats sunk. The PFs were cut off from the people, even from travel with their own families. The VC then were free to tax all who used the river, while the PFs lost face among the people.

That afternoon when the trading boats had wallowed in half sunk with the dead PFs and the wounded and the screaming villagers, Minh had feared 1964 all over again. But because of the seven pursuers, the Viet Cong could not claim a victory. They had suffered equal losses. The people had seen the bodies and the boat race.

Three PFs. Three VC. A small incident on a warm spring afternoon on a flat river full of boats. A one-line entry in the I Corps daily situation report. Nothing but a few added statistics at the Saigon level.

On May 7, trading boats again set out from Binh Thuy, carrying PFs and villagers alike.

# 24

The PFs and the Marines were often seen in each other's company during off-duty hours—a PF hitchhiking with a Marine to Quang Ngai City, a Marine sitting behind a PF on a motor scooter, a PF handing a Marine a family shopping list for the PX, a Marine drinking hot tea in a PF's home on a lazy afternoon. The disagreements which arose were generally those one expects among men who share cramped quarters for a year: a blaring radio when someone else wants to sleep; a tasteless practical joke; neglect in returning an article loaned; selfishness in the use of commonly shared items such as rifle-cleaning materials.

But on two occasions incidents of serious physical strife did occur between the Marines and the Vietnamese. In one instance the PFs solidly supported the Marines. One afternoon Joe came limping into the fort, quietly slipped into the squad tent and lay on his side with his face toward the canvas, his shoulders shaking. Observing this, Garcia called out to McGowan, "Hey, Sarge, you better come over here. I think Joe's hurt."

McGowan came over and sat on the edge of the boy's cot.

"Joe? What's the matter, Joe? Want me to get the doc?"

"No."

"Well, what is it? Come on, why are you crying?"

Between sobs, Joe told of leaving the fort that morning to play with some other boys over in one of the My Hué hamlets. They had been kicking a ball along the main trail when a man rushed out of a house, screaming at them to get out of there and to stop making so much noise. The resentful homeowner was the brother of the wealthy official who had been taken away by the police the morning after the fort had been overrun. Seeing Joe among the boys, the man reached out and grabbed his arm, cursing at him while swatting him on the head with his free hand. Joe said the man smelled of Ba Xi De, a strong, home-brewed rice liquor, and was ranting about the Americans and PFs. When Joe ducked to avoid the blows, the man kicked him hard in the buttocks. Joe was knocked down, and before he could scramble away, the man had kicked him repeatedly in the back.

The man was lucky. Wingrove was not at the fort when Joe limped home. Wingrove probably would have killed him. Instead, it was McGowan who left the fort on the run. When he reached the man's house, he found a crowd had gathered, having anticipated that someone from the fort would come. His arrival was greeted by murmurs of approval, as the villagers congratulated each other on their knowledge of American, or just human, behavior.

The man who had struck Joe was quite tall, almost six feet. Still McGowan had the advantage of two inches, forty pounds, a dozen Golden Gloves fights and uncounted brawls in New York City and in the Marine Corps. It was not much of a fight. McGowan insulted the man and spat on the ground. The man, drunk enough to be reckless, pawed and kicked ineffectually at McGowan, who then stepped back, planted his feet and let go a right cross which knocked him out.

It was the only time that McGowan struck a Vietnamese, and he worried about possible resentment among the villagers. But Trao told him that what he had done was all right. The villagers understood. In fact, they would not have understood if the Americans had done nothing.

In the second instance of serious physical contact, some of the PFs blamed the Marines, while some of the Americans blamed the PFs. A Marine new to the unit caught a PF walking out of the squad tent with a transistor radio. The Marine accused the PF of stealing and brushed aside the PF's response in Vietnamese, which he could not understand. He snatched the radio back and tried to slap the PF across the face. The PF ducked and drew a knife. The Marine lunged, grabbing the PF by both wrists, and in the ensuing tug-of-war the PF was slashed across the forearm.

When the fight was broken up, the PF claimed he had intended only to borrow the radio. Most of the Marines and PFs believed his story, although some PFs blamed him for the fight because he had not asked permission first, while others blamed the Marine for his short temper. Suong did not hold the PF in high regard.

McGowan had little respect for the Marine, whom he considered to be one of the three Americans in the fort who were barely squeaking by, either because of strained relations with the Vietnamese or tactical sloppiness on patrols. When he learned that a man would not even try to understand the Vietnamese, and clung to a belief that his only job was to shoot people, McGowan had him sent back to the line outfits. This he had done twice, in addition to his flat rejection the previous March of the five Marines on the truck.

In the case of the knifing incident, he and Suong agreed that the blame rested with both parties, and so they put both the PF and the Marine on probation. Any more trouble from the Marine, and McGowan would transfer him out. If the PF persisted in his sly ways, Suong was going to bring him to Captain Dang, the mere mention of whom impressed or frightened most people.

But there were some who didn't respect Dang, especially those in the VNQDD who, among other things, controlled the rice market in Binh Son and paid the farmers one low fixed price, despite the excess demand in I Corps for rice. Dang had worked with Robert Ressugie, his U.S. AID adviser, to break the VNQDD hold over the farmers. At the same time, he and his military adviser, Lieutenant Colonel Jarvis, were pressuring the Vietnamese and American authorities to take action against the black market operations being run in the district town by the Korean forces who had moved into the province in late 1966. As Third Country nationals, the Koreans were not subject to Dang's jurisdiction. They were stealing mainly from the

American bases around Chulai and using Binh Son town as a storage and trade depot. Dang had no authority to confiscate the truckfuls of cigarettes, C-rations and medicinal supplies which were unloaded and stored in houses less than a quarter of a mile from the district headquarters. The provost marshal of the Americal Division told Jarvis bitterly that the Army could give no American the authority to move against the Koreans.

In the end Dang was defeated in Binh Son district not by the Viet Cong, but by a corrupt element of the VNQDD or Nationalist Party and a coalition of Vietnamese and Korean racketeers. In late spring there were banners flying in Binh Son, saying in Vietnamese: "Down with Dang, Despot and Oppressor of the People." Quang Ngai radio reported that spontaneous, simultaneous demonstrations had broken out in several of the larger villages in the district, Binh Nghia being prominently mentioned.

The morning of the demonstrations McGowan saw a group of about fifteen people carrying banners walking in from Highway One toward Binh Nghia along the main trail which passed directly in front of the fort. The PFs were greatly disturbed, yelling back and forth to each other and looking toward Suong for instructions. Suong and Trao huddled briefly with some of the village officials, and then Suong walked over to where McGowan stood waiting, shrugged and in a resigned voice said: "VNQDD."

It was as though he knew the ending was foreordained regardless of what he did. When the marchers drew abreast of the fort, the PFs had collected on the road to meet them. Both sides started shouting and arguing in the manner speakers use when they are addressing those supporting them, not those opposed. The VNQDD faction maintained their half of the dialogue for an hour, then left, having been close enough to the village to claim a demonstration.

Dang was relieved as district chief by Major General Nguyen Lam, the Vietnamese Commander of I Corps. When Ambassador William Koren, representing the U.S. Mission in Saigon, protested the firing, Lam acknowledged that Dang was a fiery, energetic and honest captain, a credit to the Army and a popular figure among the villagers. But, Lam went on, Dang had been overzealous in prosecuting other elements besides the Viet Cong and he had made enemies who were powerful, too powerful for Lam to stand behind the captain. He was sending Dang to a district which had a weak VNQDD faction and no Korean forces.

Shortly afterward Lieutenant Colonel Jarvis was transferred from the district, having thoroughly exacerbated the commanders of the Americal Division for his Dang-like attitude concerning the rights of the people. The senior province adviser had feared for Jarvis' safety, since it was widely rumored that some Koreans were offering a contract for his removal.

# 25

Jarvis was replaced by the assistant adviser, Captain Phil Volentine, a rugged, forthright person with scars on his forearms and a Southern accent which he struggled manfully to overcome when speaking Vietnamese. He had attended language school in Hawaii and spent much of his time in the hamlets, trying to improve his conversational ability. Volentine dropped by Binh Nghia to tell Suong and McGowan that, like the advisers before him, he was on call whenever the combined unit might need help or a favor.

McGowan soon called.

It was on a hot day in June. The few Marines in the fort were sun-bathing in shorts and sandals when an old lady came bustling in, dragging a young girl in tow. She marched straight up to McGowan and started yelling in shrill, rapid Vietnamese.

"Hey, Joe, tell her to slow down," McGowan said. "She's going too fast for me."

"She say Americans shoot at her in boat," Joe said. "She say her daughter lose ten thou ps. Uh, Americans steal. She say you come, you see. I think maybe you better go."

McGowan took Joe, Swinford and Nguyen Tri and followed the women back to their boat. After they had climbed in and squatted down, the old lady started the small outboard and they putted upstream. The Marines carried rifles but had not put on shirts. As they were passing the My Hué hamlets, they heard firing just above the village boundaries and saw a fishing craft sharply veer from mid-channel and head toward the river bank.

"Looks like one of those mobile check points the Army runs," Swinford said. "But those crazy bastards are shooting over the bows."

"Let's keep going and see what they say to us," McGowan said. "Di Son Tra."

With the women muttering nervously, the boat held its upstream course, the Marines looking straight ahead and ignoring the small group of Americans on the bank clustered around an armored personnel carrier with its 50-caliber machine gun pointed out at the river.

Crack! A red tracer round flew across the river several yards in front of them.

"Christ, that was a .50," Swinford yelled, jerking a round into his M-16 magazine.

"Easy with that thing," McGowan said. "They could tear us up. Let's pull in."

As they headed to shore, the fishing boat, having passed the check point's cursory inspection, glided by them outward bound. As soon as the boat bumped land, McGowan jumped out and seized the initiative.

"Who's in charge here?" he demanded of the seven Americans.

"I am," a second lieutenant replied. "Who are you?"

"I was sent down from district to talk to you, Lieutenant," McGowan said. "The district chief has a report that you're harassing and stealing from the people. And just now you fired at me. Do I look like a Viet Cong?"

The lieutenant, assuming his shirtless interrogator was Volentine, could not stammer out a coherent reply. The old lady pointed out the machine-gunner on top of the personnel carrier as the thief, and when the lieutenant ordered the man to empty his pockets, piaster notes tumbled out. McGowan told the young officer to take his men back to their battalion headquarters and that a report on the discipline of his crew would follow.

When McGowan had been a young boy, his grandmother used to tell him stories by the hour of how it was when she was a little girl in Ireland. She talked about the thatched house that she had lived in, about drawing water from the wells, of trying to milk a skinny old cow, of having to scrounge for firewood, of running through the cold winter rain to a crowded one-room school. McGowan thought Vietnam and his grandmother's Ireland had a lot in common. Frequently his grandmother had spoken about the times of The Trouble. When the English soldiers had driven by in their trucks, she and the other children never knew whether to hide or run after them. If the soldiers were in a good mood, they would sometimes throw food; but if they were returning from a sour operation, they would sometimes shoot at the farmers in the fields. As far as McGowan was concerned, American line troops were equally unpredictable.

McGowan went to district headquarters and called on Volentine for help.

"Sir, we've had it with that new battalion," he said. "Our old battalion wasn't the greatest, but at least they kept the line troops out of the village. Last week this new battalion tried to pull a sweep on Binh Yen Noi, using tanks. Thank God they never even got down the road as far as the fort before one of those monsters slipped off the bank. They wrecked the road and part of a paddy pulling the damn thing out, but at least it stopped them. And they looked at us like we were some kind of freaks.

"Do you know what Suong is doing right now? He has a work crew tearing up the road at the other end of the village, just outside My Hué, where that check point was, so only motor scooters can get into Binh Nghia from either end. You'd think we were the VC, having to build a fortified village. And just now I was almost blown out of the water by one of their amtracs."

"That battalion was in War Zone D before coming up here, Mac," Volentine said. "It may take a while to settle them down. Let me try talking to the battalion commander. Who knows? He might be reasonable."

It happened he was, and Volentine was able to call McGowan that same evening with a promise that American troops would stay out of Binh Nghia and that there would be no more check points.

This especially pleased Thanh, who considered check points by outsiders to be insulting, visible evidence that he was not doing his job. Such appearances were important to him, for he was being considered for a higher police post at the province capital. Since the job opening was a result of the wide publicity attendant on the stabilizing situation in Binh Nghia, he wanted the village to appear as peaceful as possible. This struck McGowan as ironic, for during the spring Thanh had seemed displeased with the lessening action, since a prominent criterion of efficiency in the National Police was the number of arrests made.

In late June, Thanh was formally offered the job he had sought, and announced he was leaving. A cruel, fanatical, strange, hate-filled man, in his year in the village he had arrested about 150 out of a total population of 5,000. Some were dedicated Viet Cong and about two dozen were never seen again. But most were part-time helpers or reluctant abettors of the Viet Cong and had returned to Bihh Nghia after short terms in the district jail.

The National Police let it be known that they were not replacing Thanh with anybody else; the situation in Binh Nghia no longer required a full-time policeman, of whom there were not enough to go around. The unanimous choice of the village council to fill the vacancy was Trao. So before leaving, Thanh turned over to him a list of agents and informers in the village, with instructions for drop procedures to pay them and collect information. Thanh had been proud of his agent net and claimed no one could take out of the hamlets an excessive amount of rice or materials without detection and arrest. The central market at Binh Yen Noi was especially watched, and each trading day two or three of Thanh's agents would keep track of who bought which large orders.

In the spring the Marines had briefly tried their hand at

information gathering. They had authority to pay cash rewards for intelligence, an incentive system the Vietnamese did not have. In late March a woman had come to the fort complaining of a stomachache, but once alone with Corpsman Blunk, had asked to see Suong and McGowan. In return for 2,000 piasters, or $18, she drew a sketch of a field near My Hué hamlet which contained a hideaway. The next day the PFs probed the spot with long, sharp poles and discovered two bunkers, each neatly lined with bamboo and large enough to hold two or three men for weeks on end.

But McGowan soured on buying intelligence when he learned that another combined unit habitually bought weapons for $25 apiece from district officials and then turned them in at Chulai, claiming they had paid informers $50 for each weapon. Worse still, Thanh had complained that the high American rates threatened to undercut his system for gathering information. So McGowan had abolished the practice of payment and subsequently relied upon the arrangements of the village officials for local information.

Trao seemed relaxed and casual about his new additional job, but his easygoing manner was deceptive. If it seemed at times that he was not aware of what was going on, it was because he had others watching for him.

One morning in mid-July two old ladies bustled into the fort claiming they had important news for Trao. While a PF pedaled off to fetch the hamlet leader, the old ladies sat on a bench in the fort's main room, enjoying the curious glances of the Marines and the frequent questions of the PFs. Much to the exasperation of Suong, they would not tell why they had come until Trao arrived. Then they burst out with the news that two women whom they did not know were shopping in the market and had bought over sixty kilos of rice. Trao, Suong and McGowan hopped on bikes and set out for the market, Suong as he left yelling at the old ladies for their dalliance.

In response to inquiries at the market, people pointed to a side trail which ran down to the river. Trao was at the bank in less than a minute and there were the women, poling a boat toward mid-channel. Trao shouted at them across the flat water while Suong fired a few shots in the air. The women came back.

Stacked in the boat were several bags of rice. Suong questioned them on the spot, while they were still trembling. They readily admitted being from the Phu Longs and buying the rice for the P31st District Force Company, both facts being self-evident. Trao wanted something more.

For over a month the Viet Cong had been stockpiling rice in the Phu Longs, preparatory to moving it into the mountains for the main forces. Unable to penetrate Binh Nghia in force and organize a major takeout, the enemy was trading closely stitched bamboo mats and carefully woven fishnets for small quantities of rice. Women from the hamlets of Binh Nghia had only to find the contact and in the evening stash their rice at a certain spot along the river bank, returning in the morning to pick up well-made goods. Trao did not care about a piddling amount of smuggling. Obviously, enough rice had not been crossing over; otherwise the Viet Cong would not have risked a large purchase in the open market.

But he did want the name of the contact in Binh Nghia, the man or woman who was whispering to certain women where along the bank they should hide their trading rice. Justifiably fearing beating or torture, the women from the Phu Longs told him. Trao then gave the women a choice: they could sell back the rice in the market, pocket the money and settle in Binh Nghia without their boat, or they could go to the district jail for ricerunning. The women chose jail, where they were held for two weeks and then released, a normal district sentence for small acts.

While Trao and Suong rode off in search of the VC contact, McGowan lingered on the bank, looking across toward the Phu Longs, and the three tiny scrub islands sticking up just short of mid-channel. He was thinking of mounting a private interdiction effort against the P31st. When the sergeant returned to the fort, he saw that Trao had arrested the VC contact, a man whom Trao had known for years.

The man had been beaten, but refused to talk. Trao wanted to know where the VC were crossing, and when they were next due in. Suong yelled at him, Trao screamed at him, he was slapped back and forth. Not a word. Trao drew out a pistol, cocked it, grabbed the man by his hair, jerked his head back and pushed the muzzle against the man's nose. Still he did not speak. Why should he? Trao was not a real police chief. He was a gentle man who won real elections because people could talk honestly with him. Trao was not like Thanh. Trao would not shoot.

Trao did shoot, roaring with rage and shaking with fear, seeking to scare the man and succeeding in scaring himself, pulling the revolver aside and jerking when he meant to squeeze the trigger, intending for the bullet to miss and for the man to talk. Instead, the bullet creased the man's cheek and tore his ear off. Blood gushing, the man stood petrified. Trao was trembling.

Suong offered to take over.

"No," Trao said. "Get him out of here. Send him to district. It's over. Get him out."

# 26

That evening McGowan took out the first patrol, intending to wade to the nearest of the three tiny islands he had been looking at that afternoon. He asked nobody's advice at the fort; in fact, he did not discuss it with anyone, not wishing to make a big thing out of a routine ambush which would probably prove fruitless. With Tri, Norwood and two new Americans named Loring and Moskel, McGowan left the fort quietly under a soft night sky.

The beaters at the outer gate were blabbering and clacking their bamboo sticks; none of the patrollers paid them any attention. The PF at point took the main trail through the village to the hamlet of Binh Yen Noi Number 3. The path was clearly visible, with the lamps from villagers' homes shining like street lights under the small trees. The clatter and the smell of evening meals hung in the damp air, and practically every house had its door open and windows and sometimes a whole thatched wall raised. Music blared from dozens of transistor radios at a horrid pitch, as next-door neighbors competed to drown out each other's stations. Children laughed and mothers scolded and old people gabbed. Some villagers glanced at the riflemen; most did not. There was no detectable change in voices as the patrol moved by. The patrol was part of the scenery on a normal evening.

When they reached the market, McGowan took point and led them down the side trail to the river bank.

"There it is," he whispered, pointing to the islands which loomed small and black and far, far out in the glistening water. "That's where we're headed."

"You're kidding," Moskel whispered. "We'll drown. I'm not going."

"The tide's out."

"So am I."

"Screw you then."

"I'll go," Loring whispered. "I've done a lot of swimming."

"O.K. Loring and I will cut across. We'll signal if it's not over our heads," McGowan whispered. "Thi—coi ao."

"Toi so. Toi so. Dung bi bac Song Tra Bong. Ba do. Ba do."

"Did you catch that?" McGowan asked Norwood.

"He doesn't go for your act."

"Thanks. I got that much without your help. But what's bugging him? What's this 'Ba do' bit?"

"You're our leader, Mac. You figure it out."

"Screw it. I can swim. You guys cover us. Let's go, Loring."

Naked, with their boots and cartridge belts draped over their shoulders, the two Marines slipped off the bank. The night had no wind and stars covered the sky, permitting those on the bank to watch the waders move outward, their vulnerable white skins steadily disappearing into the black waters as though they were being slowly sucked under.

McGowan had no way of knowing if he could reach the island without swimming, and he inched his way out, scuffing with his feet to follow the trace of the sand bars. It was a trial-and-error process, with many slips off the bars into twenty feet of water, his rifle serving as a life stick by which Loring could drag him back after each slip. In this bobbing manner, it took them half an hour to make two hundred yards. Their zigzag course had taken them to within fifty yards of the island when the water level rose from their chests to their necks and the bar narrowed so that it was like walking a railroad track.

So intent was McGowan on gaining the island that he did not notice the stirring of the water directly in front of him. From the channel close by his side it happened again—he distinctly felt the waters part and rush together again at once, as if they had been disturbed by the passage of a very large fish. McGowan turned to Loring, but before he could say anything Loring hissed: "Let's get out of here."

Both had seen sharks in the river. In the nets downstream at the river's mouth a thirteen-foot hammerhead had been caught the previous week.

McGowan pressed forward and again the fish passed close by. He felt like he was walking the dotted white line on a freeway while cars hurtled by within inches. He knew all he had to do to test his wildly racing imagination was veer off the bar and plunge into the deep water once more. His toes gripping like hands, he treaded his way forward.

A few more yards and it was over. The bar widened and tilted upward, the water fell to his chest, his waist, his knees—he was on the island, cold from the warm waters. A step behind him came Loring.

"Spread out," McGowan whispered.

The island was less than thirty yards long, and they concluded their search for a Viet Cong sentry or small boat team in a few minutes.

"Loring," McGowan asked, "do you think we have company out there?"

"I don't know. I sort of felt there was something. Now I'm not as sure. What do you think?"

"I thought so, too, but I guess you're right. It was probably just some trick current or something. I'll signal the others."

He took a flashlight from his cartridge belt and blinked it on and off a few times. Then he and Loring sat down to watch for traffic on the river. After what seemed to them almost an hour, Tri, Moskel and Norwood floundered onto the island.

"Man," Moskel said, "that's too hairy. Do you know what's out there?"

"Maybe," McGowan said. "But how could we have lived with the PFs this long and not know there were sharks here? The PFs go swimming all the time."

"They don't swim out here," Loring said.

"I think they thought you'd check with them, Sergeant," Norwood said sarcastically, "before you pulled a stunt like this. I have a feeling we're going to find out Tri was saying 'Shark! Shark!' back there on the bank."

"Let's get into position," McGowan replied, ending the conversation.

They walked the few yards to the southern tip of the island and settled in to wait for any traffic crossing downstream. McGowan set the patrollers in among the scrub growth so that they covered both shorelines as well as directly downriver. At midnight a dull light began dancing along the far shore opposite My Hué.

"They're moving," Norwood whispered.

In the black, McGowan could hear careless splashes but see nothing. Then came a lucky break. A few miles to the south, artillery illumination blossomed out and etched the surface of the water like a mirror catching the sun's rays. In the clear reflection McGowan saw six sampans two hundred yards downstream, moving in column toward Binh Nghia. Each held two men standing erect to pole. McGowan's guess was right; the Viet Cong were crossing to pick up the food their wives could not bring them.

"Bunch in," McGowan said. "We all fire at once. Start right and swing left. Tri—tay phai. Re tay trai."

A pause.

"Ready? Now."

The line opened up from the prone position with four M-16s and an automatic carbine. The weapons fired almost all tracers. The first bursts knocked the two men out of the lead sampan, and the line shifted to the next target.

For a moment the boats lay dead in the water, their rowers having dug in their paddles and backwatered when the tracers started whipping in front of them. The five ambushers swiftly changed magazines and poured their fire into the second boat, the streams of red dots bursting on the boat like flicks of flame.

The dull clacking of magazines. Fresh rounds. Onto the third sampan. Only now the boats were moving with the speed of terror, surging forward under frantic strokes, scattering out and splashing away.

"Which one?"

"Any one. Just fire."

McGowan's wet rifle jammed on the fifth magazine. As he knelt to clear it, he heard the roar of engines and looked up as three helicopter gunships bore down on his position. The helicopters had been flying a Firefly mission, designed to rove the rivers at night, with one helicopter every so often flashing huge spotlights while his rocket-laden brothers hung off the side waiting to strike. Attracted by the tracers, the Hueys were on top of the Marines before they knew it. McGowan was scared that the Hueys would chop them up if they couldn't identify themselves, and Norwood's radio was out, the batteries soaked.

The blinding lights went on, pinning the patrol to the

earth. McGowan ripped the tape from a hand flare and
fired a green starcluster, the symbol for a friendly unit.
One Huey dropped lower. McGowan stood up and waved
frantically, pointing downriver. The helicopter hovered for
several seconds not twenty feet over his head as the crew
looked over the naked, waving man and his four naked
companions.

Then, fully satisfied that the figures on the ground were
some sort of Americans, the Huey fell off and swooped
downriver. Over the spot where the boats had been a few
minutes earlier, the light helicopter dropped flares and
swept back and forth with his searchlights. After a few
seconds, he fastened on a sampan farther downriver and
one of his companions pounced with machine guns and
rockets. The other gunship was diving on some object
beyond the ambushers' vision at the edge of the flare light
near the Phu Long shore. The ambushers couldn't see the
helicopter, only steady streaks of red slanting like rain
toward the river.

The Hueys buzzed back and forth over the river like
angry hornets but found no more target after their first
runs, although they hovered and dropped flares and
skimmed so low McGowan thought their wheels were in
the water. After fifteen minutes they tired or sickened of
the scene. One after another made a final machine-gun run
on the wreckage and flew upriver. As they passed near
McGowan's island, one Huey winked with its searchlights.

After the roar had faded, the ambushers waited to hear
a splash or see any moving object, but there were just bits
of flotsam on the calm surface of the water.

"I think that's it," McGowan said. "Let's go back in."

"What about him?" Norwood asked, gesturing at the
water which lay between them and shore.

"I'll bet that was just a fluke. Besides, he won't bother us as long as we're on the bar."

McGowan's guess proved correct. They were not bothered by any inquisitive shark on their wade to shore.

# 27

By summer the mood of the village had changed. The perceptions of the chief protagonists—the villagers, the PFs, the Marines, the guerrillas and the enemy main forces—had altered. In July of 1967, Binh Nghia was no longer the scene of nightly battles, with the forces of both sides struggling for local suzerainty. The enemy, clearly dominant in the spring of 1966, had tried to keep control of the village both by contesting with his guerrillas the passage of each small patrol and by assaulting with main forces the source of the patrols. He did better with his large-scale efforts and twice had almost forced the Americans out (and with them the PFs), once in September of 1966 when the fort was overrun and once in March of 1967 when it was nearly abandoned. Despite tactical victories, the enemy had to cope with the capacity of the combined unit to endure, to stick after making mistakes. By the summer of 1967 the enemy had accepted the persistence of the unit, whereas his own determination to defend Binh Nghia had waned.

Suong claimed that many Viet Cong still visited the village, and that the potential for violence remained high. Any respite was only temporary.

Trao felt differently. He believed the strength of the

local guerrillas and Party members had been sapped in the many firefights. Their losses meant fewer articulate voices to argue in intervillage and district meetings for more outside help. For almost a year Binh Nghia had been a focal point of fighting in the district. Yet it was but one of seventeen villages, eleven of which by mid-1967 had PF platoons and five of which had combined units. The Viet Cong district leaders had other problems besides Binh Nghia, and other Viet Cong village chapters were requesting aid.

The actions of the villagers displayed their belief that the time of the peak fighting had passed. In the hamlets no longer did a family sleep in the stale blackness of the household bunker. Lights could burn all night and the fishermen broke morning curfew habitually and noisily, so a lurking ambush would let them pass. Not one PF had deserted from the combined unit, although there were French leaves. The PFs would go anywhere in the village at almost any time. The only times they tried to avoid patrolling were when the Army sent over a new Western movie. The unit would then give the villagers an hour's notice at dusk that a Western was being shown and the marketplace at Binh Yen Noi would be packed by the thousands. The second largest drawing card was color comedies filmed in the United States. The villagers would demand reruns of shots of the skyscrapers of New York City. On the few times that there would be a shot of the Hollywood version of a typical modern American kitchen, the women would shout until the projectionist gave them a second and a third look.

The Americans in the combined unit loafed in the sun in the summer and thought of home and guzzled beer and went for boat rides. But at night they set out to kill, and even during the day they carried their rifles because they knew the price of becoming cocky or lazy or stupid. Although Binh Nghia was quiet, they heard the stories from other places, such as the hamlet of Son Tra, at the mouth of the river. In May district had wanted to start a combined unit there and McGowan was asked to recommend a leader. He enthusiastically endorsed Colucci, second only to Luong in tactics, adept at Vietnamese, well liked by the villagers and respected by the Marines. He had risen from boot camp to sergeant in fifteen months. Colucci went to Son Tra, drawing a few Americans and PFs from each of the established combined units.

First reports indicated everything was going well, then an incident happened which shook Fort Page from its summer complacency. One of the Marines sent to Son Tra did not pan out. He was more interested in drinking and whoring than in patrolling. His surliness finally ended in a fistfight with a PF, after which Colucci threw him out of the unit. While awaiting orders to Da Nang, the man was temporarily kept at another combined unit, just north of Fort Page and directly across the river from Son Tra. One afternoon after several beers, he decided to revisit Son Tra and hitched a ride to the other side of the river. Colucci saw him and put him back on board a boat, telling the helmsman to drop him off near the other fort. This was done, but instead of returning to the fort, the Marine sat in the sand drinking a bottle of the local rice wine. About dusk he passed out.

He was not missed that night, since each unit believed he was staying with the other. When the man awoke at dawn, his rifle was still at his side. Missing were his boots, grenades and magazines. It was assumed that the man had learned a lesson at a cheap price.

Incredibly he hadn't. Shortly thereafter he repeated

the idiocy, drinking alone on the beach in the afternoon.
The Viet Cong took him without a struggle and he was
led off to the Phu Longs. He was stripped naked and for
four days he was displayed in a succession of hamlets.
Through rumors from villagers a special U.S. prisoner
recovery team was able to follow his passage, but always
too late. He was seen in Ton My, in Dong Le, in Phu
Long, in Nam Yen. At each place the story was the same.
His captors were from the Phu Longs, and in the hamlets
they made him stand naked in the sun with his arms
bound behind him while they urged the people to hit him
with sticks. His captors would speak of the day when
they would kill all the Americans in the combined units.
Then they would lead him away by tugging on a rope
attached to a bamboo stick which had been jammed
through both cheeks. The man's mouth was black with
flies. He was given no water.

The villagers said he died on the fifth day after his capture.

So even on the quietest summer day each American in
Binh Nghia lugged his rifle with him wherever he went.
Often the Marines went out with the fishermen, who thus
could chug by U.S. Navy patrol boats without stopping for
inspection and beat competitors to the better fishing
grounds. Although no one dove overboard near the river's
mouth where the big fish and predators ran, farther
upstream there were deep pools into which the Marines
could jackknife from the bank and escape the stark sun.

The Army ran a river patrol with two thirteen-foot
fiberglass Boston Whalers, mounted with 50-horsepower
Mercury outboards. In return for local gossip about traffic
in and out of the Phu Longs, the Marines used the boats
during lunch and dinner hours, racing to the river's mouth,
trading their hot beers for cold ones from the crews of the

Navy Swift boats, then skimming back upriver, shirtless, beer cans in hand, grinning. Alfano wanted to take up a collection to buy water skis, but the idea was quashed for fear some general flying overhead would not appreciate water skiing in a war zone.

Visits to families in the hamlets became more frequent after McGowan loosened the security regulations upon which he had insisted during the early spring. Captain Volentine had instructed the Marines to be meticulous in material matters on such visits. Four bottles of warm beer cost a PF one-tenth of his monthly salary. As host, a PF could be put in debt after a few visits by a thoughtless, guzzling American friend. So the Marines bought the beer for such visits. Enterprising small merchants quickly saw the profit potential, and by midsummer there were five small concession stands crowding each other for first spot where the main trail from the fort cut into Binh Yen Noi. At a dollar a bottle, a Marine could buy beer and a chunk of dirty ice. The same price was charged to the villagers. Credit was accepted, and some Marines ran up bills of $60 a month.

The combined unit enjoyed daily an evening meal, helicoptered in by the 196th Light Infantry Brigade, who at the end of April had assumed responsibility for Fort Page. The food was good and plentiful; it was a luxury not previously provided by Marine headquarters. The unit's standard of living had improved under Army care and they were able to save their C-rations for visits in the hamlets. The families with whom the Marines ate sold such canned goods in the district town, after setting aside the choicest items, such as thick chocolate, for home consumption.

The Americans visited where they were welcome, which was not everywhere. Some families, with relatives in the Viet Cong, hated them. Some could single out one or two Marines and PFs for special blame for a particular firefight. Other families feared the presence of any sort of government authority in the village, be it RDs, PFs or Americans, because it might attract a main-force attack. Still others would take their chances with the combined unit rather than have the VC in control and be threatened by American bombers and the terrible swift helicopters; but they sought to minimize retribution by obeying commands of both sides while voluntarily befriending neither.

Still, after a year many families had invited the Marines to their homes. Some had relations who fought against the Viet Cong; others had girls or young boys who knew the Marines; and some invitations were the result of chance meetings. Whatever else they may have been, the summertime invitations were a signal that the inviters did not expect Viet Cong retribution for their actions. Nor were the invitations given out of fear of the Americans. There was no awe of the unknown in the villagers' dealing with the Marines. They were not the anonymous giants of the tanks, jets and helicopters. These Americans lived in their village, ate their food, worked with their men, died in their paddies. If a villager had a complaint about a Marine, he could tell Trao the man's name and what he had done. Or he could take direct action.

McGowan found that out when he dropped in at Missy Top's for lunch one day. The house was large, with three rooms, two hearths, and sturdy wooden columns supporting a sloped thatched roof fifteen feet above a clean stone floor. Wingrove and Swinford were sitting on the edge of a wooden bed, chatting with Luong and Khoi. The Americans had each brought a box of C-rations and several warm beers, and soon the five of them were belching loudly and rehashing old patrol stories, kidding each other about mistakes made. Top and her mother were busily preparing a lunch of steamed rice topped with duck's eggs and sprinkled with dried shrimp, with side dishes of peanuts and bananas.

Drinking steadily and regaling each other, the men ignored the women, accepting as their due the food served to them, mumbling a perfunctory "Cam on, ba," and returning to their beers and sea stories. Top sat down with them and tried to look bright-eyed and interested, but her presence went unnoticed by her guests and she retreated to the kitchen, where she broke down in tears.

Her mother tried to comfort her, then walked to the doorway to glare at the men. She arrived just as McGowan spilled his rice bowl, splashing egg on the floor and squishing it around in a vain attempt to toe the yolk out of sight behind the leg of the bed. Mrs. Top stormed back to the kitchen, seized her bamboo broom, swept out into the front room, yelling "ingrate" and "ill-mannered" in Vietnamese, and proceeded to beat McGowan about his head and shoulders.

McGowan ran from the house, pursued out of the yard by Mrs. Top, who was shouting that he could not come back until he learned how to behave himself. The others had followed Mrs. Top from the house, her daughter giggling through her tears, the Americans and PFs laughing and cheering until Mrs. Top turned on them, saying they were no better than McGowan was and to get out of her house and not come back for a week.

# 28

One burning noon in late July Mr. Lee, the district census grievance chief, rode his bicycle into the fort. It was Lee's task to wander about the hamlets and talk privately with individual villagers, guaranteeing anonymity and asking about grievances against both the Viet Cong and the government officials. When the grievance taker was true to his pledge and not afraid to travel afield, he sometimes received valuable information, which, when reported to higher Vietnamese headquarters, was sifted for political acceptability before being acted upon. The Chinese Mr. Lee was an honest man, and he came to the fort because he had a piece of information which required immediate action. He was supposed to report only to district headquarters, but he told Suong and McGowan he had pedaled to Binh Nghia instead because he was tired of the slow, ineffectual, bureaucratic responses at higher levels.

"What is the information?" Suong asked.

An officer from the NVA 409th Battalion had come to Binh Son to discuss dwindling food supplies. There was a plan afoot for the main forces to come in and pin down several PF units while the local Viet Cong moved a massive rice shipment upriver. It was to be a twenty-four-hour operation and Binh Nghia was one of the villages involved. Lee had been told that the liaison officer from the 409th would sleep the next night at the home of a ranking member of the Viet Cong district executive committee.

At the mention of the 409th Battalion, which had participated in the attack upon the fort the previous September, Suong had sprung alert.

"Where will he be?" Suong asked.

Lee had known Suong would respond.

"Dong Binh," he said.

McGowan had to laugh. Dong Binh was at the foot of Charlie Company's old position, on the back side of the sand dunes, right next to the Chulai airfield fence. From Suong's expression, McGowan knew they were going there. It was useless to tell Suong that the district chief would be upset, or that Lee worked for the CIA, or that Dong Binh was a mile outside their patrol boundaries. Suong was not going to allow either the National Police or the CIA to deprive him of revenge. McGowan also sensed that Suong, although he did not come right out and ask for help, wanted the Marines' aid in working out a foolproof plan.

They worked at it all day, consulting with only a small number of Vietnamese and Americans in order to avoid a leak. First they talked of hiding two men with shotguns inside the suspect house and trapping the man when he came through the door. Luong squelched that idea by pointing out that the cadre's wife might have a secret signal to warn her husband not to enter.

Garcia suggested waiting until three in the morning and then, with the assistance of the Army, surrounding the entire hamlet. They could then arrest the men in the morning. Trao said no, he knew of tunnels which had been dug in Viet Minh days that extended for hundreds of yards. It was possible, even probable, that at least one such escape route had been redug and the cordon troops would walk right over the men.

Colucci, who was visiting from his new unit, suggested combining the ideas. He pointed out that the ground

around Dong Binh was sandy and a small patrol of good
tacticians could move right up to the house and wait for
the men, while the Army could ring the hamlet with obser-
vation posts and keep a company-sized reaction force
ready to cut off escape routes if the small ambush failed.

McGowan borrowed a motor scooter and drove to
Army brigade headquarters, where he was warmly
received. The operations officers listened attentively to his
plan and told him they were more than a bit envious of his
information. They kidded him, pointing out that the combined unit was already patrolling a six-square-kilometer
area, and now he was proposing to advance their boundary
another kilometer, which were the dimensions generally
given two rifle companies. Perhaps he intended to patrol
all of Chulai eventually? McGowan explained why the
409th was so important to the PFs and to the Marines who
had been at the fort the previous September.

"The 409th NVA reinforced the P31st District Force in
that attack. Suong and Lee figure the NVA liaison officer
who planned that hit is the guy who's coming back
tonight. There are a lot of people at the fort who want him,
sir," McGowan said. "They figure they owe him."

"Well, Mac," the army operations officer said, "in that
case we'd better give you some help. It will be your show,
but let us revise a few aspects of this plan, O.K.?"

With the completed plan, McGowan returned to the fort
and went over the details with an excited Suong. The two
sergeants thought the plan looked good. They could only
take the best tacticians in the unit and together selected six
Americans and ten PFs, an acknowledgment that several
PFs were better than Americans.

They thought security had been tight, with only those
selected being briefed. But the next morning when Brown,
one of those who had been picked, strolled into the mar-

ketplace, a girl asked him why the Marines were not going to ambush in My Hué that night. Flustered, he asked where she had heard the news. She told him her PF boyfriend had just told her. Brown dragged both the girl and the PF back to the fort, where Suong privately questioned the PF. He found out that the PF, a good fighter, just could not resist bragging to his girl and teasing her with his superior knowledge. Suong was furious at the breach of security. The girl said she had told no one else until Brown came along. That Suong did not believe any woman could have done. Still, he decided to stick to the original plan, while holding the girl and the PF at the fort for the day.

An hour after dark on that night of July 24, sixteen men left the fort in two separate patrols. They met again near PF Hill and climbed into the back of a covered Army truck. They drove north through Dong Binh without attracting suspicion, for vehicles passed through dozens of times a day and the brigade that day had ensured that at least one truck rumbled through the hamlet each half-hour. As the truck neared the far outskirts of the hamlet without slowing down, the patrollers jumped out and rolled into the bushes. They lay quiet for a few minutes, then sneaked into the hamlet.

Splitting into teams of three and four, they crawled toward their preassigned ambush spots. The hamlet was not strange to any of them. It held less than fifty houses, almost half of which were strung out along the road. The air hung heavy with heat and thick with the smell of food, and the sweat dropped off the patrollers as they moved on their hands and knees along the hedgerows. The silent sand was their ally, and the teams crept undetected to their ambush sites, where they settled in, prepared to spend all night.

Suong, McGowan and Colucci crawled up to the house of the district committeeman. They heard the woman inside puttering in her kitchen and inched forward until they were at a corner, with a clear view of the short path which ran from the front door to a slatted wooden gate in a high thorn hedge. They sat down, their backs against the wall of the house, and waited.

Within an hour the hamlet had quieted down as most of the children and many of the adults went to bed. After the woman in the house had finished eating and cleaning her dishes, she had blown out her lantern, but McGowan had not heard her climbing into bed and he could imagine her sitting in the dark, waiting. He could only hope that the dark house was not the signal for danger. He did not think so. Their approach, he was convinced, had been utterly silent in the sand. And yet . . .

At the far end of the hamlet, a dog barked—one uncertain, testing bark; then a series of quick, challenging yips which stopped suddenly, as if his owner had jerked on the rope around the dog's neck and dragged him indoors.

McGowan peered into the blackened face of Colucci, who was leaning forward, genuflecting on his right knee, with his sawed-off pump shotgun balanced across his left thigh. Colucci nodded vigorously to McGowan. Suong, still sitting, was glaring at the hedge as if he thought that, with just a little more concentration, he could stare right through the bramble tangle. On impulse, McGowan pointed at the gate and the three slithered forward until they were right under the hedge. Colucci, being farthest back, wiggled past the other two and snuggled against the hedge on the other side of the gate.

It didn't seem that they waited any more than five minutes before they heard a murmur of voices followed by the slight scuffing of loose pebbles on the hard-packed road and then the men were there, two of them, standing at the gate, chatting, like neighbors on a gentle summer weekend night pausing in the soft dark before going inside to drink a cold beer.

As one of the men fumbled to unlatch the gate, Suong stood up and shot him in the face. The Marines had no warning. He just did it. One small bang from his carbine, no louder than a cheap firecracker, had broken the spell of a peaceful summer evening.

The other man stood frozen for an instant, gaping at Suong and at the black faces of the Americans who had popped up on either side of Suong. For that moment no one fired, and McGowan was sure they had a prisoner. He was still thinking so when the man bolted, turning and running in one blur of motion. Suong, thrusting forward over the gate, sent his shots wild and blocked McGowan out of the action. The man was a second and a step away from a deep drainage ditch and a chance to run a gauntlet of ambushes. But Colucci was raising the shotgun and squeezing the trigger, and the hamlet reverberated with the ugly, final sound, like a sledgehammer on glass.

"Damnit, Suong," McGowan shouted, "why didn't you wait? Once inside the gate, we could have snatched them. Truoc vao—hang oi."

Suong did not bother to reply. He had intended from the first to kill the North Vietnamese officer.

The woman from the house ran by them, flung open the gate and knelt beside one of the dead men, keening.

A few days later a silver-gray helicopter fluttered down unexpectedly in front of the fort. Two Americans and two Vietnamese men hopped out, all dressed in neat civilian clothes. They were followed by an attractive Vietnamese woman wearing an ao-dai, the graceful pants and gown costume favored for everyday dress in Saigon and in the more prosperous district towns and suburbs. In Binh Nghia the Marines had seen ao-dais only at weddings and funerals, and then only a few.

McGowan received a call from district telling him not to bother the visitors, who worked for the CIA. The unusual entourage strolled into Binh Yen Noi and stayed for three hours, chatting with various people and wandering about the paths. When they were returning to their helicopter, one of the Americans walked over to the fort's gate, where McGowan was sitting.

"Nice village here," he said.

"We like it," McGowan replied.

"That feeling seems to be shared by the villagers. We've gathered you get along here. Get much dope on what's going on?"

"Too much," McGowan laughed. "Most of it's just scuttlebutt. You know, gossip. It's what Nguyen's cousin said his mother-in-law heard when she talked to a fisherman from My Hué."

"What do you know about taxing?"

"Our acting village chief, Mr. Trao, says his opposite number has a list of who should pay how much. Last month we got the word he was on the trail up by My Hué stopping anybody who came along. Naturally he bugged out before we got there. He'd only been able to shake down a couple of people. They don't tax in this village any more."

"Why not?"

"We patrol, so it can't be done on a regular basis. The villagers would bitch, we'd get tipped off, and bang!— there go your tax collectors. And if we missed them, the VC families would be forced to make up the losses. These PFs aren't fussing around."

"Yes," the man said dryly. "We've noticed. . . . You are aware that we have special teams trained to do the sort of thing you did the other night? Lee was supposed to report to them, not to you."

"Sir, that was something personal which goes pretty far back. The PFs wanted that guy bad. So did we. His battalion did a job on this fort once. We owed him.

"I hope you're not thinking of sending any of your people around here. As far as this particular village is concerned, no friendlies come in but us. No Marines, no soldiers, no medcaps. Not anybody. Your special teams will get blown all away to hell if they come sneaking around here. One Marine from a line unit got accidentally killed that way. Nobody from the outside hunts in here. We'd appreciate it if you'd keep your people out. This is our village."

"Well, it seems a lot of people here agree with you, so I won't argue the point. But aren't your boundaries a bit big?"

"We just sort of go where we have to."

"All right, I'll pass the word that it's O.K. for Lee to work with you—not that he hasn't been doing so. Good luck, Sergeant."

# 29

Helicopter visitors were not rare. Fort Page was known as the combined unit that wouldn't die. The village had been written about in *Time* magazine, as well as in several books and articles. The fort became a fifteen-minute stopping place for high-ranking commanders and for VIPs on two-week tours of Vietnam.

The Marines and the PFs did not mind. In fact, they were flattered, and McGowan felt it was good for morale for his men and Suong's to see that the top command was personally interested in them, although sometimes McGowan found the interest too personal.

When the commander of all U.S. forces in the Pacific, Admiral U.S. Grant Sharp, visited Binh Nghia, he said that as a Navy man he knew little of ground tactics and instead wanted to spend his time questioning the men about their backgrounds and their relationships with the Vietnamese. The men found him easy to talk with, and McGowan regaled the admiral with tales about his father's bar in New York City. Upon his departure, the admiral thanked them for the job they were doing and for their courtesy toward him. He said their parents would be proud of their sons. When the admiral had flown off, McGowan commented to the others, "He was a nice old gent," and thought no more of the visit.

But the admiral did, and while still in his helicopter he dictated a letter to his aide to be sent to Mrs. McGowan. It was a warm note, expressing the attitude of a father, signed by a four-star admiral with a command of almost a million men. The sergeant himself had not written home in three months, and when the admiral's letter arrived in a stark, official envelope, Mrs. McGowan feared the worst. She could not bring herself to read it. She called her sister, who lived nearby, and asked her to come over.

"Here," she said, her hands trembling, "you open it. Something's happened to Vinnie. I just know it."

When her sister read her the letter, they both wept in relief and joy.

Soon afterward McGowan received a blistering note

from his father for the anxiety he had caused his mother by not finding the time to write, when Admiral Sharp could.

The Marine generals who visited Binh Nghia were, of course, interested in the nature of the ground combat. Under severe criticism from the Army for wasting manpower in Combined Action Platoons, the Marine command wished to clearly demonstrate the wisdom of combined units. This they were never to do to their own satisfaction, let alone that of the U.S. Army. The combined units seemed too fragile, the American role too temporary, other demands for U.S. manpower too powerful.

Almost all the generals, whether American or Vietnamese, asked the question: What would you do if attacked by a battalion? To McGowan the question was foolish, since anyone surrounded during attack had no option but to fight back. He felt depressed by the question because it indicated there was no history of the fort, that no one knew the combined unit had twice fought a battalion, once failing and once driving their would-be attackers away. And he felt angered because the question implied that combined units working in villages were too vulnerable to be undertaken on a large scale. To McGowan this attitude showed that some of his senior commanders did not understand the nature of the war. There were not enough enemy battalions to be attacking the fort continuously. The Americans who lived in Binh Nghia had grown to understand that the Viet Cong could triumph only if the threat of such an attack cowed the small unit into leaving. The Americans at Fort Page were determined never to leave because of Viet Cong pressure. Partly this was a matter of personal pride, and partly it was a feeling of obligation to the PFs and to the villagers. But McGowan and his men could only vaguely explain to generals and ambassadors what they were doing or why they were proud of it.

The U.S. Army commanders who visited Binh Nghia showed marked reserve in listening to the briefings McGowan and Suong would deliver. They rarely asked a hard or critical question. Regardless of what they believed wrong with allowing Americans to live and work with the Vietnamese, they respected the efforts of the PFs and Marines in Binh Nghia and, with the innate courtesy of the military, would not think of criticizing a sergeant's tactics in order to show disagreement with a general's strategy. In fact, quite the opposite occurred.

During a September visit by General Harold K. Johnson, Chief of Staff of the U.S. Army, McGowan found himself being drawn out on a variety of subjects, ranging from his educational background (high school; no college) to his marital plans (none) to his career plans (none). Before leaving, Johnson offered him a commission as an officer in the United States Army. The sergeant thanked the general and declined the offer. It was not being an officer as opposed to an enlisted man that made him shun a military career. It was not the Army versus the Marines. He did not know what he wanted to do, but he wanted to keep on moving. When he left the village, he would leave military service altogether.

One visitor who did not fall into the easy briefing pattern was General Creighton Abrams. McGowan considered his visit a disaster. The general hopped out of his helicopter, strode into the fort, sat down in front of the briefing map, lit a cigar and fixed McGowan with a steady stare. With easy confidence, the sergeant commenced his routine briefing, describing the physical layout of the village, the nature of the enemy, the sort of contacts encountered. There were several points in the briefing where McGowan had learned to pause, inviting an obvious question from his visitors, one which allowed him to describe a pat anecdote praising either the PFs, the villagers or the Marines. McGowan would repeat this technique until he had said a good word for everyone and used up the fifteen minutes which marked the extent of most VIP visits.

With Abrams, the technique failed, and McGowan's smugness turned to fear. At each pause in the briefing, Abrams said nothing but stared at McGowan intently. The sergeant felt himself growing nervous, stumbling over points and stuttering over words. The briefing ended on a lame note in less than eight minutes. Abrams got up, turned and strode back to his helicopter, having no more time to waste with a nervous, cocky, know-nothing sergeant. McGowan afterward was better able to sympathize with Suong, who stammered and stumbled when called upon to brief Vietnamese VIPs.

# 30

On August 13 the combined unit again arbitrarily extended its patrol boundaries to take care of what they considered to be a village responsibility. That afternoon Suong had asked McGowan to look after things for the evening; he, Trao, Lee and most of the other village officials were going to a big card game in Nuoc Man—a kilometer south from Binh Nghia across the paddies. Nuoc Man was a twisted congestion of ramshackle wooden, thatch and tin huts flung up on either side of Highway One. Stocked by the Koreans, it was a typical boomtown which catered to the American units. Business was brisk and boondock prices high: cold Cokes were 75 cents, bundles of laundry $1.50, girls $3. The

Marines from Fort Page were charged the same prices as were the line units, an equality which they deeply resented, and out of hurt pride they shunned dealings with the town. Not by accident, the squatter town had sprung up at the bottom of a hill holding a U.S. battalion, and conditions within its dusty, claptrap borders were deemed so safe that soldiers on liberty were not allowed to carry rifles. MPs sauntered from bar-girl shack to bar-girl shack during the day to keep the peace. Although the town had been receiving desultory night sniper fire for a week, no one had paid much attention. Things were so comfortable many store owners had stopped giving a cut of their earnings to the VC.

That night McGowan had sent out his usual three patrols and, finding it too muggy indoors, had climbed on the roof of the machine-gun bunker to sleep. It was near midnight and he had just dozed off when Nuoc Man exploded.

The first fusillade came full and sharp in steady volume. Its lack of raggedness or swelling crescendo told McGowan a surprise attack had been pulled on the little PF outpost at the town. Next a few rounds smacked into the sandbags beneath him, and he ducked inside the bunker as Marines and PFs lurched from their sleeping quarters, expecting attack. The sentries strained to spot movement on the flat paddy lands to their west.

"It's just stray incoming," the radio sentry said. "They must be attacking the ville itself. Man, look at that."

The horizon above Nuoc Man was dancing with fire as from all directions the Viet Cong lit and hurled kerosene-soaked rags into the timber town. Homemade gasoline bombs were bursting successively, their cascades of sparks and darts of flame mixing in the blackness with the trails of fire left by the streaming rags.

"Monitor battalion," McGowan said, referring to the radio channel for the Army unit on the hill behind Nuoc Man.

"No traffic, Sarge," the radio operator reported.

"What the hell! Try company."

An infantry company sat on another hill east of the town, with one platoon outposting PF Hill. Still picking up no traffic, the sergeant broke radio silence and asked the company what was going on. Company replied that they didn't know but were trying to find out.

Out of patience, McGowan grabbed the handset and yelled, "Don't find out. Send people in there—those PFs need help."

"Wait—out," came the reply.

McGowan waited ten minutes while battalion and company talked undecidedly back and forth—then he broke in again.

"Captain," he said, "if you're not going to do anything, I'll take some men in. Those are my people in there. They need help—now."

"Get off our net, Lima Six," came the reply. "You have the wrong freq. That fight is outside your AO. I don't have time to gab with you. Out."

McGowan changed channels to the PF frequency and called the district headquarters at Binh Son, two miles down the road from Nuoc Man. He spoke to Volentine.

"Sir, Trao and Suong and half the honchos of Binh Nghia are in Nuoc Man. If they're lost, it's all over. Someone has to do something."

"How many men do you have?"

"Enough."

There were in the fort at that moment six Americans and eight PFs.

"Mac, we've lost touch with Nuoc Man," Volentine

said. "You go ahead and act on your best judgment. I'll back you up."

Most of the Marines were clamoring to go in. There was a firefight, and most of them liked to shoot. It wasn't a time for stealth and movement; it was a time for firepower and rifle marksmanship. McGowan selected four Marines and two PFs. He dared not take more men lest one of the unit's own patrols in Binh Nghia run into trouble and need a reaction force from the fort.

He radioed to the Army platoon on PF Hill.

"We're coming west, around your hill in two minutes. Don't shoot us. Out."

Each man was carrying the combination weapon of the M-16 and grenade launcher, fifteen to twenty magazines, and four to eight grenades. They were ready to move as soon as McGowan put down the phone. The seven dogtrotted the quarter-mile down the road past PF Hill, talking loudly so they wouldn't be shot. Still at a lope, they cut across the paddy dikes until they neared Highway One.

Everyone at the fort had agreed that the Viet Cong would set ambushes astride the road north and south of the town. So rather than run that gauntlet, the seven stopped short of the road, slid off the dikes and waded through the paddies parallel to the road until they were abreast of the center of the town. There they turned in, cut through a few backyards and stopped in the shadows at the edge of the main street.

The scene before them was one of chaos and terror. Many of the shacks which lined the road were blazing and the fire bathed the street in weird, flickering light. The alleyways and the walls of the buildings seemed to catch and echo the din of the screams and cries of people fleeing amidst the crash of timber, the furious crackling of the flames and the pop-pop-pop of small-arms ammunition cooking off. The families of the prostitutes, barkeepers and store owners were pouring past the seven riflemen, who could see the Viet Cong off to their left about a hundred yards down the road pitching torches and darting in and out of shacks.

At first the people kept running right by McGowan's men, as though they didn't—couldn't—exist. Then an old lady stopped and pointed back down the street toward the Viet Cong and yelled something at them, the tone of which was: "Don't just stand there gawking, do something!" Almost instantly the riflemen were surrounded by people, all pointing toward the Viet Cong and shouting, some pushing at the Marines, urging them into battle against the men who were burning their homes and businesses. Still McGowan hesitated, seeking assurance that he would not be trapped from the rear, finding it when Ho Chi, the Binh Nghia schoolteacher, elbowed his way through the crowd to say that all the Viet Cong were at the southern end of town.

McGowan's men stepped out into the glare and stood abreast looking down the street. The crowd which had been around them a minute earlier was gone, having ducked into the alleys to avoid what they knew was coming. Intent on their torch work, the Viet Cong never looked back, probably under the reasonable assumption that they would not be attacked without warning from the center of the burning town.

The seven riflemen fired together, first with the grenade launchers, then with their rifles. The first volley was all theirs and they made the most of the surprise, firing as fast as they could change magazines. McGowan's men had the initiative and they went in, moving by bounds to cover one another and firing their rifles in long bursts. They drew abreast of the cement house of Mr. Bun, a contractor working for the Army and, seeing two five-gallon gasoline cans sitting on the front porch, promptly broke into a run before the explosions went off. With the shacks blazing and crumbling on both sides of the road, the heat seared their faces and they ran faster, closing on the enemy.

The Viet Cong had a huge edge in numbers, but the flames kept them from spreading out and those who could shoot, being closest to the seven riflemen, were outmatched in firepower. Their return fire was scattered and ill-coordinated since their leader had to cope with uncertainty. Was he fighting just seven men, or was the rest of the American battalion drawing near, perhaps encircling him?

The Viet Cong pulled off, their main body plunging into the brush south of town while two stayed to hold back the attackers. But McGowan's men were rolling with the momentum of battle, past an enemy soldier sprawled in the street, past yet another, and the two rear guards loosed but a few desultory bursts before the seven riflemen were on them, too, passing them, outflanking them, killing them and running on, plunging into the bush, and there in front of them, crossing a twisted railroad track, went the Viet Cong company. McGowan had the fleeting impression that he was looking at more than fifty in one bunch, but he had no time to count or shoot as the enemy stopped and turned, like a bear harried by a pack of small hounds, and McGowan and his men were falling flat with the bullets whipping around them. The seven of them lay there, panting for breath, knowing they were safe as long as they didn't raise their heads high, knowing too that the enemy were scampering safely away, scattering bullets behind them like fistfuls of sand.

When the firing sputtered out, they turned around and walked to the tiny PF outpost at the edge of the town. They weren't about to enter a dark ravine in pursuit of an enemy company, and without a radio they had no means of calling an artillery mission. Once the enemy were out of the town and away from the PF fort, McGowan's men had no more interest in them.

Their concern was for their friends in the fort. The Viet Cong had surprised the PFs, most of whose leaders were drinking and playing high-stake poker at the bimonthly gathering. The enemy had surged through the wire and carried the fight into the bunkers. Mr. Lee, the census grievance taker, was killed by the blast from a hand grenade, his body shielding Trao, who was crouched beside him, and saving his life. Two PFs were killed and four wounded. The others had formed and held a ragged perimeter but had been unable to help the villagers, twelve of whom were killed.

McGowan found the Nuoc Man PF leader in critical condition, his buttocks ripped off. With his shirt the sergeant bound the massive wound, then grabbed the PF radio and called Binh Son. Captain Volentine in turn wasted no time calling the Army, and soon a platoon came trotting down the road to help.

The lieutenant in charge set about in a brusque manner to organize a defense when McGowan brought him up short by saying: "I don't need you—now—Lieutenant; I need a medevac for this man. Where is it?"

The lieutenant took one look at the PF leader and hastily called his battalion.

The medevac was refused because the area was called "insecure." So McGowan called Fort Page and Bac Si Khoi ran the full mile, bringing a bottle of intravenous fluid which he injected into the PF, but his condition did not improve. Khoi recommended they carry him to Fort Page, where he could care for him better. So those who had come from Binh Nghia returned that way.

Passing through the smoldering village, McGowan saw a girl who sold Cokes and other things to the soldiers standing outside her untouched hut. Those shacks on both sides of hers lay in ashes. In response to McGowan's question, she said she had to make a living and stay alive, so she just paid her taxes to the VC regularly.

When the portaging party arrived at Fort Page, Khoi used two more bottles of fluid to keep the PF leader alive. At dawn a helicopter came in and lifted him out.

By then McGowan was in serious trouble. His temper rubbed raw by the night's events, his messages to battalion from Fort Page in the early morning hours had been framed in ill-concealed disgust. The helicopter had not been dispatched during the night because Binh Nghia was not considered secure either—and because the wounded man was not an American.

The next morning the battalion commander went to the division commander and requested McGowan's immediate relief for insubordination and refusal to obey orders, to wit: entering Nuoc Man after permission to do so had been denied. The division commander listened to the story, then blasted the colonel for his failure to act. The general said McGowan had been right and he wrong.

The battalion commander left Task Force headquarters and drove to Binh Nghia, bringing with him a case of cold beer. Taking McGowan aside, he apologized for his inaction the previous night. He thanked the sergeant "for pulling a slight victory out of what otherwise would have been defeat."

Still peeved by the situation, McGowan asked why the colonel hadn't acted. The officer replied he didn't really know—the country and the people seemed strange and he wasn't sure what his men could do, or would know how to do, in a situation like that. That answer McGowan could understand from his own days in an infantry battalion.

The seven riflemen from Fort Page had gone into Nuoc Man for Trao and Suong. They had had no use for the town or its people, who cheated and overcharged them. The town rebuilt quickly and was soon back to its normal corrupt practices. But afterward the PFs and Marines from Fort Page could not buy a Coke or a beer.

"There is no charge," the merchants would say.

# 31

The end came quietly in October of 1967, after two and a half months without a firefight or even a sighting of a Viet Cong within the confines of Binh Nghia. Although the village officials insisted the enemy still skulked in the shadows after midnight, the savage struggle for Binh Nghia was over. The PFs were patrolling in the My Hués in teams of two, like cops on a beat. The enemy had placed his priorities and his manpower elsewhere. The Marines were no longer needed; the PFs could do as well. It was time for the Americans to leave.

District and Marine headquarters had agreed that McGowan's men should be transferred to Binh Thuy Island, three hundred yards out in the river from Binh Yen Noi, a world away from Binh Nghia. Trao and the village council vehemently disagreed. District's arguments that the shift was for the greater common good of the war effort fell on deaf ears. These Americans belonged to Binh Nghia; let Binh Thuy find their own Americans.

McGowan's men were of two minds. The newer ones were anxious to go to a place where the Viet Cong came in every night, and the PFs were afraid to leave their fort. The older ones had seen all that; Binh Nghia was their village. They wanted to stay. So did McGowan. But when in September Lieutenant General Robert E. Cushman, who had replaced Walt as commander of Marine forces in Vietnam, had asked him if the PFs could stand alone, he had felt obliged to say they could. That reply had marked the Marines' remaining time in the village. The last few days his men were at the fort, villagers kept coming up to them and urgently, desperately insisting that the Viet Cong would come back if they left. McGowan believed them. He considered it preordained that the PFs would be tested. He was betting they would hold.

Seventeen months after they had arrived, the Americans left the Vietnamese village of Binh Nghia. There was a flurry of good-byes, and the dozen Marines climbed into the boats from Binh Thuy and paddled away.

McGowan lingered after the others had departed, searching for Suong, who had not come to the fort that morning. All the others had been there—Trao, Bac Si Khoi, Luong, Tri, Missy Top, even Mr. Buu—all except Suong. It was no use looking for the PF leader when he did not want to be found. Nevertheless, McGowan tried, going to his house, going to the marketplace, sending boys out looking for him, making an effort before admitting it was useless. At last he headed toward the river bank, shaking hands one last time with the throng of villagers walking with him, stopping and turning around for one final look when he reached the boat. And there was Suong, pushing his way through the crowd.

McGowan looked at him.

"I have to go, Suong," he said. "The Americans have to go."

"I know," Suong replied.

They shook hands, strongly. No smiles. No playful shoves.

"Chao, Suong."

"Chao, McGowan."

# EPILOGUE

# 1967

In December of 1967 I revisited the Chulai area. I checked in with the staff of the Americal Division, where a Civil Affairs colonel and a major, who was the Public Information Officer, offered to drive me to Binh Son district headquarters. They did not want me to go to Binh Nghia without permission. At the district hill fort, we were greeted by Captain Volentine, so I knew there would be no difficulty in returning to the village.

Volentine didn't like the way things were going. In the three months since I had last been there, he said, both the Army and the Koreans had moved in more forces. But their deployment concepts, in his opinion, had not improved the security of the district. He said most Army troops were far out in the hills and the Koreans were behind a massive defensive barrier.

The VC did not appear to be hurting, yet the district had been so quiet he felt the enemy was up to something big. He considered the Revolutionary Development (RD) teams a liability since, by Saigon order, they required a high degree of PF protection and had done nothing he could judge to be of lasting value. When hard-pressed, many broke and ran. Although several hamlets had been labeled "Ap Doi Mois" (pacified New Life hamlets), he said he had never seen one where the people were actually organized or where they expressed in any way a spirit of hostility toward the VC. The people in the district town volunteered no information; he felt the VC could move into town and he wouldn't know it. He said his conviction of deterioration in security was a gut feeling and that he hadn't proved it to the brass.

Binh Nghia, he said, had been doing all right since the Americans left. Although Buu, the village chief, had moved back in once McGowan had gone, Suong and Trao seemed to have things under control. A PF had been blown up one morning by a booby trap set near the fort, but aside from that there had been no serious incidents in the locale.

In the town of Binh Son PX goods, liquor, narcotics, medicinal supplies, American cigarettes, silk and prostitutes were being sold. The Americans could not take action because Binh Son was in a Korean sector, and the Vietnamese officials did not want to act because they were getting rich. Volentine did not believe U.S. AID was much help to the people, but the rake-offs—up to 50 percent—were making the middlemen and the contractors wealthy. He considered the district chief a middleman who looked out only for himself, in no way comparable to Captain Dang.

Volentine was convinced the level of accommodation between the VC and Vietnamese officials was both high and foolish. He thought it was high because the district police chief was so corrupt that only a poor man stayed in jail over three days, and neither the police chief nor the district chief would arrest the known NLF members who worked in Binh Son. He thought accommodation was foolish because the VC broke it at will.

The colonel from Civil Affairs, listening to our conversation and becoming more irritated as the hours went by, objected to the use of the word "accommodation." Volentine reached under his chair and picked up a burlap bag. A few hours before our arrival, he said, a little boy was walking with the bag across the highway bridge eighty yards from district headquarters, when he saw two combined-unit Marines walking up the street toward him. He stopped short, looked around, then smiled at an

American soldier walking past on his way to town for an afternoon's liberty. Hand in hand, the little boy and the soldier, who was new in the country, walked off the bridge past the two Marines.

When the Marines asked what he had in the bag, the boy tried to run away. They caught him and opened the sack. It was filled with shotgun and carbine ammunition. They gave the sack back to the boy, who ran straight to the house of a PF official. The Marines followed, broke the door down, and caught the man and the boy stuffing the bag into a corner.

They then sent for Volentine, who searched the house and arrested the PF. The district chief arrived, however, said Volentine had no such authority and ordered him to leave the house immediately.

The Civil Affairs colonel said he should go through channels with his complaints. Volentine laughed and said Binh Son was a showcase for pacification. It was one of the most heavily American-advised districts in Vietnam, with four officers and five NCOs. There were ninety PFs guarding the seven-room compound, which was so close to the main highway from Chulai that some of the outer strands of barbed wire straddled the road's drainage ditch. Due to the accessibility of the compound, all sorts of official visitors arrived every week, and Volentine had told his story straight. In turn, a very high-level pacification official told him he was perhaps not fit for the job because he was overly critical. That worried him because he wanted to get promoted. He was told large rake-offs were a normal part of aid distribution and that he should not buck the system. He was convinced his superiors listened to him but accepted only the optimistic parts of what he said. He had been ordered to pay off the police chief to collect more information, rather than try to get him relieved.

The colonel told Volentine to cheer up, that we were winning the war and that the Americal Division had the NVA regiments out in the hills completely on the run. Volentine looked at him for a full ten seconds before replying. Then, the burlap bag still in his hand, he said, "Colonel, that's your war, not mine."

Volentine invited me to stay the night, so that we might talk at length about some of the enemy intentions and about the situation, village by village. The next day we would catch a boat to Binh Nghia. The colonel hastily interjected that I had been invited to the senior officers' mess as the general's guest. It was agreed that I would come back the next day to stay over and go back to Binh Nghia.

I took my leave, accompanied by two very glum staff officers. Anxious to allay their obvious displeasure with him, Volentine added as we left, "Don't get me wrong, Colonel, I'm all for the little guy—the PF. But he needs good leadership, and I mean that word the way we use it; you know, a guy who watches out for him, and goes to bat for him, gets him his pay and his food supplement, trains him and leads him. Right now he doesn't have it. But I'm behind that little PF 100 percent."

The colonel saluted but did not reply. On the way back in the jeep, the major said, "Boy, that guy was pretty pessimistic—sounded like sour grapes to me."

The colonel responded, "I'm not sure about Volentine; maybe he's been out here too long."

At dinner that evening, the three generals were interested in discussing security strategies in response to enemy capabilities. I related what I had seen farther north in Dai Loc district, where one night in early November the VC had laid waste several villages with the thoroughness and savagery of Apache raiders, despite the nearby pres-

ence of a Marine battalion. As a consequence of the fear
thus instilled, the people afterward refused even American
medcaps for their wounds. One general thought that the
disruption proved his point that the people went with the
winner—the incident at Dai Loc had happened because
the people had not been provided security.

"Give them security," he said, "and they'll give you
information and cooperation."

He thought Binh Son was an example of this, where the
PFs "can hold out by themselves because no enemy are
there." Through ceaseless battalion operations, the enemy
was being pushed back into the hills and losing the initiative. The colonel from Civil Affairs was sitting next to me,
but he said nothing throughout the meal. It was he who
had mentioned to me the recent refusal of medcaps in the
Chulai area, but he had also mentioned that there were certain things the general did not want to hear.

While we were talking, Captain Phil Volentine was
dying. A mixed NVA/Viet Cong battalion came in on one
of the routes Volentine said they habitually used. At six
that afternoon, 150 of them were seen moving east down
the valley toward Binh Son. District was warned, but
someone thought they were going to hit some outpost, and
so the district headquarters took no special precautions.

General Vo Thu, commander of Viet Cong Military
Region V, had personally ordered the attack against Binh
Son district and his men were thoroughly prepared. It was
windy and raining when the bangalore torpedo went off
and the enemy rushed through the wire. The senior adviser
later said the PFs were awake, but no Americans had
checked the watch and if the PF sentries were awake, they
weren't alert. The VC came through unopposed, methodically shot their way through the PFs stumbling in the
trenches and blasted the buildings. All the Americans

except one huddled together with several Vietnamese in a bunker. Alone, Volentine raced to the command bunker to direct operations and there was killed when satchel charges crumpled the structure.

The attack started before midnight and went on until dawn. Helicopter gunships arrived half an hour after the first call for help; Korean and American troops converged on the town at dawn, six hours later. There was no pursuit of the enemy forces; no one bothered to even ask in which direction they might have gone. As they always do, the VC mined the main approach route (in this instance, Highway One), and the first two Americans to drive up in a jeep the next day were blown to bits.

The district chief was not killed, but fifteen PFs were. Volentine was the only American casualty. The few people in the jail were freed. And the district headquarters was completely leveled. The next morning it was a black, smoldering clump of earth and charred corpses at the top of a little hill, separated from clusters of silent, staring Vietnamese by three rows of barbed wire.

In the town itself, one section of six houses was reduced to charred stubble, but no one asked why the VC had singled them out.

The American advisers were "proud of those little PFs. They really fought like hell." In the Saigon English newspaper there was a three-line blurb about an attack on a district headquarters in Quang Ngai, with one U.S. adviser killed and fifteen PF casualties. At the Army division headquarters, those working on the after-action report were trying to tabulate the final count from the rumors that the helicopters and artillery had killed "35 or 40 of them" in that battle. So in the monthly summary, the Binh Son attack could go down as just another enemy-initiated incident; the overall kill ratio was about three to one favoring

the PFs, statistically indicating continued allied effectiveness.

The province senior adviser was putting Volentine in
for the Silver Star.

I did not get to Binh Nghia that trip.

# 1968

With unfortunate bureaucratic predictability, American
and Vietnamese officials devoted their energies to rebuild-
ing the district compound—at the expense of providing
reaction forces to the outlying PF platoons in villages such
as Binh Nghia. Suong was ordered to leave Fort Page and
take his platoon to the top of PF Hill. When he objected to
moving away from the village, he was told district could
not guarantee support if he was hit. What district said, the
Viet Cong knew. Suong moved.

The district and the village were quiet during the early
part of 1968. The Viet Cong shifted south the P31st
District Force Company so that they could aid in the Tet
attacks against Quang Ngai City. They battled with the
ARVN forces for three days and failed to take the city.
When they limped back to Binh Son district, they were in
no condition to fight again for several months.

The most egregious event in the district during 1968
occurred at Son Tra hamlet, where Colucci had established a combined unit. The people in Son Tra were
refugees moved from the Phu Longs. There were among
them few, if any, Viet Cong families, who had preferred to
stay in the area controlled by the P31st. Le Quan Viet, the
VC district chief, had warned the people not to move, and

the lack of Viet Cong families among the refugees allowed him to punish the people directly without fear of retribution.

There were over seven thousand people in Son Tra, and sharing responsibility for security arrangements were Colucci's combined unit, a U.S. Army platoon and a fifty-man Revolutionary Development team. Between the three units there was bad blood, and since they could not agree to patrol together, they divided the hamlet into three separate security sectors. On the night of June 28 the RDs were supposedly guarding the western approaches to the hamlet. The guards, however, had deserted their posts to join a large poker game.

The Viet Cong knew of the game and came through where the guards were supposed to have been. The enemy moved swiftly toward the center of the hamlet, using flame throwers on the houses and shooting the people as they ran outside. From the southern end of the hamlet Colucci's combined unit counterattacked, passing by the Army platoon's hill position without radio contact. Mistaking the PFs for VC, a machine gunner on the hill opened up on the Marines and PFs, keeping them pinned down for twenty minutes.

That was all the time the Viet Cong had needed to blast and burn their way down the main street and cut their way back out of the hamlet, leaving behind eighty-five dead civilians.

Also in late spring, the P31st attacked the Binh Nghia PFs. They crossed the river and stole through the back sections of the Binh Yen Noi hamlets, creeping up undetected to the foot of PF Hill. They had their attack route plotted and their bangalore torpedoes and satchel charges ready. All they needed was for their lead sapper to clear a path through the wire. The man stripped off his clothes and plastered himself with mud and dirt so he would blend with the bare earth beneath the barbed wire and wiggled forward, holding a dozen strips of bamboo cord between his teeth. He had to worm his way through five separate rolls of concertina wire. He inched up to the first strand, grasped a coil of wire and tied it back to its neighbor. He did the same with the adjoining coil, opening a gap of about a foot, and slithered through. He was at the second roll. Through. The third. Through. The fourth. Through. The fifth. He tied back the coils and looked up.

There was Suong, squatting on his haunches, his elbows braced against the inside of his thighs, his two hands wrapped around the butt of a 45-caliber pistol. Suong shot the sapper between the eyes. Nobody else tried to come through the wire that night.

I visited Binh Nghia several times in the summer and fall of 1968, usually accompanied by Charles Benoit, a Yale graduate who had spent four years in Vietnam and had extraordinary fluency in the language and a deep compassion for the people. Suong would not believe that Benoit, speaking Vietnamese as well as he did, did not work for the U.S. government and so he made a strong effort to convince us that things were going badly and that he needed the Marines. Speaking to Benoit in Vietnamese he said:

"The Viet Cong have come back. They go to My Hué every night. We're not afraid of them, but if we get into a firefight in My Hué 1, we're not going to get any help from district or from the U.S. Army for several hours. My men and I know this for a fact. We got into a fight out on the sand dunes last month and it was two hours before we had illumination. We captured an M-79 grenade launcher anyways. If we have to fight alone, I want it the way it was last year. With the Marines we had enough firepower to

fight anybody, and we could always get helicopter medevacs."

"Why not recruit your own People's Self-Defense
Force," Benoit asked, "like they are doing in the hamlets
near Saigon?"

"That is Saigon," Suong laughed. "How would I pay
them? Or arm them? Besides, they'd be a bunch of ama-
teurs and my men would have to spend months training
them. We wouldn't be able to rely on them. They'd get lost
in the My Hués, and they might run away.

"No, it would be a lot better if Sergeant Mac and the
Marines would come back."

"But the Marines you knew are gone," I said. "Mac is a
civilian in a university in the United States."

Suong spent several minutes digesting that piece of
information. He found it hard to imagine a sergeant in any
army being admitted to a university. After a pause, he
spoke again.

"Well, Garcia is on Binh Thuy Island and he still visits
the village, and there are a few others. Perhaps you could
all spend the night with us in Binh Nghia?"

A boat ferried us from Binh Yen Noi to the island,
where we met Garcia. He said he had gone back to the
United States but after six months of garrison duty he
"couldn't hack it any more" and asked to be sent back to
the combined unit. He did not like what he had found on
Binh Thuy. The replacements for McGowan and the old
group had brought with them the antagonistic attitude of
line troops toward the villagers. The only Vietnamese
whom they liked was Joe, who was still with the unit and
doing very well in school. Garcia said he spent a lot of
time in Binh Nghia, away from the other Americans.

The only other American from the old group in Binh
Thuy was Foster, whose stolen watch had been returned

after the intervention of Captain Dang. Like Garcia, he enthusiastically responded to Suong's invitation. But there was something he had to do along the way.

So the four of us set out to walk the short mile back to the ferry crossing to Binh Nghia, Foster in the lead and taking us by a roundabout way, across the green paddies under a hot July sun at a leisurely pace, Benoit stopping often to chat with villagers, we others envying the ease of his tongue and the grace of his manner.

We came out on the river bank just south of Binh Nghia at the tiny hamlet of Chau Tu, and Foster stopped and stood for a minute looking at the quiet, tree-shaded houses in front of him and the people bent over in the paddies and the water buffalo wallowing in the mud at a low spot in the river and the dragonflies droning in the summer afternoon.

"This is my hamlet," he said. "I'm the only American who comes here. Watch this."

From a pocket in his utilities he drew out a snowball wad of plastic explosive with a short piece of fuse.

"The people here are really poor," he said. "They have to go the farthest, so they get the worst fishing spots out at sea. I try to help out by bringing fresh fish."

With that he ignited the fuse and dropped it in the water. The explosion brought black mud bubbling to the surface and boys streaming out of nowhere shouting "Gene! Gene!" even before they could see him. To the bank they raced, shed their clothes and plunged laughing in. Soon their dives recovered several small fish, but many boys were still empty-handed. So the corporal walked the bank with a dozen naked urchins traipsing behind. He would peer into the water and locate schools of minnows, raise his M-16, and fire into their midst. The concussion would shock them, and the boys would jump in and scoop them out.

In the midst of this laughing, giggling procession, we entered the hamlet. The shooting and the shouting had brought the people to their doorways and, when they saw Foster, they simply waved and went about their business. One small, sturdy lad, his breeches stuffed with minnows, was allowed to carry Foster's M-16, now unloaded, and he walked at the head of our small procession, turning constantly to joke with Foster, finally running pell-mell up the trail and disappearing into a small grove of banana trees. Foster did not seem concerned about his rifle and we ambled up the trail, turning in where the boy had gone.

In front of us stood a small, thatched house with Foster's rifle propped against one of the outside walls. The boy had his back to us, tugging at his young, attractive mother, who stood in the open doorway, looking pleased and flustered and trying to shoo her son away while smiling. The smile was all for Foster, who grinned back, said a few words and settled comfortably into a chair beneath a palm tree, gesturing to us to sit down on a bench nearby. The young woman had gone inside and was bustling about preparing hot tea and snacks. While we waited, Foster talked.

"Everybody has sort of his favorite place and favorite family. This is mine. Nguyen Co was in the combined unit with me. He was a good man with a BAR, and one morning after a long night he took me back here to meet his wife and boy and have breakfast. Co and I were tight. It got so I spent as much time here as I did at the fort. He got killed in a firefight near My Hué about four, five months ago. A grenade got him.

"That was pretty tough on the family. I mean, there's no one to look out for them. The government didn't give them too much, so I sort of drop around and help out. Little Nguyen's a real good kid. We have a lot of fun together.

He's the best swimmer in the hamlet. You saw him diving for those minnows. He and Joe are best buddies, so he stays at the fort with me a lot."

The mother came out of the house with a tray of food and drinks. When we had each taken our cup, Foster put the empty tray on his knees and from six different pockets drew C-ration cans of fruit and meat, along with several packets of cocoa and sugar. He piled them all on the tray and handed it with a wink to the boy, who winked back and walked into the house.

"It's not what you might think," he said. "I'm not shacking up here. I don't think I could if I wanted to, which I don't. Besides, if I did, I might spoil her chances of remarrying. And the Cong around here are mean bastards. I don't want to give them an excuse to fuss with this family. So I never go inside that house. Whenever I visit, I sit right out here. If I'm going to eat, I eat off a tray, right here."

We finished our drinks, thanked the woman and walked the short distance to Binh Yen Noi. There the villagers fed us well, and there were several bottles of beer drunk while old anecdotes were retold for the fifth or tenth time and Benoit almost succeeded in convincing me to swallow a red pepper whole. In the growing dusk we left the hamlet and trudged up PF Hill, looking forward to a full night's sleep.

But Suong was on the radio.

"Do you know what he said?" Benoit asked. "He just told the district chief that he has a strong American squad at his position and he would like to send an ambush to My Hué. Now if we don't go, he'll lose face, almost like he was lying to the district chief. I think he's determined to show us that things aren't going well."

"Don't worry," Foster said. "We'll protect you."

With four PFs and two Marines, we walked off the hill at eleven that evening. Luong was in charge of the patrol and he took point, stopping at every trail intersection to run his hand through the dust for possible trip wires. As we cut across dunes, he cast for tracks in the sand. When we waded swollen paddies, he went first and left ripples without splashes. We set in at a river crossing point in My Hué, and, sure enough, the enemy were signaling with lights from the far shore.

Luong grinned and the PFs and the Marines lay down in a row and waited for a boat to cross. And waited and waited. The light kept flashing on and off, on and off, while somewhere near us a contact man with a lantern must have sat inside his house and, having seen or heard us, was not about to commit suicide by striking a light. Luong thought they might try to cross regardless, but they didn't. We waited until dawn, when the fishermen and their sons stumbled sleepy-eyed to their boats and, upon seeing us sitting in the foliage, set off with haste down-river. It was obvious the PFs weren't visiting as frequently as they had the previous year.

Garcia had snuggled in the shadows of a doorway, and when the hamlet started to stir, a fisherman opened the door and Garcia lurched sideways. Thinking Garcia was some drunk who had not made it home after a bad night, the fisherman gave him a hearty kick. Surprised and shaken to find himself sprawled in the dust, Garcia sprang up, giving his wide-eyed and dumbfounded antagonist a shove which sent him reeling back into his house. That set off the fisherman's wife, who was not about to be intimidated by some grubby American, and Garcia found himself evicted from the premises in a torrent of verbal abuse, despite his best efforts to strike back with single-syllable swearwords. That confrontation ended any hope for the ambush and we left, Luong being soundly pummeled on the way back by a pretty young miss when he kidded her about a possible pregnancy.

At the edge of the Binh Yen Noi hamlets we met Suong, who was taking his platoon into the My Hués in the hope that some Viet Cong had entered after we left. He asked if we were satisfied that the enemy were trying to come back into the village. We said yes, but we thought he could handle it. Suong growled and said he could handle it a whole lot better with even a few Marines, meaning he would like to have Garcia and Foster if there were no chance McGowan would return with a full squad—an allusion to the echelons of support he knew were guaranteed by the U.S. military if even one American was in danger. After a half hour of discussion, Suong finally and reluctantly accepted the notion that we were civilians and could not order Marines back to Binh Nghia. We said good-bye, promising to visit again.

On our return to the area in October, we learned that Foster had become a hero and a legend. The people told us first—the boatman who was taking us from district upriver to Binh Thuy and Binh Nghia, and his other passenger, an old grandmother who wanted her picture taken. Later the PFs and village officials filled in the story.

It seemed that during September enemy activity on Binh Thuy Island had picked up considerably. At night small bands would circle near the fort and fire their newly acquired AK-47 Russian automatic rifles to scare the defenders and impress the villagers. A Viet Cong with a megaphone, nicknamed "Rudy Vallee," came three times a week to exhort the PFs to desert and to curse the Marines in pidgin English. Unable to ambush Rudy, the Marines acquired a German shepherd and Rudy had not returned since. The PFs were bringing in reports of VC movements in every hamlet.

Then on a routine patrol one evening, Foster, who was walking point, had the uneasy feeling that he was being stalked. He was on a well-traveled trail hemmed by houses, and each time he paused to listen he had the prickly sensation that another person was pausing opposite him in one of the backyards. Worse still, Foster was convinced he was outclassed. The man was moving through backyards and over fences at Foster's pace and with less noise.

Foster wanted to give it up, to quit before he found out just how good the man was, to turn around and go back. But behind him there were two Americans and two PFs, and he didn't know how to tell them he was afraid without being laughed at. He was uncertain. He didn't want to go on.

So he stopped, gesturing to those behind him to keep their distance. With his safety off, his finger on the trigger, his body in a slight crouch, he stood ready to fire at the slightest sound or movement. He stood and refused to budge, and the man came looking to kill him and brushed ever so slightly against the side of a house and Foster tore loose a full magazine of tracers.

The man screamed as a searing bullet cut into him, while Foster in his fear slammed another magazine into his rifle, sending twenty more bullets spitting forth in search of the sound. Then the other patrollers joined in and the man was driven into the ground.

The man was alone. Foster picked up an AK-47 which lay beside the body and turned to leave. But the highly excited PFs would not hear of it. They insisted on carrying the body back to the marketplace at Binh Thuy. All the next day, villagers came from both Binh Thuy and Binh

Nghia to stare at the dead man in disbelief. Mr. Minh, the hamlet chief, presented Foster with a case of cold beer. The people smiled and bowed when he walked by; the children swarmed after him; and the son of his dead PF friend from Chau Tu came to the fort to share in the glory of his American foster father.

It was no ordinary VC who lay in the marketplace; it was a man whose reputation was feared throughout the district, a killer who had been the PF leader in the village but who in 1963 had gone over to the VC and had since risen to become a company commander. He had long terrorized his former PF colleagues, for he liked to hide in their houses at night to catch them alone when they came to visit their families. At first he would try to persuade them to join him, but later he came just to kill. Mr. Minh estimated that over the years the renegade had executed close to two dozen PFs. Foster was a hero.

He repeated the shooting performance a few weeks later, when he was taking a patrol along a treeline bordering some paddies swollen with rain. It was fairly open terrain and, ahead of him several meters, Foster saw a few men with weapons, chatting idly. Thinking they might be PFs out where they shouldn't have been, he whispered, "Nghia Quan? PF?" The group froze, then lit out running. Foster raised his M-16 and fired, saw a man go down, crouch back up and hobble on. A general firefight ensued, each side testing the strength and position of the other. At first Foster thought his five-man group might get the worst of it and was preparing to pull out, when the enemy fire slackened. Foster's group then decided the enemy were just trying to provide cover and time for their wounded comrade, and so pressed in. Two sides fighting for the life of a man.

When the VC flinched first and pulled out, the fight

became a search in the paddies. A PF found a weapon lying in the open, left perhaps in the hope that its souvenir value might be enough and the PFs and Marines would turn back. But they knew the man was near, and that his friends had left him. The searchers were passing by a dark mudhole filled with water when they heard a splash close at hand. The Marine at rear guard wheeled with his shotgun, firing as he turned. Alone, with a leg mangled by bullets, the man had sought refuge in the hole. But he slipped and splashed and died in the mud on a warm summer's evening.

The villagers knew that man also, and news of his death added to Foster's prestige. It seemed for the first time to the villagers of Binh Thuy that Americans could fight in a way that meant something and that their PFs were beginning to hunt the VC, instead of the other way around.

Pressure from the enemy side slackened significantly in the hamlet adjacent to the fort, but remained high in the outlying areas. The rice was high and the VC wanted the harvest. Word was passed to the fort that a band of thirty were taxing each night in Chau Tu, Foster's hamlet.

So he set out that same night to protect that hamlet, taking two Marines with him. Their trip across the paddies and through the treelines went quietly enough, but as they neared the hamlet, a series of flares silhouetted them. They hunkered down to wait for the illumination to flicker out. But it persisted, along with the dull sounds of artillery, for the Viet Cong were harassing the district headquarters, four miles to the southwest.

The Marine at point had just decided to move on despite the light when he saw a face peering at him from some nearby bushes. Just as he turned to warn the others, Foster, hearing something, stood up and said, "Nghia Quan? Nghia Quan?"

That was how Foster died, making sure he did not shoot one of his PF friends by accident. The Viet Cong who shot him ran away.

# 1969–70

It was growing dark on a cold, drizzly evening a year later when Benoit and I walked back into Binh Nghia. We had planned to spend the night with a combined unit across the river, but at five that evening Marine headquarters had called, refusing to allow two unarmed civilians to stay in a hamlet where there were Marines and PFs. A colonel in an air-conditioned office said it was too dangerous. Having been evicted, we hitchhiked part way and walked the rest into Binh Nghia, only to find PF Hill deserted.

"What do we do now?" Benoit asked.

"Find some bushes and hide until dawn?" I said.

"I think we might be a little bit too late," Benoit replied. "Look behind you."

We were standing at the foot of the hill, with open paddies on three sides, and out of the treeline on the fourth side about fifteen yards away had stepped a group of men dressed in black pajamas with a few odd bits of khaki, carrying assorted types of weapons and staring hard at us.

"Know any of them?" Benoit asked.

"No. They're not PFs. If they're Cong, I want to see you talk us out of this."

"It's simple. I'm going to tell them there's a reward on you and I'm turning you in."

Not one had raised his weapon, and as they crowded in around us, they were staring the way one does when trying to recall the name of a person he has met casually once or twice. I stood, as usual, dumb and foolish while Benoit carried on his usual rapid-fire conversation, but I was damned if I was going to ask him what our status was, and at length, when he thought he had kept me on tenterhooks long enough, he said:

"Remember last year Suong told us he couldn't be bothered with a people's self-defense force? Well, you're looking at part of them. They say Suong has over one hundred of them under arms. They remembered us from before. They knew we looked familiar. They just couldn't place us."

We found Suong together with his PF platoon near the marketplace in Binh Yen Noi Number 3. He greeted us warmly and told me he had a surprise for us: we were going to My Hué. I said, "Oh no, we're not; I know the VC are still there. He doesn't have to prove it each year we visit him." When Benoit phrased my objections in colorful Vietnamese, the PFs howled with laughter. Suong said they were going to My Hué. We could stay where we were, alone. We would be safe—probably.

So we all went to My Hué, arriving shortly before nine while lights were still on and the children were playing along the main trail and radios were blaring. Suong didn't even have a point ten yards out in front of us and Luong was carrying his rifle casually by the barrel. We came to the cluster of houses where Colucci's RD friend, Truong, had been killed almost three years earlier and Suong turned off the path.

Amid smiles of welcome we entered a medium-sized house and sat down to thimbles of whiskey. I looked at Suong to see if he had already been drinking. He caught my disapproving glare and laughed delightedly, explaining to Benoit that this was his surprise. How did I like being treated like an old grandfather in My Hué, where, when he had first met me three and a half years earlier, we had fought our way in and out, night after night?

He told me not to worry; his men were everywhere. Not the PFs. The PFs were special. They didn't handle ordinary security patrols; they were the praetorian guard, reserved for the most difficult missions. Each of Binh Nghia's seven hamlets now had an armed self-defense group of ten to twenty men. The PFs had no fort. They roamed from hamlet to hamlet at night, Suong deciding on the spur of the moment where they would go so the Viet Cong did not know where they were or what to expect. On the other hand, he usually knew when the Viet Cong were coming. One night a small group of Viet Cong had sneaked into Fort Page and blown up the empty adobe building, but Suong said that was a trivial matter, since the fort had already been abandoned for several months. He generally had advance warning of serious attacks through his intelligence net of deserters and draft dodgers. He did not report them to the district officials as long as they kept their eyes and ears open. The new police chief—Bac Si Khoi—agreed with the method. Trao had not had the time to manage the village and keep up with police matters. The village council had not thought the village needed another Thanh, so Khoi it was, although he spent as much time at the dispensary as at the village office.

But then the enemy threat had diminished. The P31st was not what it had been. American planes had caught the company in the open somewhere over in the Phu Longs and the villagers said the company was hurt terribly. Le Quan Viet, the district leader with one hand, had been captured. Suong did not know how, but he had heard that for the five days he was held at district he had refused to eat or drink and had not spoken one word. Suong had not heard about him since he was taken away from district in a helicopter.

In early November, the 95th Sapper Company, a mixed NVA/VC unit, had attacked Binh Nghia. Suong said it had been like the old days. His intelligence was so exact he knew which trail they were going to use and all his PFs and self-defense forces were clamoring for one of the select ambush sites. The PFs waited until the 95th's lead platoon was part way across a small paddy before springing the ambush. Suong claimed that the 95th didn't even try to fight back. He thought that was rather disgraceful. The PFs buried the men they killed because all were strangers to the village and had no kinfolk to care for them. Suong stored away the seven AK-47s his men captured. He said each was worth one M-79 grenade launcher from the Americal Division. The district chief had given a party at Binh Son for Suong and his men.

During the night, as PFs and self-defense troops wandered in and out of the house, Benoit and I heard from at least thirty different individuals that they had been part of the paddy ambush against the 95th. Suong had told us privately that it had been Luong, as we expected, and about five others who had done the greatest damage to the Viet Cong. But Suong also smiled tolerantly when the others boasted to us and never said a word to contradict them. The victory was shared by all.

Inevitably, the conversation drifted back to McGowan, White, Brannon, Sullivan and the others. Suong said that he would like them, those that were still alive, to see the village again.

But Suong would not have been there to act as host. In a sense, the PFs had done their job too well. By 1970 Binh Nghia was so peaceful that the new American district adviser had termed it an "R & R" (Rest and Recreation) center. He and the district chief had agreed that Suong and his well-armed PFs could better be used elsewhere. There was no need of them in Binh Nghia; the self-defense force could look after things. So the Binh Nghia PFs were transferred to the Phu Longs. They could visit their own village and families on weekends, maybe.

The village council was reorganized. With relative peace, a new splinter political party emerged and vied with the VNQDD for local control. They triumphed and Trao was thrown in jail for two months as a draft dodger. The PFs tried to defend the man who had worked so steadfastly in the dark days, and their loyalty to him was a strong reason for their transfer. Trao was released from jail on the condition that he go with the PFs. Naturally, Khoi was sent back to the PFs.

# 1971

The war has passed Binh Nghia. To be sure, there are still secret Viet Cong agents and villagers sympathetic to their cause scattered through the seven hamlets. And there is a self-defense platoon and a village government in Binh Nghia. But the savage struggle of 1966 and 1967, the months when the fight went on night after night after night, when neither side would quit or admit defeat, that period has long since gone. That was when the Marines fought there and lost nine dead—Page, Brannon, Sueter, Glasser, Fielder, Sullivan, Lummis, Fleming and Foster. The Americans are gone, the living and the dead. And the PFs who fought beside them and carried on after them—

Lam, Thanh, Suong, Luong, Khoi, Tri—they are gone.
And the leaders of the village council—Phuoc, Trao,
Buu—they are gone. And the Viet Cong who were the
guerrillas and who were in the local force companies,
they, too, are gone. All gone, some dead, some replaced
by others.

Fort Page is gone, too. The adobe building still stands,
but only as a cracked, crumbling shell. Its walls are
streaked and forlorn, like the World War II defenses
along the coastlines of the United States. Once the
weather frayed the sandbags along the trench lines, the
wind blew the sand away. Over the seasons, the rains
beat on the sides of the moat and caved them in eventually, washing away the punji stakes. The villagers took
away the wood from the village office built for old Mr.
Minh and from the dispensary built for Blunk and Khoi;
once the fort was abandoned, there were other uses for its
wood.

In the decade of the 1970s, one would have to look
twice to see where Fort Page had once stood. But if you
know the trail through the paddies, you can walk among
the weeds, cross the shallow dip which was a moat, pass
by lumps of rain-pressed earth once called breastworks
and stand on a flat place so hard packed the grass does not
grow. At the far end of the flat place, which was a courtyard, squat the crumbled remains of a building and in front
of the remains sits the stump of a flagpole. In front of the
stump, a square stone thrusts up from the hard ground just
high enough to stub your toe. A few weeks before his
death, Volentine had presented the stone to the PFs as a
memorial to their departed American friends—the living
and the dead. Screwed to the top surface of the stone in
Ozymandean solitude is a salt-crusted bronze plaque. On
it are chiseled the words:

CAP LIMA——ONE
FORT PAGE
DEDICATED IN HONOR OF PFC L. L. PAGE
KILLED IN ACTION——21 JUNE 1966
7 JUNE 1966——14 OCTOBER 1967

If it is late in the day when you stop to read the plaque, the sky behind you might be soft in a sunset of pink and purple, orange and red. Toward you from the hamlets will drift the full smells of evening: wood smoke and steamed rice, chicken broth, fish sauce and fried shrimp. The sounds, too, will wash over the fort—a baby crying, crickets calling, a farmer shouting to his neighbor, children laughing, frogs croaking, a mother screeching at her little boy who is dawdling on the back of a huge water buffalo while supper goes cold. If you linger, you will see warm yellow lights begin to wink on amid the darkening green of the treeline.

The village is intact. The village has endured.

# THE VILLAGE, 2002:
# THE KINDERGARTEN MARINES

What happened to the village after Saigon fell in 1975? Over a quarter of a century later, Charlie Benoit, who had been with me on patrol in the village, and I went back to find out. Charlie had gone on to become an old Asian hand, living in Shanghai, speaking four languages, owning property in Thailand and China, and specializing in software consulting. An all-American guard at Yale with a

Ph.D. from Harvard, Charlie looked like a former professional football player and it was a continual delight to watch the astonishment of Vietnamese when he flawlessly conversed with them.

My own career had remained in national security, where I went from the RAND Corporation to serve as Assistant to the Secretary of Defense during Saigon's last days. Later, I was appointed Assistant Secretary of Defense for International Security in the Reagan administration. I continue to write, my most recent novel being *The Pepperdogs,* published by Simon & Schuster, January 2003. See www.westwrite.com.

Charlie had made over a dozen trips to Vietnam since 1975 and invariably the secret police questioned closely those who spoke with him. He is not CIA, but his fluency is suspect to the Hanoi government. He warned me to be prepared for silence in Binh Nghia, or for denials that Americans had ever lived there. The trip, he said, might be a bust. He reminded me that in 1976 we had traveled throughout China after Mao died and, despite Charlie's fluency in Mandarin, no one on the streets would speak to us. The same might happen in Binh Nghia.

While waiting for our flight up-country, we visited Tu Do Street, Saigon's tiny version of Fifth Avenue, a strip of upscale hotels and shops unfortunately shorn of their old French colonial charm. As we walked, Charlie chatted with the cyclo drivers and street urchins, a network which warned him about the whereabouts of the secret police. Yesterday, Charlie had knocked out a pickpocket and the street people joked that he was a secret policeman. A ten-year-old girl selling last year's Christmas cards offered condolences about "that bad in New York." There were perhaps a dozen Westerners browsing along Tu Do and the beggars—the cripple, the woman with three children, the orphan boys and girls—were trying only halfheartedly. Business, they complained, was nonexistent. Few foreigners had come this year.

The same iron will which enabled the Lao Dong Party to persevere in war, regardless of cost, has prevented the communists from changing. There are stifling regulations, too many fingers in any investment pie, pervasive corruption. As a woman wanting to restore a two-hundred-year-old antiquities site for tourism put it, the local authorities "won't talk to me about a permit unless I bring cigarettes."

That afternoon we flew 400 miles north to Da Nang, a city of half a million people and perhaps ten cars. The traffic was a mix of bicycles and motor scooters. On several blocks were Internet cafés, with half a dozen old computers, all in use.

At seven I was awakened by church bells. At the spacious pink-hued church down the block, Mass had begun. The pews were packed and the faithful spilled out the doors. The attendants lining up the bikes and Hondas said the congregation had grown about ten percent a year, since the regime had somewhat loosened its restrictions on Catholic Vietnamese.

The eighty-mile drive to the village down Route 1, Vietnam's main highway, took three harrowing hours. It seemed our small van shared the two-lane, semipaved road with four cars, three thousand trucks, five thousand schoolchildren, and twenty thousand bicycles and scooters. It was a never-ending game of chicken. Will the next truck crush us, or will we run over a little girl on a bicycle? A state trooper from the United States, before having a nervous breakdown, would have issued reckless driving tickets to all drivers, period. The roadside shop signs told the barren economic tale: tire repair, electric coil rewind, ice, cigarettes, beer and soda, insect repellent chemicals, bicycle parts. The signs bore a striking resemblance to photos of rural America during the Depression of the 1930s.

After we passed the abandoned Chulai airport, I tried to get my bearings. The village lay to the east, along a river so swollen by winter monsoons that the paddies were a vast lake, submerging any landmarks. There were no roads to the village, so Charlie and I walked in at a brisk pace on the mud trail, anxious to put distance from the highway before the secret police got on to us and followed us. We took one trail after another, cutting back and forth as the layout of the hamlets came back to me. The smells were the same, the pervasive wood smoke, the pungent benjo ditches, the heavy scents of jungle decay. The palm and banana trees overlaying the trails deflected the sheets of rain which came and went.

After 1975, the village name of Binh Nghia—"Just Cause"—was changed to Binh Chuc— "Just Peace." The meaning is about the same, but the change showed who was in charge. Many of the thatched huts had been replaced by cinder blocks held in place by a thin layer of cement, with tile roofs. Since the war, many more dwellings had been erected, jammed side by side, separated by thin hedges, each with a small courtyard and a single strand of electric wire running along a set of haphazard poles. We shared the mud trail with water buff spooked by our smell, scraggly cows, and people, people, people.

The schoolchildren swirled around us, exclaiming and following. In the swollen paddies, pant legs rolled up and barefoot in the muck, the farmers were stooped over, planting seedlings underwater. A man stood on a dike throwing fistfuls of manure into a paddy. In each small paddy, marked off by dikes of brilliant green, there was a peasant farmer hunched over. As we passed, each would straighten up, stare for a moment, then stoop and return to the eternal business of farming.

I had forgotten the village was so large, surrounded by a vast array of sand dunes, impossible to irrigate. The squad's area of operations had been five square miles. Walking along, looking at all the people, all the houses, all the trails and alleys and ambush sites, all the cover and concealment, I wondered if our military today would risk plunking down one squad among thousands of Vietnamese and issuing a simple order: Control this area, day and night. Use your rifles but no artillery or air power. It seemed unlikely; today's infantry uses lasers to guide bombs onto targets a thousand meters away.

Charlie stopped an old man to inquire.

"Anh (Older Brother), were there American soldiers here, many years before Liberation?"

"Yes, a few Marines were here. They paid hard sacrifice. They lived right there." He pointed to a small yellow building with a tile roof grown brown with age and a commanding view of the paddies. It stood a few feet taller than the land around it and the location seemed familiar.

A woman yelled from the paddy, "What do they want?"

"They're from the kindergarten," he shouted back.

The woman yelled to the next paddy, and as we walked up the trail, we heard the shouts echoing from paddy to paddy. In the grass courtyard in front of the small kindergarten, I found the foundation stones outlining where the fort had once stood. But the stone memorial to the Marines, set in the ground thirty-three years ago, was gone.

An old farmer stepped forward from the crowd.

"We welcome you back," he said in Vietnamese, as the crowd grinned and called to neighbors. Soon we were sur-

rounded by smiling farmers, each with a comment or
query. I had brought pictures from *The Village* and they
were passed from hand to hand. The English came creak-
ily, like a gate not opened for thirty years.

"You know Mister Bill? . . . Marines number one . . .
Where Larry? . . . You know Monty? . . . Bob, he throw
bomb. VC no get him. . . . Where Sergeant Mac? . . . You
stay my house tonight? . . . You old now, *dai uy.*"

The *dai uy*—the captain—had returned as the Ancient
Mariner. Most in the crowd had been born after I had left.
Whatever they had heard about the Marines had been
passed down. They were all smiling.

"If the ghosts of those little guys in khaki and pith helmets, covered with leeches after a two-month trip down
from Hanoi, are looking down," Charlie said, "you can bet
they're complaining about this reception."

We avoided asking questions which would jeopardize
anyone, knowing that Party cadre were among the crowd.
No one was hostile or stone-faced, and the grumbles
Charlie heard were directed at those hogging the limelight
and not giving others a chance to talk. People tugged at
our sleeves, inviting us to their homes. Some village history was gradually filled in.

The village chief, Trao, had drowned in 1972 while
fishing in a storm. The village medic and later the police
chief, Bac Si Khoi, had moved away when his wife died in
the early '70s. He was in failing health and not expected to
live much longer. Joe, the ten-year-old orphan who lived
with the Marines, had been killed fleeing in a boat when
Da Nang fell in 1975. Of the teenage girls who flirted with
the Marines, Missy Tinh had married and moved to Quang
Ngai City. Missy Top lived in a province farther to the
south.

The military leader in the village had been Suong. In

1974, he was on patrol in My Hué hamlet when he tripped a wire attached to a grenade. What Suong liked most about the Marines was their immediate medevacs. There were no Marines to help when he died.

Regular military units—American, Viet Cong, or North Vietnamese—have periods of rest and stand-downs between engagements. For Suong as a village militiaman, there was no rotation, no surcease. Suong completed roughly two thousand patrols. An American soldier with one hundred patrols would be highly respected among his peers. Suong had engaged in the close-in combat of the hamlets for twelve years. In comparison, over a thirty-year career, an American soldier may be in a "combat environment"—near enough to hear shooting—for two or three years. At no time in our history has an American soldier been asked to endure twelve years on the line.

What a tale Suong could have told. The closest parallels are our Indian wars and our Mountain Men of the Old West. Suong died because the war had gone on too long. No man, no matter how skilled and experienced, can survive continuous combat. Sooner or later, the bell will toll.

From the fort we moved down the trail to the central market. We passed five old (my age, about sixty) women who rushed to the bramble fence. We stopped and they giggled and grasped Charlie by his shoulders and asked if he needed a Vietnamese wife. To include me, they reverted to the pidgin English of their youth.

"Me good girl. No go boom-boom. . . . Marine *dai uy,* you learn how talk, we find you good wife. . . . You stay long time this time?"

Here they were, grandmothers, their grandchildren gawking as they flirted shamelessly, taken back to their youth when the young Marines walked through the market every day, stopping to talk and joke. They looked at my pictures, trying to sort out the women and the Marines from their teens. Led by a handsome older woman in orange-print pajamas, they clustered together, puzzling as to which of them is smiling shyly at Sergeant White all those years ago. A teenage boy peeked over their shoulders and was soundly smacked on the ear. These weren't his memories.

Before returning the next day, we made a trip to My Lai, four miles to the east, where American soldiers had massacred over one hundred villagers. A place of careful gardens, pitiful statues, and gruesome pictures, the memorial grounds felt like a cemetery. Throughout Vietnam there were instances of Americans killing in the hamlets, driven by anger or fear, terrified and ignorant, believing every villager was a Viet Cong.

"That didn't happen in Binh Nghia," Charlie said. "The Marines couldn't destroy their own village. What would they say? Sorry, we forgot we live here?"

After leaving My Lai, we had lunch in Binh Nghia with a landowner dispossessed in 1975 of thirty of his thirty-one hectares. His father had been the village chief, assassinated in 1962. Dozens of his extended family clustered around as we sat down to rice, green sprouts, pork, tea, and bootleg rice wine, all grown on his half acre. The family lived in four bare rooms with a dirt floor; a fluorescent bulb—the single change since 1966—dangled from a tattered electric wire we carefully avoided.

He had done two years' "service" after 1975. His friend the police chief had been "sent away" for seven years. Now they were back in the village and we noticed the schoolchildren crossed their arms quickly as they walked by him, a sign of respect for an elder with stature. When he said that he hoped to run for village chief, his wife shook her head, suggesting she had heard that dream before.

After lunch, he walked ahead of us down the village trails, joking that the Americans had taken him prisoner. One villager laughed and shouted in English that "Victor Charlie's (Marine radio slang for Viet Cong) in charge here now. Where you go?"

"I'm taking them to Quat's and Suong's," he replied, referring to the Communist Party chief and to the widow of the man who fought so fiercely against the Party. That sentence summed up the complex skein of village politics. Marines used to say, "If the VC were on our side, we'd wrap this war up in a week." Yet the same basic, tough soldier was on both sides. Communism wasn't a better way of life or a better ideology. Rather, in Vietnam it proved to be a better military system, more capable of insisting upon sacrifice without end.

The Party chief, like everyone else, lived in a small house; the old term was "hootch." Handsome, with a trim mustache, he had been ten when the Marines were at the fort. At first he was formal, using the salutation "ngai" (exellency), meant to establish distance. Gradually, he warmed up, switching to "anh" (older brother), and explaining the village had grown from 6,000 when we were there to 12,000. Fishing had somewhat expanded, but the land hadn't. Every child went to school, but after that, what? No one had a solution. The village was on its own. The central government had no money to send. Prospects for employment outside the village were grim.

His family listened in the background. Soon the women tired of politics and infrastructure development.

"You know Ppbill?" asked the older sister. She was the older woman in the orange-print pajamas who had flirted with us near the market.

"Phil," corrected the Party chief. "Pph."

His sister tried to say Phil and made a face. After all,

which of them had really known Phil? Corporal Phillip
Brannon had died in the village in 1966. Her brother had
been ten, playing soccer behind the fort; she had been
eighteen. It wasn't much of a mystery which one had
talked to Bill/Phil.

The Party chief nodded at several other names and left
for a meeting. We stopped by Mrs. Suong's home, which
showed obvious signs of disrepair. She was sitting in the
courtyard peeling strips of bark which are pounded into a
paste to add color and preservative to the cement exterior
of the huts, or hootches. We said we admired her husband
and offered a solatium, modest by our standards but perhaps a bit large in the village. It seemed to overwhelm her,
and as we walked off, she stood smiling while a dozen
crones gathered around her, jabbering away.

At the fort, there had been a small cement marker with
a bronze plaque in remembrance of the Marines. In 1975,
when the guerrillas came down from the mountains, they
hauled the marker a few hundred meters away to the courtyard of a militia soldier. Why they didn't dump it in a
paddy or break it into pieces was not explained. The
plaque was beaten into a trowel. The villagers wanted to
give it to us, but its owner had thrown it away years ago.

A stone's throw north of the marker was the village
shrine, a simple cement room, dyed yellow, with four pil-
lars and an open front facing the paddies. Inside, surrounded by joss sticks, was a bright wooden altar honoring
the spirits of the village. Once a year, the villagers gather
to pray for good crops and no floods. Behind the building
is a cement well bearing a Vietnamese inscription to the
Marines who built the well and the shrine in 1967.

A crowd led us to the marker, which was resting
between two palm trees, overlooking an expanse of rice
paddy as green as the world's finest golf course. It was a

fitting spot for Sergeant Sullivan, Corporal Brannon, and all the others who fell there. We looked out over the paddies as farmers half a world away from the United States talked about Americans dead thirty-five years.

A few miles distant, there is the memorial to the Vietnamese dead at My Lai. These two memorials symbolize the contradictory faces of America in that tragic war, the one fearful in polished marble, the other resolute in rough cement.

W. H. Auden once wrote, "Teach the free man to praise." For that freedom, America has generously praised the generation of World War II. But of their Vietnam progeny, of those who returned to jeers rather than parades, the press has projected the face filled with fear, unworthy of praise. It is left to others in unlikely places to trace callused hands over rough cement and to remember the faces which were stalwart.

The village remembers.

SIMON & SCHUSTER
PROUDLY PRESENTS

# THE PEPPERDOGS

## BING WEST

Now available in hardcover
from Simon & Schuster

Turn the page for a preview of
*The Pepperdogs*. . . .

> *If one falls down, the others will lift him up.*
> —Ecclesiastes 4:10

# I

To the half-drunken Serb soldiers in the tan Toyota pickup, the farm looked inviting. Its orange slate roof, untouched by mortar blasts, glistened in the thin sunlight. No shells had burst against its whitewashed walls and most windowpanes were intact, the few broken ones sealed neatly with white tape. A stocky woman in a blue mantilla was draping bright quilts over a rope strung to a nearby tree, taking advantage of the fickle winter sun to air out some bedding. The rich farm was war's joke, like a tornado that spares a single mobile home.

Holding their rifles carelessly, four soldiers hopped from the pickup, laughing back and forth like teenagers going to a party. Their leader had a full black beard and wore a shaggy black-bear coat with torn, floppy sleeves. His girth was so wide it looked like the bear was still inside. He didn't try the handle on the front door. Instead, he raised back his foot and kicked, splintering the frame. Unhurried, he plodded up the stairs, trailed by his men.

The woman had scurried inside when the pickup veered off the main road, but she found no place to hide. When they had finished with her, she lurched out the kitchen door, stumbling through the mud toward the privy, a stone's throw to the southeast, where the wind seldom blew the stench toward the house. Her skull had fractured at its base when they slammed her on the boards and threw her skirt over her head. The blood streaming from her nostrils was vivid red and darker rivulets seeped from her ears. She walked dizzily, lurching while everything whirled around and around her. Then she vomited and crumbled gracefully, settling down, folding her parts within herself.

The soldiers paid no heed to the dying woman. They had wiped themselves, passing around a grayish towel, stiff as cardboard. Now they were wrestling onto the back of the pickup a Blutner piano, with two broken ivories and several snapped strings. The woman knew several melodies which avoided the broken keys, including a little Liszt, but the men hadn't asked her to play.

Sergeant Saco Iliac, head bodyguard to the commanding general of the Tigriva Division, picked up one end of the piano, smirking as his men struggled with the other end. He was thinking how he would arrive before the general's luncheon. The general would set the piano in the middle of the great room and pound Saco on the back of his thick fur coat.

Sometimes Saco lumbered like a bear to remind his men how he had won the coat. After they took Srebenica, they disposed of most of the *hadjuks* the first night and blood caked their uniforms. No longer stupified by drink, their heads splitting, the soldiers were anxious to get back home and wash up. Gathered in the barn, there were fewer than a hundred to go, but no one wanted to go back inside.

That was when the adjutant thought of the contest. Three officers held watches and five finalists entered the barn where the last Muslims milled around like cattle. A Croat, who had been a wrestler before the war, did two more males than Saco. But so what? The small ones Saco went after wriggled like eels. His trick was to grab the ankles and swing their heads against the roof poles. *Whack!* and it was done. One girl bit his thumb, costing him several seconds. Still, he won the coat in an honest contest. The Croat did fifteen, while he, Saco, snapped eighteen necks to win the coat.

Saco sat next to the driver in the Toyota. The legs of the piano hung over the sides of the pickup and the soldiers sat at odd angles, their rifles swinging wildly as the truck bounced down the hill toward the paved road at the far end of the pasture. The tarp thrown over the piano flapped and billowed, as though waving at the American Cobra gunships buzzing over the main road.

The Toyota was the muscle kind advertised in glossy car magazines, with high axles and four rear wheels, ideal for heavy farm work or driving around a small town with the radio blasting. The left front tire soon caught in a pothole. They were five minutes in front of the general's convoy; it wouldn't do to arrive late at the Castle. Four sets of shoulders set to rocking the overloaded pickup back and forth to push it loose.

Captain Tyler Cosgrove, U.S. Marine Corps Reserve—very reserved, he would laugh—handled the motorcycle with easy skill. It was his turn to be scout and Sergeant Neff and the two corporals a quarter mile behind in the humvee would have to wait their turn. This was the first morning in a week without rain or sleet but—*Hey! I didn't make out the duty roster.* Cosgrove had that medium build and sharply handsome, slightly vulnerable, face seen in advertisements for Prada and other upscale stores. Upbeat by nature, his spirits lifted to be on a fast bike on a Sunday morning. He tried not to think of his mother in the hospital. He would see her soon enough, his tour eight hours from ending. He would be at the airport by five. He swung the bike in short half-loops, enjoying the pull of gravity as his body leaned first one way and then the other.

One final hour of playing Marine before coming to grips with his mother's mortality.

He had studied the overhead photos, the radio intercepts, the reports from locals. The route was secure. This close to Christmas, Cosgrove considered Fifth Avenue more dangerous. Wall Street commandos, flush with bonus money and guilt about missing their kids' soccer matches, would trample you on their way to FAO Schwarz. Here in Kosovo, NATO soldiers had pulled guard duty year after year. Nothing ever happened. That's why reserve units like Cosgrove's were sent over for three-month stints. The shooting war was in Afghanistan. Nobody worried about the reserves in the Balkans, an afterthought among the Pentagon planners.

So what if the confab with the Serb general was overprotected? For Cosgrove, riding a motorcycle was better than sitting around waiting for the evening flight to the States. This was the last U.S. sweep and he was nearing his turnaround point, with the Serb convoy only a few miles to the north.

He glanced casually at the farm to his left . . . smoke from a farm . . . that Toyota?

"Arrow Five, this is Six," he spoke into his head mike. "I have eyes on one pickup with a piano in back. It's Tesch on tour, the cows twitching their tails to the beat."

"Six, this is Five. Can you get us tickets?"

"SRO. First pasture around the bend. I'll save you a space near the stage."

"Roger. Three mikes behind you."

The bike was fast. One moment, an open road. And now the bike was coming right at the Serbs in the truck. They barely had time to grab their weapons before the American stopped in front of them. He pushed his goggles back and spoke, like a fighter pilot, into the voice mike projecting from his helmet.

"Arrow, this is definitely weird," Cosgrove said.

"Hey!" Saco smiled. "Is nothing. We help move."

Cosgrove was sitting back, his hands on the bike's crossbars, the 9mm pistol secured in his shoulder holster. Saco moved closer, eyes on the pistol. Cosgrove looked past him at the house, his gaze wandering until it came to rest on the crumbled woman. He stiffened abruptly and reached for the pistol.

Saco didn't think. He rushed forward, knocking Cosgrove from the bike. He hit him once, then again, in the neck, on the side of the helmet, on the cheek. The great blows stunned Cosgrove and he offered no resistance. Saco lifted the Marine's head, helmet and all, and slammed him against the ground. Cosgrove saw dazzling light, then black.

"Quick!" yelled Saco. "Throw him in back. And the bike. Move!"

The Marine hummer had started into the turn and taken the first path, twisting and bouncing toward the farm two pastures above. It took several minutes to reach the front step, where a farmer and his wife and a few children greeted them curiously. It was a few more minutes before Sergeant Neff realized he had turned off at the wrong farm. With slightly growing anxiety, he turned the vehicle around, bounced and lurched back to the highway and looked for the next cutoff. He soon found it and once again bobbed across rocks worn smooth by decades of wagon wheels.

When the hummer came around the curved face of the next tilled field, Neff saw the piano tilted forward in the rutted track, kneeling in cow dung as though awaiting execution, its keyboard legs broken and splintered. Another two minutes passed before the frustrated sergeant could bring himself to report that Captain Cosgrove was missing—plain missing, nowhere to be seen, no bike either, and farther upslope there was a dead woman and a farm on fire.

By then Saco's pickup was two kilometers south down the main road, with the Serb convoy coming into sight behind it.

MITROVICA VALLEY, KOSOVO
NOON, SUNDAY

Serbian Lieutenant General Ilian Kostica gave no particular heed to the tan Toyota pickup as it recklessly cut in front of his lead escort vehicle. That was Saco showing off. Childish. The general's mind was on the meeting ahead, determined to impress the American, who also played childish games, such as arriving early for negotiations. *Only today, Mr. Ambassador,* Kostica thought, *I am the early one.*

The small castle was the town's strong sentinel, blocking entrance to the valley from the north. For centuries, it had shielded the farmers from whatever raiding bands made their way south along the only road, which twisted for dozens of kilometers among the hillocks, narrow ravines, and steep slopes of the mountain ranges on either side. Built in the seventeenth century, the castle was part fortress, part manor. Typical of the old Middle Europe style, it closely abutted the road, its massive stone facade indifferent to the occasional sideswipes of the tractors of drunken farmers.

Tanks were another matter. When Kostica's armor— Soviet junk from World War II shoddily reconditioned in the factory which manufactured the tinny Yugo auto—first clattered toward the town, the castle looked like a massive bunker, its minarets and cut-glass windows only softening the thickness of stone walls which had withstood sieges a half-dozen times in the previous six hundred years. Kostica considered smashing it. Why take a chance?

The trembling proprietor persuaded him otherwise, running into the road in his hostler clothes, aware the tanks were taking aim, shaking but determined, offering the general an aperitif, a petit déjeuner for his staff. The meal was excellent and Kostica had returned often. A good location for negotiations, too, right in the middle of the neutral zone between Kosovo and Serbia.

When Kostica pulled up, the security details of the two sides had already dismounted, the Americans robotlike in their oversize armored vests and helmets. He had told his guards to wear three sweaters under their jackets and not to shave for four days, so they, too, looked bulky and menacing. Saco had parked the Toyota around a corner. The other bodyguards grinned and nodded to him, and stepped aside to let him approach the general.

"I had a piano for you," he said, "only an American came along, so I took him instead."

It had to be a stupid joke. The general heard the words and his body reacted before his brain. For a moment, he thought he was suffering a stroke. His heart stopped for a beat. He could feel his blood pressure drop to his toes, as if falling suddenly in an elevator. For a few seconds he said nothing, aware of those around him.

Images were clear in his mind—a cannibal offering to share his meal, a dog mouthing a putrid fox and expecting to be patted. And this—this dancing bear shitting in the village square and expecting a pail of berries. General Kostica waited a moment, half-convinced Saco would raise his paws in the air and pant with his tongue hanging out, waiting to be scratched on his swollen stomach.

"Where is this American?"

"Right here." Saco grinned. "In the back of the Toyota. He's out. I hit him good."

Good? Good? The general pictured American helicopters

taking off, tanks blocking road crossings, satellite cameras zooming in—all because of this *papak,* this idiot.

"Get him out of here, now. He's not to know you're part of this command. Get across the border and release him. Go away. Get out."

The general turned away. He had weathered the Tito years, outlasted that lunatic Milosevic, outfoxed the Americans at Dayton. The first of his family to have a villa along the Amalfi, an apartment in Prague. He wasn't going to be brought down by this brute's stupidity. Was he responsible for the bull in heat, for the weather in December? This wasn't his business.

THE WATERGATE CONDOMINIUMS, WASHINGTON, D.C.

The secure phone to the White House rang with a discreet purr, a courtesy to the mates of high level officials who relished being summoned at any hour. Political power was more a narcotic than an aphrodisiac. The White House Chief of Staff, a large, balding man, glanced at the Caller I.D. and lifted the receiver, while his wife fluffed her pillow and continued to slumber.

"Plane crash or terrorists?" He prided himself on his crisp manner, his voice abrupt even at seven on a Sunday morning.

"Good morning to you too," the Secretary of Defense said. "Don't be so grumpy."

"OK, so how many did we lose?"

"Less serious, a Marine missing in Kosovo. May be kidnapped."

"We still have people there? And that's it—one missing?"

"Want me to add Armageddon?" the SecDef said. "I'm called when this stuff happens, and I call the White House. Now that you're awake, you can go to church. My good deed, like spotting you a couple of points."

"Don't let one lucky squash game go to your head," the Chief of Staff said. "OK, at least it's not a reporter or a spook or something with a press angle. I'll tell the President after he's up. When he was governor, I didn't wake him every time a cop had a bad day and I'm not going to start unloading small stuff now. What's the next step?"

"We're searching. We don't know who has him."

"Damn, this is bad timing. We have to keep the decks clear for the health bill."

"Right, it's an HMO plot to shift votes," the SecDef said.

"All I'm saying is we have to stick to our game plan. It took a year to get back on track after the Twin Towers," the Chief of Staff said. "Every military incident can't end up at the Oval Office. We've agreed the domestic agenda is the focus for the next Congress. You'll keep this across the river?"

"It'll be managed from Brussels or Kosovo."

"Good, the farther away, the better. It's a distraction," the Chief of Staff said, "and we can't do anything to help from here."

25TH MARINE REGIMENT, MITROVICA VALLEY
NOON, 21 DECEMBER

The security patrols for the meeting were to the north, inside the two-kilometer Red Zone marking the Kosovo-Serb border. To the south, the highway followed the river toward the open valley and the railhead at Pristina. There was a downward pitch to the road, as it paralleled the river rushing through ravines and gullies carved out of the limestone hills by centuries of spring snow thaws and heavy fall rains. Returning to the brigade compound the road was deceptively steep, and most trucks shifted into a lower gear. So did the three Marines running uphill with rifles slung over their right shoulders. They ran along the shoulder of the road, taking short, choppy strides at a fast shuffle, faces down, concentrating on a steady, grinding pace, no wasted motion, their boots barely clearing the surface of the thin snow.

They wore soft covers, not the German-style helmets adapted by the Americans, and none had on the flak jackets required of all U.S. troops outside the base. The three ran as if connected by a giant elastic band, sometimes stretching apart, then snapping back into a tight triangle. Each had an ALICE pack on his back, plus a large canvas water sack with a long, strawlike tube so he could drink as he ran. They were running up the grade, not jogging, the strain showing on their faces and in their stiff, quick stutter-steps.

They had left the base after full light, not wanting to be hit in the early-morning gloom by some bleary-eyed truck driver hauling in CDs or Gucci knockoffs or BMW parts from some chop shop in Albania. NATO forbade training in the mountains—it was too politically dangerous to train like soldiers— so the recon team had to stay on the main highway to Pristina, racing down out of the foothills to a turnaround point at twenty kilometers, then facing the grind back to the base, uphill the last ten kilometers. A full twenty-six-mile marathon carrying thirty-pound packs, four hours the target time. Not likely they could achieve that, but hey, what else to do on a Sunday?

For three hours the captain—the twin black cloth bars prominent on the lapels of his camouflage jacket—had been running with the single-minded lope of the Alpha wolf, sometimes allowing one of the other two to slip into the lead for a mile or so. As long as the lead shifted back and forth, all three stayed energized, a pack confident that together they could not be stopped.

Lang forced the pace, even when he wasn't in the lead,

pushing so that the pain in his lungs blocked out his thoughts, shut out the world. He'd first learned to do that in boarding school at thirteen, when he would sneak into the gym after study hours and lift weights until he couldn't lift his arms, then press his face against the cold metal of his locker and cry.

How does the son of the captain of an oil tanker, with a divorced mother who never writes, fit into a New England boarding school? Work was Lang's escape. A few classmates had snickered about his fanaticism. That subsided when, at fourteen, Lang was named starting linebacker and Cos decided to be his roommate. Mrs. Cosgrove swept him into her orbit as another son, and between sports, studies, and school breaks spent with the Cosgroves, Lang learned how to smother his loneliness. Even then, Lang punished his body to distract his mind. And now he didn't want to think.

"Six miles to go," Lang said, glancing at the GPS receiver held outside his breast pocket by a strip of Velcro. "Eight mikes for the last split."

The other two said nothing, conserving oxygen. Eight minutes for a mile was excellent this late in the run, but could they hold that pace for six more miles?

Lang glanced at the sergeant clipping along feverishly at his side. Sergeant Herbert Caulder was a head shorter than Lang and looked a bit cartoonish, with a face too small for a neck and shoulders absurdly thick from too many workouts with heavy weights. He had the coiled energy of a downed power line. For Caulder, patience was torment. In the sniper championships at Lejeune, in half the allotted time, he put ten rounds into the black from the thousand-meter line, capturing first place and promotion below zone to sergeant E-5. A most unlikely sniper, he always wanted to get on with it, whatever it was. Now he was pumping his legs furiously, trying to sprint past the others, get out in front, gain the lead, get inside Lang's mind, and slow down the pace.

The upgrade worked against his strategy. He couldn't suck enough oxygen to open a lead. Each time he struggled ahead, Lang's long legs would pull him even. It wasn't fair. God should give everyone the same size legs. His pulse was at max. After the third fruitless sprint, Caulder eased off, gasping. *I'm a sniper,* he thought, *not an antelope.*

"I have a life after this death," Caulder said, his stride shortening, "I'm reining it in."

His face was pasty gray, slick with sweat. Lang slowed, trotting beside Caulder for several seconds, watching him. The third Marine did likewise. He was as tall as Lang and, like Caulder, had the three black chevrons of a sergeant on his lapels. He reached out and pulled Caulder to a halt.

"That's it. You're done," he said. "Two pitchers last night, dummy. Drinking's not your thing."

Caulder didn't reply. He leaned over and vomited as his companions jumped back.

"That's good. Solid test. I hope the monitors caught that," the other sergeant said. "You should have seen him at Tun Tavern last night, sir. Standing on his head with a shot glass in his teeth, ass in the air. The troops were barking. The colonel was laughing. Totally embarrassing."

Caulder breathed deeply and stood erect. "Don't listen to him, sir. Last night was a glorious moment. We're the dogs. No one can run with the big dogs."

"Drinking upside down?" Lang said.

"My old man owned a bar," Caulder said. "Learned that trick when I was ten. Some Saturday nights I'd get twenty bucks in quarter tips."

"Now you've learned not to drink and run," Lang said. "Sure you're old enough to drink?"

He flagged down a passing hummer, gesturing as though hailing a cab in New York City. After eleven weeks in Kosovo, everyone in the regiment knew all the officers. The humvee driver agreed to take Caulder back to the base.

Lang and the other sergeant resumed the run, matching each other stride for stride, agreeing to deduct a minute from their elapsed time because they had been so solicitous of Caulder.

"Caulder's crazy enough to take off after us, sir," the sergeant said. "He doesn't know he's nuts."

"Right," Lang said. "Let's pick it up, Blade. That way Caulder can't catch up and totally dehydrate."

In New York City, the reserves trained on the Combat Decision Range—a computer program which played combat missions. Sergeant Paul Enders made the right decisions so fast that throughout the regiment, he was called Blade. His hard body and relaxed manner—and family connections—had earned him an expanding clientele as a personal trainer to New Yorkers rich enough to be encouraged to sweat. Five hours of aerobics and weights a day gave Blade an advantage over the other recon reservists. And that's what he lived for—the weekend missions, the four hundred mile adventure races, the team against the elements.

His father the banker was forever urging him to stop wasting a first-class mind, chiding that five years ago he had wanted to be a ski instructor and now it was this "Marine Corps business"—another passing fad. Blade knew he was the classic spoiled only-child from East Side wealth, everything coming too easily. Except this. Making the team hadn't been easy. Still, this wouldn't last. Doc Evans said the experiment would be over after the deployment. If the team broke up, maybe he'd apply in January—Williams, Columbia, possibly Lewis & Clark, the flower-child college. He smiled, thinking of his dad's face going red. But now he had a race to run.

Even for Blade, the pace was harsh and he looked sideways at Lang, trying to read his expression. The captain was a big man, larger than Blade, with a body shaped by decades of weights, runs, and solitary weekends. His face was long, with the marathoner's anemic lack of flesh, cheekbones pulled taut like a bird of prey. His tight haircut exposed the back of his head, flat as the bottom of an iron, a gift from a mother who never picked him up or shifted him in his crib.

Around another bend they went, giving each other room, neither hogging the spots where the footing was firmer. Blade was determined not to let Lang gain a step. If Blade fell back, Lang would pick up the pace, sap his confidence, break his will to win.

Worked the other way too. Hell, the skipper was an old man, over thirty, and ten pounds heavier. That Lang won at long distance, as Blade saw it, was due to mental harassment. Lang distracted you, made some weird comment about a hot new actress or the Jets, took your head out of the game. Only not today. Sooner or later, he could beat Lang, he was sure of it.

Blade knew he couldn't think too much about Lang, who had been acting strange all morning. He had to run his own race, force the captain to worry about him, not the other way around. He wondered when Lang would try to unnerve him. Oh-oh, he was doing it to himself, letting his mind drift. Concentrate.

"Let's do seven thirties," Lang said.

"Let's not," Blade said. They were training, for God's sake, not trying to break their bodies. Seven and a half minutes for a mile, with a pack on? After twenty miles? Forget it.

His lungs felt like a blast furnace. "We can't hold that pace. It'll take us a week to bounce back."

He looked at Lang. Lang sped up without replying or turning his head. *He's in his own world,* Blade thought, *I don't exist.* He looked back to where the hummer was trailing them, three hundred meters behind. Caulder, plodding next to the vehicle, fluttered his hand, palm down, signaling Blade to fall back. Blade shook his head no.

Lang unslung his heavy rifle and held it at port arms, left hand under the barrels, right hand over the stock. It was an experimental design, ugly, with too much weight in the barrels. *This is it,* Blade thought, *Lang's latest psyche trick.* Blade reached for the sling of his M16A3, with its bulky telescopic sight, and imitated Lang—left hand under the barrel, right hand over the black stock aft of the trigger housing. Now they were even.

Lang didn't challenge Blade to exhaust himself, just lengthened his own stride, looked at the dull gray rock slabs bordering the road, and set off to punish his body. Wherever his mind was, it wasn't on the road.

"Caulder's on the road, skipper," Blade said. "I'm dropping back with him. I can't hold this. You got it today, but you're going to be whipped for a week."

Lang nodded, without breaking stride or looking to the side, in his own world. The run was a tunnel and the light at the end was the base gate. Four miles. For thirty more minutes of fire in the lungs, he could run away from what was hurting him.

Blade dropped to a slow jog, letting Caulder catch up. They were professionals out for a workout. They could go the distance when they had to, and they knew when to back off.

Lang hit the main gate in under four hours and slowed to a jog, then a walk, circling near the guard gate, waiting for the others. The base looked like a mini high-rise complex set inside a maximum security prison, with its perimeter of guard towers, berms, and chain-link fences topped with curled rolls of razor barbed wire.

"Did you do it?" Blade asked, when he trotted up several minutes later.

"Yes." There was no enthusiasm in Lang's voice. The other two wanted to tell him they were impressed, but the captain held himself at a distance.

"Doc will want your time," Blade said, looking at his watch. "I'll send it to her."

"Three fifty-seven," Lang said, sounding flat. "See you in the mess hall."

Lang walked the few blocks to his brick and mortar BOQ room, opened the portable fridge, and guzzled down a quart of Gatorade. There were two narrow beds in the room, one with a footlocker shoved at the end for Lang to rest his heels, and two scratched metal bureaus with too many books and pictures piled on top. One was a black-and-white photo of a striking woman in her midfifties, with long hair, high cheekbones, a bright smile, and light eyes which shone with warmth and intelligence, leopard eyes. A gentle leopard.

Lang looked at the photo, at a stuffed duffel bag lying askew on the bed next to his, at the whitewashed cinderblock walls, and back at the photo. For a moment his shoulders slumped. He didn't know why it was hitting him so hard. Seventeen years, that's why. He'd been going to the Cosgrove home for seventeen years. So maybe he should go home now with Cos. And leave the team behind? That was bright. Cos would keep him informed. She'd already fought it for a year; he'd see her next month. He didn't want to think about it.

He stripped off his sopping clothes, walked into the tiny

bathroom and vomited. He felt his insides rush, voided himself, flushed, left the bathroom for a second bottle of Gatorade, returned and vomited a second time. Too weak to stand, he lay facedown on the cold tiles, weight on his chest and forehead, his overheated body glad for the cold.

When his body had cooled down, he showered, gulped a third quart of Gatorade, and cleaned his ugly rifle, with its two barrels, twin magazine holders, and heavy optical sight. Then he walked slowly to the mess hall.

It was after eleven and the cavernous room, with its shatterproof glass windows and tables bolted to the floor, was nearly empty. The three of them sat at a long table, a dozen glasses with different liquids spread out, trays heaped with sausages and eggs. Caulder had bounced back and was wolfing down the eggs. Blade and Lang were too exhausted to eat much.

"Staff Sergeant Roberts sleeping in again?" Lang asked. "Second Sunday in a row."

The Sunday runs were optional. Still, the absence of a team member was unusual.

"Maybe he sensed you were going to go wild, sir," Blade said.

The excuse was flat but Lang didn't pursue it. They were enlisted and he was the commanding officer, but that wasn't why they were holding back. You couldn't choose your parents or where you lived. And if you didn't go to college, forget about becoming an officer. But who chose to become a Marine, who went recon, who *liked* going thirty hours with no sleep on two canteens to reach a checkpoint eighty miles away while the wind cut like a whip—who became one of the dogs—that you decided for yourself.

They were a team. If the staff sergeant was off somewhere, that was like your older brother not showing up for dinner.

When your father asked where he was, who'd ever answer that question?

Caulder changed the subject.

"Me and Blade are hitting the souk, sir. Wrap up our Christmas shopping," Caulder said. "You and Captain Cosgrove want to come along?"

"Meaning will our Intelligence Officer get a hummer for you?"

"That would help."

"Cosgrove's on security patrol," Lang said. "Then he's leaving on tonight's flight to Dover. His mother's been readmitted. So the souk's out."

The sergeants said nothing for a moment. The team, together for two years, had talked with Mrs. Cosgrove a dozen times, at parties, marathons, training exercises. They considered her good people, always interested in what they were doing. She never said it, but they sensed she gave them high marks. Especially nice from a professor, finely dressed, with a striking face and a direct gaze. She stared into their eyes when she asked questions in a clipped accent which made each word stand up straight. She really wanted to hear their answers, and as each man replied, he stood a little taller, like her words, his muscles swelling a bit under his trim uniform.

"Thought she was in remission," Blade said.

"Happened out of the blue," Lang said.

"We just sent her our pic," Caulder said, pursing his lips.

Mrs. Cosgrove had always asked about his latest score on the range and congratulated him on concentrating so single-mindedly. Not many people appreciated the thousands of hours which went into that split second of squeezing the trigger. He thought of her wasting away and his features puckered up like a little boy's, almost comical against the bulk of his shoulders.

"You going home too, sir?" Blade asked. "Knowing her and all."

"I'm not family."

"You almost are. The regs allow it."

"Captain Cosgrove will keep me up to speed."

"Well, you'll catch up with her after Christmas," Caulder said.

Lang kept his eyes on his tray.

"You will," Caulder repeated, holding a glass of orange juice close to his chest, as though he were cold.

"Who's filling in for Captain Cosgrove?" Blade asked. "They're not putting us under some squid, are they?"

Lang shrugged and they resumed eating. The silence lasted several minutes, until a corporal from Operations noticed them. He hesitated before slowly approaching their table. What if they already knew? Sergeant Caulder would chew on him. No, they wouldn't be just sitting there. Not the dogs. They'd be moving, doing something.

Blade looked up. "What's going on, Corporal?"

"I—I wasn't sure whether you all had heard—about Captain Cosgrove."

Now they all looked up and the corporal knew he had made the right choice.

"He's missing on patrol."

They were out the door in ten seconds, running toward the Operations Center.